DATE DUE

NOV 0 6 2007	
APR 2 2 2008	
MAY 0 4 2009	
MAY 0 4 2009	
AUG 0 9 2011	
AUG 2 2 2011	
NOV. 28, 2011	
MAR 0 2 2012	
FEB 2 4 2014	
FEB 1 6 2017	
MAR 2 3 2017	

BRODART, CO.   Cat. No. 23-221-003

Previous Jossey-Bass books by Stephen D. Brookfield

Discussion as a Way of Teaching: Tools and Techniques for Democratic Classrooms, 2nd Edition (2005, with Stephen Preskill)

The Power of Critical Theory: Liberating Adult Learning and Teaching (2004)

Becoming a Critically Reflective Teacher (1995)

Understanding and Facilitating Adult Learning: A Comprehensive Analysis of Principles and Effective Practices (1991)

Developing Critical Thinkers: Challenging Adults to Explore Alternative Ways of Thinking and Acting (1991)

The Skillful Teacher

Stephen D. Brookfield

The Skillful Teacher

On Technique, Trust, and Responsiveness in the Classroom

Second Edition

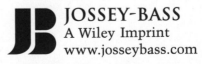
JOSSEY-BASS
A Wiley Imprint
www.josseybass.com

Published by Jossey-Bass
A Wiley Imprint
989 Market Street, San Francisco, CA 94103-1741   www.josseybass.com

Jossey-Bass books and products are available through most bookstores. To contact Jossey-Bass directly call our Customer Care Department within the U.S. at 800-956-7739, outside the U.S. at 317-572-3986, or fax 317-572-4002.

Jossey-Bass also publishes its books in a variety of electronic formats. Some content that appears in print may not be available in electronic books.

Library of Congress Cataloging-in-Publication Data
Brookfield, Stephen.
  The skillful teacher : on technique, trust, and responsiveness in the classroom / Stephen D. Brookfield.
    p. cm.
  Includes bibliographical references and index.
  ISBN-13: 978-0-7879-8066-5 (cloth)
  ISBN-10: 0-7879-8066-8 (cloth)
  1. College teaching. I. Title.
  LB2331.B68 2006
  378.1'25—dc22
                                    2006016499
Printed in the United States of America
SECOND EDITION
HB Printing   10 9 8 7 6 5 4 3 2 1

The Jossey-Bass
Higher and Adult Education Series

Contents

Preface

In 2005 I celebrated my thirty-fifth year as a teacher by finishing
this second edition of *The Skillful Teacher,* a book that had first
appeared on my twentieth teaching anniversary. The first edition
had been typed on a small portable typewriter during my sabbatical
in France, so no computer files existed of that manuscript. What
you have in your hands, therefore, is truly a completely revised edition. Although many of the ideas from the first edition have found
their way into this one, I have had the chance to rethink and then
rewrite everything I wrote fifteen years ago. What surprised me was
how much of the first edition still rang true. I have not altered my
conviction that the essence of skillful teaching lies in the teacher
constantly researching how her students are experiencing learning
and then making pedagogic decisions informed by the insights she
gains from students' responses. The predictable rhythms of student
learning, the importance of teachers' displaying credibility and
authenticity, the need to have a well worked out philosophy of
teaching and to know what you stand for—all these themes were
highlighted in the first edition, and they continue to inform my own
thinking and practice. But other things have crept into the mix of
this teacher's life, such as the increasingly diverse student body most
teachers work with today and the explosion of online education,
both of which needed wholly new chapters.

My intention in writing *The Skillful Teacher* is to tell the real story
of teaching as I live it. It is the story of teaching as an activity full of
unexpected events, unlooked-for surprises, and unanticipated twists

and turns that take place in a system that assumes that teaching and learning are controllable and predictable. Despite the system's apparent rationality, the one thing teachers can expect with total confidence is uncertainty. I want to tell this story of uncertainty in a way that communicates the passion and panic of teachers' emotional lives so that readers can recognize themselves in these pages. My intent is to show that teaching is a highly emotional reality, a marvelously and frustratingly complex mix of deliberate intent and serendipity, purpose, and surprise. As I explore this mix, I hope to show college teachers as flesh and blood human beings full of passions, foibles, and frailties. I want to understand how we can celebrate the messiness of teaching and how we can thrive in ever more diverse classrooms.

To me, then, *The Skillful Teacher* is a survival manual to help readers navigate the recurring and inevitable dilemmas, problems, and contradictions they face in their work. It is designed to reduce the mistaken and unjustified sense of guilt many of us feel when things don't go as they should and our classrooms seem out of control. There is nothing worse for a teacher than feeling that everyone else in your institution is in complete command—cool, calm, and collected paragons of pedagogic virtue—while your own classrooms never seem to conform to the plans you have developed for them. You think that everyone else's students are diligent, smart, and cooperative, while your own are truculent saboteurs, and that any problems you face have been created by your own incompetence.

So this is a book meant for difficult days—days when confusion and demoralization reign supreme in your world. On those days I want a book I can turn to that won't lie to me about the complexity I'm facing, that will tell me honestly how difficult it is to teach well, and that will give me some insight into how I might analyze and respond to my problems. The point of such a book would be to help me find the energy and courage I need to get back into class the next day fired by a renewed sense of purpose. That's a tall order for any book—and I know I'm bound to fall short—but *The Skillful Teacher* is my best shot at meeting it.

In writing this book I have set myself some difficult problems as an author. First, I've tried to ground whatever I write in easily recognized vignettes of college teaching. I've also attempted to write in a way that would encourage, strengthen, and even inspire. I've done this knowing that writing with a desire to inspire is usually a death knell that ensures the opposite happens. I've also tried to display enough understanding of the diverse contexts and problems of college teaching to allow me to offer some insights, advice, and practical suggestions that would go beyond reassuring clichés or banal, supposedly inspiring generalities. In effect, these three motifs—the experiential, the inspirational, and the practical—run through the entire book. They dominate its organization, comprise its major themes, and represent its chief purposes.

On the experiential plane I want to present a picture of teaching that is recognizable and truthful to readers. I draw this picture partly based on my own experience but also on accounts of college teaching provided by numerous researchers. These accounts emphasize unpredictability, ambiguity, and frustration just as much as they do fulfillment, success, and satisfaction. Chapter One focuses explicitly on these themes, but they resurface constantly throughout the book. I want, also, to place students' experiences of learning and teaching at the heart of the book, since it is knowing what these are, and responding well to them, that is the essence of skillful teaching. In different ways Chapters Two (on the core assumptions of skillful teaching), Three (on how we can understand our classrooms), Four (on what it is that students appreciate about us), and Five (on the emotional rhythms of learning and teaching) all explore this idea. I also try to address the noninstructional dilemmas teachers consistently raise in faculty development workshops I have conducted in colleges and universities across North America. Chapters Twelve, Thirteen, and Fourteen on facing student resistance, navigating the political dynamics of college life, and surviving the emotional roller coaster of teaching are my attempt to do address noninstructional dilemmas.

On the inspirational plane, I want to assert the importance, meaning, and effect of college teaching in the face of the barrage of criticisms college teachers have endured in the last few decades. College teachers—and their students—change the world in small, and sometimes big, ways. Although I am strongly influenced by critical theory and its belief that colleges are part of what Louis Althusser (1971) called the ideological state apparatus, I don't believe that teachers are blind to this fact or that they inevitably function as smooth, seamless agents of ideological indoctrination. Like Herbert Marcuse (1969) I think higher education is potentially an agent of liberation, opening students up to ideas and perspectives that had previously never occurred to them, and developing in them the requisite confidence in their own abilities and opinions that allows them to act on and in the world. So while I believe that colleges function in ways that reflect structural inequities in the wider society, I also believe that many teachers fight against, and do their best to subvert, this tendency. In writings such as those of Shor (1992), Daloz (1999), and Greene (2001), we find examples of how teachers can act creatively to develop their students' powers of critical thinking and to increase their sense of agency.

I also reject those conservative, almost apocalyptic analyses of higher education that ring the alarm bells of relativism, multiculturalism, and political correctness to argue that in the face of moral disintegration what we need is to hark back to an era of classically derived verities. These analyses fail to match the complex ambiguity of contemporary adulthood and serve to support the wishful thinking of those who believe that college teaching boils down to the inculcation of universally agreed-on facts and the appreciation of higher (usually Eurocentric) truths. This is a cocktail party view of academe that has as its rationale helping students to acquire a stock of culturally approved concepts, dates, facts, and names. In this view the purpose of higher education is to learn to impress peers by the number and variety of culturally sanctioned terms one can drop into the conversation, thereby demonstrating one's cultural literacy. From my standpoint cultural literacy requires the ability to critique the Eurocentric dominance of higher education curricula rather than being an uncritical mouthpiece for its continuation.

Finally, on the practical level, I have tried to write a book that takes the major demands, dilemmas, and problems of college teaching and analyzes them in an informative and helpful way. It is easy to write a book long on experience and inspiration but short on practicalities. To avoid that danger I have analyzed the questions, issues, and concerns that have been raised most frequently by teachers in faculty development workshops I have run over the past twenty years. Answering these questions, issues, and concerns provides the focus for the chapters in this book. Most of these questions have had to do with practical issues, but a significant minority also deal with matters of political and emotional survival, which is why I have included chapters dealing with those themes. I provide plenty of suggestions and advice and give lots of exercises and techniques that I hope will help readers negotiate their way through the problems they face.

One difference in emphasis that *The Skillful Teacher* has when compared to many other texts on college teaching is that it is written from an adult educational perspective. I have often been puzzled by the absence of adult educational literature in books on college teaching. After all, college teaching is focused on learners who are partially or fully immersed in adulthood. In this sense, it is part of adult education. Also, teachers are themselves adult learners engaged in a continuous analysis of their practice. Yet the rich literature on adult learning and education is rarely acknowledged, let alone built on, in most works on college teaching. In my years teaching students in a variety of college settings, I have, to my mind, been practicing a form of adult education. So one distinctive emphasis of *The Skillful Teacher* is the recognition of college students and college teachers as adult learners who need to be understood from the perspective of adult learning research, theory, and philosophy.

Because I wanted to write in a sympathetic way about the travails, pleasures, and serendipities of college teaching, I have adopted a particular prose style in the following pages. I have tried to cut down on citations of literature and to communicate as directly as possible using a conversational and personal tone. The book I would want to read for sustenance, advice, and encouragement after a bad day in the classroom would not be peppered with scholarly references and written in an academically formal manner. It would speak to me directly and concretely. So in *The Skillful Teacher* I have tried to write as I would speak, using the familiar *you* and the first person *I* throughout the text in an effort to cut down the distance between reader and author.

Audience

The audience for this book is teachers at all levels, and in all settings, of higher education. Hopefully some of the book will also be interesting to upper-level high school teachers. But there is no "typical" reader for this book. I don't have in mind a particular kind of teacher in a particular kind of college teaching a particular kind of subject. Instead, I hope the book can be read by a variety of people for diverse reasons. I hope it will be helpful to beginning college teachers who (as I was in the first years of my career) are wondering how they are going to get through the next day, much less the rest of the semester. I hope that teachers who are expert in their subject matter but who have not really thought much about issues of teaching and learning will find that it focuses their minds on things they need to attend to and how to do accomplish these. I hope that relatively experienced teachers who are caught in dilemmas they seem to encounter again and again will find insights or suggestions on how to respond to these situations.

I hope, too, that readers who have been teaching for a long time and suffer from a sense of torpor or routine will find something to renew them and remind them why they became college teachers in the first place. Finally, I hope that teachers everywhere who are dogged by the suspicion that they fall woefully short of being the calm, controlled, skilled orchestrators of learning spoken about on faculty days (and featured in texts on teaching) will feel reassured by the common experience I have depicted.

Overview of the Contents

The book begins with a chapter on the experience of teaching that emphasizes its chaotic unpredictability and the ways this is viscerally experienced. I argue that skillful teaching resembles a kind of contextually informed "muddling through" classroom experience that involves us negotiating moments of surprise as we grow into our own truth about the realities we face. Chapter Two explores the three core assumptions that inform the book: that skillful teaching boils down to whatever helps students learn, that the best teachers adopt a critically reflective stance towards their practice, and that the most important knowledge we need to do good work is an awareness of how students are experiencing their learning and our teaching. Chapter Three explores this third assumption in more depth through an examination of various classroom research approaches, particularly the classroom Critical Incident Questionnaire (CIQ).

Chapter Four continues the review of college learning through students' eyes by considering the two characteristics of teachers that students say they value the most—credibility and authenticity. Specific examples of each of these characteristics are given so that readers can recognize when they are displaying them in their own practice. In Chapter Five I explore the typical emotional rhythms of student learning and how teachers can respond to these. Chapters Six through Twelve focus on some of the practices most common to college teaching across disciplines and levels. These are lecturing (Chapter Six), discussion (Chapters Seven and Eight), teaching in diverse classrooms (Chapter Nine), giving helpful evaluations (Chapter Ten), teaching online (Chapter Eleven), and responding to student resistance (Chapter Twelve). In all these chapters I try to give examples of specific classroom exercises that will be helpful and to provide advice on when to judge which of these are most appropriate.

Chapter Thirteen examines the ways in which political factors—both inside and outside college—affect the practice of teaching. I

argue that teaching is an inherently political activity through which
people learn how to treat each other democratically or autocratically. I also offer some strategies for political survival and conclude
by analyzing the political values and purposes of college teaching.
Chapter Fourteen argues that all teachers have a working philosophy of teaching that needs to be acknowledged and examined. I
believe that honing and refining this working philosophy is personally, professionally, and pedagogically crucial. The book closes
with fifteen maxims of skillful teaching that summarize the main
themes that emerged in the previous chapters.

Acknowledgments

My greatest acknowledgment must go to those various college teachers who have come up to me at conferences and workshops to tell me
how useful they found the first edition of this book. Their encouragement provided the motivation for me to write this second edition.
Mary Hess of Luther Seminary in St. Paul was generous enough to
read and critique the first draft of the manuscript. For two years Mary
was a member of a faculty reflection group at Luther Seminary for
which I was an external consultant, and I am honored that she would
devote her precious time to helping me make this a more honest
book. I know that thanks to editors often appear ritualistic, but I hope
that my gratitude for David Brightman's supportive yet critical perspective is read as genuine. As always, David was full of useful ideas
and provocative questions that helped me reshape the second edition
of this book. Molly and Colin Brookfield, along with Kim Miller, were
always generous and understanding in allowing their father and husband the time and space needed to rewrite the whole manuscript from
scratch; even when the writing had to fit round the recording of our
family band's (The 99ers) first two albums—"On Southport Pier"
(2004) and "Bob's Your Uncle" (2005).

About the Author

The father of Molly and Colin, and the husband of Kim, Stephen D. Brookfield is currently Distinguished University Professor at the University of St. Thomas in Minneapolis-St. Paul, Minnesota. Prior to moving to Minnesota, he spent ten years as professor in the Department of Higher and Adult Education at Teachers College, Columbia University, where he is still adjunct professor.

He received his B.A. degree (1970) from Coventry University in modern studies, his M.A. degree (1974) from the University of Reading in sociology, and his Ph.D. degree (1980) from the University of Leicester in adult education. He also holds a postgraduate diploma (1971) from the University of London, Chelsea College, in modern social and cultural studies and a postgraduate diploma (1977) from the University of Nottingham in adult education. In 1991 he was awarded an honorary doctor of letters degree from the University System of New Hampshire for his contributions to understanding adult learning. In 2003 he was awarded an honorary doctorate of letters from Concordia University for his contributions to adult education practice.

Stephen began his teaching career in 1970 and has held appointments at colleges of further, technical, adult, and higher education in the United Kingdom, and at universities in Canada (University of British Columbia) and the United States (Columbia University, Teachers College, and the University of St. Thomas).

In 1989 he was visiting fellow at the Institute for Technical and Adult Teacher Education in what is now the University of Technology, Sydney, Australia. In 2002 he was visiting professor at Harvard University Graduate School of Education. In 2003–2004 he was the Helen Le Baron Hilton Chair at Iowa State University. He has run numerous workshops on teaching, adult learning, and critical thinking around the world and delivered many keynote addresses at regional, national, and international education conferences. In 2001 he received the Leadership Award from the Association for Continuing Higher Education (ACHE) for "extraordinary contributions to the general field of continuing education on a national and international level."

He is a four-time winner of the Cyril O. Houle World Award for Literature in Adult Education: in 1986 for his book *Understanding and Facilitating Adult Learning: A Comprehensive Analysis of Principles and Effective Practices* (1986), in 1989 for *Developing Critical Thinkers: Challenging Adults to Explore Alternative Ways of Thinking and Acting* (1987), in 1996 for *Becoming a Critically Reflective Teacher* (1995), and in 2005 for *The Power of Critical Theory: Liberating Adult Learning and Teaching* (2004). *Understanding and Facilitating Adult Learning* also won the 1986 Imogene E. Okes Award for Outstanding Research in Adult Education. These awards were all presented by the American Association for Adult and Continuing Education (AAACE). The first edition of *Discussion as a Way of Teaching: Tools and Techniques for Democratic Classrooms* (2nd edition, 2005), which he coauthored with Stephen Preskill, was a 1999 Critics Choice of the Educational Studies Association. His other books are *Adult Learners, Adult Education and the Community* (1984), *Self-Directed Learning: From Theory to Practice* (1985), *Learning Democracy: Eduard Lindeman on Adult Education and Social Change* (1987), and *Training Educators of Adults: The Theory and Practice of Graduate Adult Education* (1988).

The Skillful Teacher

1

Experiencing Teaching

Passion, hope, doubt, fear, exhilaration, weariness, colleagueship, loneliness, glorious defeats, hollow victories, and, above all, the certainties of surprise and ambiguity—how on earth can a single word or phrase begin to capture the multilayered complexity of what it feels like to teach? This rhetorical question holds as much power for me now as it did when I first explored it fifteen years ago. And I still feel that the answer to it is that no single term or descriptor can possibly capture the full reality of teaching. Personally, I would mistrust anyone who dared to sum up the experience in a simple homily or set of rules. There are no seven habits of effective teaching, no five rules for pedagogic success, and if someone tries to tell you there is, you should steer clear of them as fast as you can! For the truth is (and now I'm going sum up in the way I just criticized!) teaching is frequently a gloriously messy pursuit in which shock, contradiction, and risk are endemic. Our lives as teachers often boil down to our best attempts to muddle through the complex contexts and configurations that our classrooms represent.

Muddling Through as the Honorable Response to Uncertainty

Muddling through a situation sounds like something you do before you've learned the truly professional response to it. It seems random, uncoordinated, and not a little amateurish. But muddling through should not be thought of as a haphazard process, nor as somehow dishonorable. Muddling through is about all you can do when no clear guidelines exist to help you deal with unexpected contingencies. When a racially motivated fistfight broke out on my second day of teaching, all I could do was try to muddle through. Because the institution in which I was working had the word college in its title (Lewisham and Eltham College of Further Education), I had images of my classrooms as gentle oases of reflection peopled by eager young minds desperate for intellectual engagement. The second day I was leading a discussion with an all-male group of sixteen-year-olds when an English boy and a West Indian boy began trading punches. Immediately the thought flashed through my mind "What would John Dewey do?" When nothing came to mind I realized I would have to muddle through the situation the best I could (an intuition that accurately describes the rest of my life as a teacher and person) and hope that I could learn enough while doing that to make sure it wouldn't happen again. Somehow (I don't remember how) I managed to calm things down enough to finish the class. And for whatever reason I had no more fights break out in class that year.

As we muddle through different teaching contexts we usually draw on insights and intuitions born of experience. Sometimes these serve us well, but sometimes we quickly realize their limitations. For example, when something that worked wonderfully in class last semester only serves to provoke anger or confusion in students this time around, the highly situational nature of teaching is underscored. Administrators, politicians, and evaluative systems often don't like to hear that teaching is situational and resolutely plow ahead assuming that standardized indicators of good teaching do exist that can be proven to be reliable and valid across multiple contexts. I have spent my life in such systems and, while they may make the administrative task of assigning annual scores to a teacher's performance easier, any correlation they have with an accurate assessment of what actually goes on in a classroom is often purely coincidental.

As you can see from the paragraph above, this is going to be an opinionated, some would say polemical, book. But the skepticism expressed above is not just my opinion. A host of ethnographic studies of teacher's lives (Connelly and Clandinin, 1999; Goodson, 1992; Cohen, 1991), collections of teachers' stories (Thomas, 1995; Jalongo and Isenberg, 1995; Logan, 1993; Isenberg, 1994), and descriptions of teachers' thought processes (Day, Calderhead, and Denicolo, 1993; Carlgren, Handal, and Vaage, 1994; Schubert and Ayers, 1992) indicate that most teachers find themselves muddling through their careers. They report their work to be highly emotional and bafflingly chaotic. Career counselors and popular films may portray teachers as transformative heroes skillfully navigating classroom dilemmas, but actual teacher narratives (Preskill and Jacobvitz, 2000) emphasize much more how teaching is riddled with irresolvable dilemmas and complex uncertainties.

Some of these dilemmas, such as how to strike the right balance between being supportive to students and challenging them with tasks they resist, or how to create activities that simultaneously address all learning styles and racial traditions in a culturally and academically diverse classroom, exist in any contemporary institution. But many of these pedagogic dilemmas are compounded by the market-driven, organizational effectiveness paradigm that has taken hold in higher education. As colleges find themselves under more and more pressure to attract students, create new programs, and move up in the *US News & World Report* standings, faculty find themselves working longer and harder than ever before. It is hard to imagine how you can make a difference in your students' lives (something most of us probably want to do) when you're teaching five to six courses a semester, have long advisee lists, and are required to serve on important committees and attend endless (and often apparently pointless) department or faculty meetings. Add to this the pressure to recruit students in the community, the expectation that you will bring in grant monies to help cover your salary, and the injunction that you publish and display other forms of professional engagement.

The problem researchers in higher education should study is not why college teachers quit but why they stay!

Part of the answer to that question may be that there is sometimes a visceral joy in muddling through unanticipated classroom situations. Everyday circumstances force us to make a dazzlingly quick series of judgments about what to do next in class, how to respond to unforeseen events, or how to translate a broad pedagogic or philosophical purpose into an immediate action. When the Internet connection fails, your PowerPoint presentation dies and you have no back-up overheads, when students viciously attack each other in a discussion or answer questions in ways that suggests they have completely misunderstood what you've been trying to demonstrate for the last twenty minutes, or when they ask you probing questions and you have no clue about the answers, you hang for a moment (sometimes for what seems like an uncomfortable eternity) above a precipice of uncertainty. Sometimes this experience is wholly embarrassing or demoralizing, and you decide then and there you were not cut out for teaching and should quit as soon as possible. But at other times an intuitive "gut" response comes to you, and you find yourself doing something you've never dreamed of doing before and being astounded that it actually has positive effects!

An example of stumbling blindly into something approaching an appropriate response happened to me one day when I had prepared a series of dazzlingly provocative questions for classroom discussion that I felt were bound to generate heated, rich, and informed conversation amongst students. I asked the first question and was met with blank stares and total silence. After counting off fifteen seconds quietly in my head, I then asked the follow-up question I had prepared. Again, silence. Now I started to panic and found myself answering the question I'd just asked. I stopped myself and raised the third question I'd prepared beforehand, the one that I imagined I would be struggling to raise about fifteen minutes before the end of the class after a vigorous and sustained conversation. Dreadful, shaming quiet met my question along with the sound of my own blood rushing in my ears.

With no forethought I found myself saying something like the following:

> I know that speaking in discussions is a nerve-wracking thing and that your fear of making public fools of yourselves can inhibit you to the point of nonparticipation. I, myself, feel very nervous as a discussion participant and spend a lot of my time carefully rehearsing my contributions so as not to look foolish when I finally speak. So please don't feel that you have to speak in order to gain my approval or to show me that you're a diligent student. It's quite acceptable to say nothing in the session, and there'll be no presumption of failure on your part. I don't equate silence with mental inertia. Obviously, I hope you will want to say something and speak up, but I don't want you to do this just for the sake of appearances. So let's be comfortable with a prolonged period of silence that might, or might not, be broken. When anyone feels like saying something, just speak up. And if no one does, then we'll move on to something else.

To my astonishment this brief speech, born of total panic, seemed to unleash the conversational floodgates and a veritable torrent of student comment (well, it seemed like a torrent after the silence up to that point) burst forth. After class that day a couple of students came up to me and told me that they never usually spoke in class discussions but that because I'd told them they didn't need to talk they relaxed to the point where they felt emboldened enough to say something. Apparently, my taking the pressure of performance anxiety off their shoulders, of their not feeling they had to be brilliant conversational actors to earn my approval, had removed a barrier to their talking in class. Subsequently, my suggestion that teachers start off discussions with a declaration regarding students' right to silence found its way into a book I published with

Stephen Preskill on *Discussion as a Way of Teaching* (Brookfield and Preskill, 2005).

I wish I could say I thought this all out beforehand, that I knew in advance about the way in which performance anxiety constituted a barrier to student participation, and had therefore worked out a shrewd pedagogic tactic to deal with this. That would be a lie. What I enjoyed seemed like pure dumb luck. And yet, to call it dumb luck is perhaps to underestimate the informed intuitive rumblings that lay behind this improvisation. The rapidly compressed sequence of judgments I was engaged in as a response to student silence can be described as practical reasoning (Brookfield, 2000). Practical reasoning (in other professions often referred to as clinical reasoning) is the reasoning we conduct in the midst of situations that call for immediate action. It is unpremeditated and instantaneous but that does not mean it is uninformed. On the contrary, clinical reasoning is highly mindful, entailing a speedy yet intentionally thoughtful response to unanticipated events. Given the daily necessity of teachers to engage in such reasoning, I want to elaborate on it a little further.

Practical Reasoning as Muddling Through

I said earlier that muddling through situations is neither random nor amateurish. Or, at least, it need not be. Muddling through can be done well or badly. When it is done well, it involves the application of informed practical reasoning.

Practical reasoning comprises three interrelated skills of scanning, appraisal, and action. *Scanning* is the act of rapid apprehension that describes the ways we speedily determine what are the central features of a situation. In scanning a situation we quickly decide what its boundaries are, which patterns of the situation are familiar and paralleled in past experience, which are in new or unusual configurations, and which are the cues we observe that most need attention. Scanning is the initial sweep or experiential trawl we undertake to diagnose the big picture. In the discussion example above, my experiential sweep diagnosed the "problem" as student silence and the contribution my behavior had made to this.

In the *appraisal* phase of practical reasoning we call on our interpretive resources to help us understand the situation correctly. These resources include our previous experiences of similar situations and the general guidelines we have learned as part of our professional preparation or in-service development. In the case of the silent discussion, I knew that I should have made sure that any questions I asked would not have a "yes/no" response. I knew too that after posing a question I should have counted silently to fifteen so as to allow plenty of time for students to collect their thoughts and gather the courage needed to participate.

During appraisal we also call on our own intuition. We attend to the instinctive analyses and responses that immediately suggest themselves as relevant. In the discussion described I had an instinctive sense that what was stopping students speaking was their perception that "good" participation meant they somehow had to be brilliant and profound. This is what the French cultural critic Michel Foucault (1980) called a subscription to invisible norms of discourse. Students had internalized an unspoken, invisible norm that good discussion participants were supposed to speak frequently and in a confident and highly articulate fashion. Something told me I had to get rid of this feeling in students, which is what my speech tried to do.

In the *action* phase of practical reasoning, we sort through the interpretations we have gathered. We decide which seem to fit most closely the situation we have scanned and, on the basis of these, we take action. Scanning and appraisal involve looking for patterns and broad similarities between a new situation and previous experiences. In action, however, we judge the accuracy and validity of the assumptions and interpretations we have gathered. This occurs through a number of interconnected processes. We sift through past experiences and judge the closeness of their fit to the current situation. We intentionally follow prescribed professional protocols and introduce experimental adaptations of these when they suggest themselves. If we are peer teaching, we consult colleagues in the midst of situations regarding which of our instinctive judgments and readings we should take seriously and which we should hold in abeyance.

As a consequence of this third phase, we take action based on the procedures and responses that seem to make the most sense in a situation. Somehow my process of practical reasoning ended up with me blurting out the comments quoted earlier in an attempt to rid students of their adherence to the invisible norm of what constituted "good" discussion participation. I reasoned that tackling head on the issue of what participation looked like, acknowledging the legitimacy of silent listening, and emphasizing that good discussants did not have to be a cross between Cornel West and Gertrude Stein was crucial. After seeing it work in that particular situation, the practice of starting discussions with such a statement then became an explicit and regular part of my practice.

Teaching as White-Water Rafting

Even the most sophisticated practical reasoning, however, cannot rid classroom life of its endemic unpredictability. Teaching is in many ways the educational equivalent of white-water rafting. Periods of apparent calm are interspersed with sudden frenetic turbulence. Tranquility co-exists with excitement, reflection with action. If we are fortunate enough to negotiate rapids successfully, we feel a sense of self-confident exhilaration. If we capsize we start downstream with our self-confidence shaken, awash in self-doubt. These are the days we vow to quit at the end of the semester. All teachers regularly capsize, and all teachers worth their salt regularly ask themselves whether they have made the right career choice. Experiencing ego-deflating episodes of disappointment and demoralization is quite normal. Indeed, being aware that we regularly face inherently irresolvable dilemmas in our teaching, and that we hurt from these, is an important indicator that we are critically alert.

Teachers who say that no such dilemmas exist in their lives are, in my view, either exhibiting denial on a massive scale or getting through the school day on automatic pilot. We will all retire, get fired, or quit being unable to resolve certain teaching dilemmas for the simple reason that these have no solution. The most we can hope for in facing them is that we settle on responses that make sense for the context in which we find ourselves, and that lessen rather than exacerbate the tensions we inevitably feel. I know I will never strike the right balance between being credible and authentic because no such perfect balance exists. I know I will never connect with everyone's preferred learning style 100 percent of the time because the diversity of my students' personalities, experiences, racial and cultural traditions, and perceptual filters (as well as my own personality, racial identity, learning style, cultural formation, and professional training) make that impossible. And I know too that I will never judge correctly exactly when I should intervene to help a struggling student and when I should leave her to find her own way through her learning challenge.

Knowing about the enduring reality of such dilemmas, I want to make sure that the people I work with are also alert to them. For example, whenever I am on an interviewing committee deciding who will be appointed to a new teaching position, I always ask candidates which of the teaching dilemmas or problems they face they will go to their grave without ever having solved. If a teacher tells me they have no such dilemmas or problems, then mentally I move a long way toward striking them off my list of "possibles." I don't want to teach with someone who either refuses to acknowledge that such dilemmas exist or, knowing of their existence, chooses to ignore them.

It seems to me that classrooms can be thought of as arenas of confusion where teachers are struggling gladiators of ambiguity. Just when we think we have anticipated every eventuality, something unexpected happens that elicits new responses and causes us to question our assumptions of good practice. Yet admitting to feeling unsure, realizing that our actions sometimes contradict our words, or acknowledging that we are not in control of every event is anathema to many of us. In our heads a good teacher is like a skilled archer with a quiver full of powerful arrows. Whenever a problem arises we feel we should be able to reach into the quiver, choose the appropriate arrow, fit it to our bowstring, and fire it straight at the heart of the problem, thereby resolving it. Appearing confused, hesitant, or baffled seems a sign of weakness. And admitting that we feel tired, unmotivated, or bored seems a betrayal of the humanitarian, charismatic zest we are supposed to exhibit.

When all these feelings arise, as they are bound to with alarming regularity, two responses are typically called forth. One is to be weighed down with guilt at our apparent failure to embody the idealized characteristics of a properly humane, omniscient, perfectly balanced teacher. This response illustrates the finding in Britzman's (1991) study of beginning teachers that those new to this work quickly learn the myth that "everything depends on the teacher." This myth holds that if the class has gone well it is because you have been particularly charismatic or motivational that day, or you have been unusually adept at diagnosing students' learning styles and designing the day's activities to respond to these. On the other hand, if the class has bombed or gone awry, you assume it must be because of your incompetence. Or maybe you deny that anything untoward has happened saying, in effect, that your performance has been exemplary but that your students, colleagues, or superiors are too narrow-minded, or unsophisticated, to see this fact clearly.

The most reasonable response when things inevitably fall apart is somewhere between these two extremes of self-flagellating guilt and self-delusional denial. It is to accept that when one is traversing terrains of ambiguity, episodes of apparent chaos and contradiction are inevitable. It requires recognizing that the old military acronym SNAFU ("Situation Normal, All Fouled Up" to put it politely) most approximates the practice of teaching. However, such recognition usually comes only after a series of profoundly unsettling experiences.

For those of us trained to believe that college classrooms are rational sites of intellectual analysis, the shock of crossing the border between reason and chaos is intensely disorienting. It is an experiential sauna-bath, a plunge from the reassuring, enervating warmth of believing that classrooms are ordered arenas into the ice-cold reality of wrestling with constant dilemmas and contradictions. What helps us in our struggle to deal with these dilemmas is the kind of practical reasoning described earlier that makes our muddling through informed rather than haphazard. Our classroom practices might seem to be contradictory (for example, sometimes the best way for me to help learners struggle with difficult subject matter is not to offer them help but to let them work through these alone), but this doesn't mean we should throw our hands in the air and succumb to numbing perplexity. As we shall see in the next chapter, when we research our practice to understand better what is happening in our classrooms, we often discover in students' comments suggestions that help us deal with the kinds of problems we encounter.

Growing into the Truth of Teaching

Truth is a slippery little bugger. As soon as someone tells me they have the truth about something I get suspicious. Yet, the truth is (are you now suitably suspicious?!) that each of us comes to certain understandings and insights regarding teaching that just seem so *right*, so analytically consistent, and so confirmed by our experiences that describing them as truthful seems entirely justified. The truth I am talking about here is not universal truth, the grand narrative of standardized pedagogy that says that everyone should think, believe, or teach in a certain way. It is a more personal truth, one smelted and shaped in the fire of our practice so that it fits the situations we deal with every day. In some ways it is close to Polyani's (1974) notion of implicit personal knowledge, the certainties that lurk in the dim corners of consciousness. Over a period of time each of us develops this personal truth to the point where we depend on it and sometimes declare it. I've been teaching since 1970, and it's only in the last few years that I've felt confident enough to do some truth telling to myself about the frustrations and fears that are always there in my work. I feel I've grown into the truth of my own teaching.

By growing into the truth of teaching I mean developing a trust, a sense of intuitive confidence, in the accuracy and validity of one's judgments and insights. Much of my career has been spent growing into truth. I now know that I will always feel like an impostor and believe that it's only a matter of time before students and colleagues realize I know, and can do, nothing. I know that I will never be able to initiate activities that keep all students engaged all the time. I know that attending to my credibility at the outset of a new course is crucial and that it is dangerous to engage in too much self-deprecation (as I did two sentences ago). I know that the regular use of examples, anecdotes, and autobiographical illustrations in explaining difficult concepts is strongly appreciated by students. I know that making full disclosure of my expectations and agendas is necessary if I am to establish an authentic presence in a classroom. I know that as the teacher I always have power in the classroom and that I can never be a fly on the wall withering away to the point that students don't notice I'm in the room. I know that modeling critical thinking is crucial to helping students learn it, but that students will probably resist critical thinking whatever I do. I know too that resistance to learning is a highly predictable presence in my classrooms and that its very presence does not mean I'm a failure. And I know that I cannot motivate anyone to learn if at a very basic level they don't wish to. All I can do is try to remove whatever organizational, psychological, cultural, interpersonal, or pedagogic barriers are getting in the way of them learning, provide whatever modeling I can, build the best possible case for learning, and then cross my fingers and hope for the best.

These truths are experiential truths, confirmed repeatedly by my own analyses, colleagues' perceptions, and students' anonymous feedback. They have not been revealed to me in a series of Road to

Damascus epiphanies; there have been no instantaneous conversions. Instead, there has been an incremental building of recognition and confidence, a growing readiness to accept that these things are true for me, Stephen Brookfield, even when they are contradicted by conventional wisdom, omitted from manuals of best practices, or denounced by authority. What has been interesting to me is that as I have grown confident enough to speak these truths publicly, I have had them confirmed by strangers. Just to take the example of the first of the truths mentioned above (my knowing that I'm an impostor), I have had countless teachers tell me that I put into words the exact feeling of impostorship that they felt. Apparently it was comforting to hear or read a supposed "expert" talk about feeling like an impostor, because it named as a universal reality something they thought was wholly idiosyncratic, only felt by them.

It's a bit depressing to think that sometimes you take seriously your own private disquiet only after a supposed "expert" names this disquiet and also claims to suffer from it. Many teachers have been tricked by the epistemological distortion of "Deep Space Nine" (Brookfield, 1995, pp. 18–20)—which holds that the answer to their problems must be out there somewhere—into believing that their concerns and anxieties are irrational or irrelevant. When a new pedagogic strategy doesn't work as it should, when the square peg of a best practice gleaned from a manual is forced into the round hole of our classroom, we often conclude that it is us, not the strategy or practice, that is at fault. If only we could be more diligent or sophisticated in applying these (we think to ourselves), we would be successful. The fact that such approaches are not borne out by our private truths is evidence (we conclude) that these truths are wrong. Many of us are so cowed by the presumed wisdom of authorities in our field (they must know what they're doing, they've written books!) that we dismiss our private misgivings as fantasies until an expert legitimizes them by voicing them.

How can we accept that sometimes *we* are the experts on our teaching? When we start to think about how to deal with the problems we face in class, our instinct is to turn to consultants, texts, or faculty development specialists to help us. The assumption seems to be that we will only stumble on useful insights or information for dealing with our problems by going outside of our own experience and consulting external sources. Far too many teachers view even a cursory reflection on their personal experience as essentially worthless. I believe that the opposite is true, that the starting point for dealing with teachers' problems should be teachers' own experiences.

In this regard we can learn a great deal from the ideas and practices of the adult educator Myles Horton (Horton, 1990; Horton and Freire, 1990; Jacobs, 2003). Myles was the founder of the Highlander Folk School in Tennessee, and he spent his life as an activist educator working with labor unions, the civil rights movement, and various grassroots organizations. Although known chiefly for his social activism, he also worked out a theory of how to help people learn from their experience. "Helping people learn what they do" is his succinct description of how to get teachers to learn from their experiences.

When I heard Myles speak this phrase to a group of educators in New York, I was taken immediately with how it captured what I saw happening in the best kind of teacher conversation groups. In these groups people come to realize the value of their own experiences, they take a critical perspective on these, and they learn how to use this reflection to help them deal with whatever problems they face. In Myles' words, "I knew that it was necessary . . . to draw out of people their experience, and help them value group experiences and learn from them. It was essential that people learned to make decisions on the basis of analyzing and trusting their own experience, and learning from what was good and bad. . . . I believed then and still believe that you learn from your experience of doing something and from your analysis of that experience" (Horton, 1990, p. 57). As I work to get teachers to take their own experiences seriously, Myles' words are always at the front of my mind.

Of course, experience can sometimes be a terrible teacher. Simply having experiences does not imply that they are reflected on, understood, or analyzed critically. Individual experiences can be distorted, self-fulfilling, unexamined, and constraining. In fact, it is a mistake to think that we *have* experiences in the sense that our own being stands alone while the river of experience flows around us. Events happen to us, but experiences are constructed *by* us as we make sense of these events. Neither is experience inherently enriching. Experience can teach us habits of bigotry, stereotyping, and disregard for significant but inconvenient information. It can also be narrowing and constraining, causing us to evolve and transmit ideologies that skew irrevocably how we interpret the world. A group's pooling of individual experiences can be a myopic exchange of prejudices. Even when cross-disciplinary groups work on the same problem (for example, when teachers of mathematics, psychology, athletics, literature, theatre, and engineering join together to look at how they can respond to the diversity of ability levels, ethnic backgrounds, and learning styles in their classes), there can still be a form of groupthink. This is caused by these teachers being drawn from the same class, race, cultural group, and geographical area, and by their having gone through similar educational experiences.

There is also the possibility that we can analyze our experience enthusiastically to help us deal with problems that we think are the chief obstacles to pedagogic fulfillment and happiness, but that this analysis can be superficial and ignore the political and cultural constraints we face. What seem to be urgent short-term problems requiring our immediate attention can divert our attention from longer-term disturbances. What looks like a little local difficulty confined to our particular classroom, subject area, or students is often symptomatic of an underlying structural problem. We can focus on changing classroom rules of procedure and ignore the fact that the organizational reward system that students and teachers follow, or the ways learning is commodified in the wider society, are what really need to be changed.

Despite these caveats concerning the uncritical celebration of personal experience, the pressures on us to disregard our privately crafted truths in favor of expert pronouncements are so strong that sometimes we need to err on the side of taking experience more seriously. If you don't already do so, then, you should begin to trust your inner voice a little more and accept the possibility that your instincts, intuitions, and insights might possess as much validity as those of experts in the field. You need to recognize the fact that in the contexts in which you work *you* are the expert. Until you do these things, there is a real danger that a profoundly debilitating sense of inadequacy may settle on you. You'll assume that plans going awry, students not being engaged, assignments not producing the learning you'd hoped for, and evaluations of your teaching being decidedly mixed are personal errors rather than predictable realities. Moreover, you'll assume that these supposed mistakes are your fault, a result of your individual inability to be smart, tough, or charismatic enough as a teacher. I hope that in the following chapters you will recognize aspects of yourself in the situations I describe, the dilemmas I pose, and the responses I suggest. Best of all, I hope that as you read my words you will find that the truth into which you are growing is increasingly confirmed.

2

The Core Assumptions of
Skillful Teaching

When the first edition of this book appeared, several readers told me that on seeing its title they assumed it would portray a particular personality type, or outline a set of behaviors, that constituted a skillful teacher. Such a portrait might embody key pedagogic characteristics or effective behavioral traits that could be incorporated into readers' own practice. In fact, this is precisely the opposite of my approach to conceptualizing skillful teaching. I am wary of objectifying the notion of good practice so that it becomes a set of standardized replicable behaviors. I believe that skillful teaching is a highly variable process that changes depending on any number of contextual factors. What does remain constant about skillful teaching is its being grounded in three core assumptions. How these assumptions frame practice varies enormously with the specific contexts of teaching, but their applicability holds true across diverse situations. These three core assumptions are that:

- Skillful teaching is whatever helps students learn.

- Skillful teachers adopt a critically reflective stance towards their practice.

- The most important knowledge skillful teachers need to do good work is a constant awareness of how students are experiencing their learning and perceiving teachers' actions.

The rest of this chapter explores these three assumptions and gives examples of how they might play themselves out in practice.

Assumption 1: Skillful Teaching Is Whatever Helps Students Learn

At first glance this seems a self-evident, even trite, truism—a kind of Hallmark greeting card of practice. If asked, most of us would say that our teaching choices are made with the interest of helping students learn. The reality is, of course, much more complicated than this assumption at first implies since a practice or activity that helps one student learn can, to other students in the same class, be confusing and inhibiting. If we take this assumption seriously, it means our teaching becomes more, not less, complex. This assumption does *not* mean, however, that we descend into a relativistic quagmire and conclude that since classroom reality can never be predicted there is little point preparing for it. The truth is that most of us approach teaching a new class with a collection of biases, intuitions, hunches, and habits that frame our initial activities. Some of these come from personal experience, some from the advice of trusted colleagues or superiors, and some from professional standards and models of practice. These inclinations suggest ways of teaching that we feel will, on the whole, benefit the students we work with.

These habits of mind and of practice can be extremely useful in helping us set up our class, and we may well find that they achieve the outcomes we intend. But sometimes they can get in the way, leading us to do things out of habit that students find unhelpful. Alternatively, we sometimes feel we ought to follow what the professional ethos in our discipline prescribes, whether or not it fits the situation we face. For example, as someone who came up through the field of adult education, my training and socialization predisposes me to move to discussion-based teaching as quickly as possible. For some students this may indeed be helpful, but for others too quick a rush to discussion may confuse or even terrify them. This is particularly true for students who are relative novices in the subject area, or who are from class, cultural, or racial backgrounds where speaking out and giving your personal opinion is viewed as egomania, as getting a bit above yourself, or even an act of cultural suicide. Where such students are concerned, a gradual, much longer period of initiation into central concepts and building blocks of knowledge prior to discussion will be what most helps their learning.

As economic challenges force many colleges to adopt what is virtually an open admissions policy, students in our classes are likely to represent an ever more bewildering diversity of racial, class, and cultural identities. They will also probably exhibit widely varying levels in their readiness to learn, their intellectual acuity, and their previous experience in the subject. In such a cauldron of difference, there will be very few standardized practices that help students across the board learn essential skills or knowledge. An approach that one student finds particularly useful or congenial may well be profoundly unsettling and confusing to the student sitting next to her. So the certainty that standardized, replicable approaches will evolve from believing that "skillful teaching is whatever helps students learn" evaporates when applied to diverse classrooms. The only way through this situation is to get the most accurate reading we can of the exact nature and range of the diversity we face, so that we can do our best to change practices as a result of what we learn. We will return to this point in our exploration of the third assumption of skillful teaching later in the chapter.

Although the apparent simplicity of this first core assumption is problematic, this doesn't mean we should jettison it. Keeping this assumption at the forefront of our mind frees us up to do things as teachers that we might otherwise avoid because we feel that somehow they are unprofessional or too deviant. There are times when a commitment to behaving in ways that we assume are professional gets in the way of helping students learn. The example I mentioned in Chapter One of beginning a discussion by telling students they did not need to speak illustrates what I am trying to say. On the face of it, it seems counterintuitive, to put it kindly, to open a classroom discussion by saying no one need speak. If I had seen a teacher do this while I was observing her as a colleague or supervisor, I would think this was risky, even foolish. Wouldn't it be obvious that by telling students they didn't need to talk the teacher was only legitimizing laziness and removing any obligation to participate? I certainly don't think I would have risked telling students this in the earlier years of my career. Yet, from the viewpoint of students who are introverted, or who come from cultural backgrounds where silence is valued over speech, a reassurance from a teacher regarding the legitimate importance of silence may well ease the terror such students feel about voicing their opinions in front of peers. Similarly, students who have been victims of the "higher education as cocktail party" model of classroom discussion (where good participation is equated with name-dropping loquacity) may be profoundly relieved to hear a teacher tell them that participating in discussion does not mean that they are supposed to be profound, brilliant, and articulate in equal measure.

Following the assumption that skillful teaching is whatever helps students learn has also changed my practice when I see students struggling with new learning. In earlier years I would have felt compelled to jump in at the earliest possible opportunity and urge the student to stick with what she was trying to do. Seeing a learner in class struggle to learn to read and write, use a concept appropriately, or practice a particular discussion skill, I would have taken on the responsibility of "motivating" the student to stick with the struggle. I would have assumed that what the student most needed, and would most appreciate, would be the teacher moving in (like a crazed pedagogic medic waving an oversized syringe full of fluid marked "motivation") to administer a hefty dose of teacher encouragement. This encouragement, I thought, would move the learner off the learning plateau on which she was marooned and on to the next level of conceptual understanding or skill development. Sometimes I was lucky and this worked; it was exactly what the learner needed at that moment.

At other times, however, my intervention caused more harm than good, ratcheting up the student's level of anxiety to the point where she considered dropping out since obviously (in her eyes) it was clear that I didn't think she had it in her to complete the learning task on her own. In terms of the assumption that skillful teaching is whatever helps students learn, the best teaching behavior is sometimes to leave the student alone and *not* to intervene. These are the times when, in the effort of moving into new and difficult learning terrain, the learner is in the regressive phase of the "two steps forward, one step back" rhythm of incremental fluctuation. In this phase learners who are exhausted with the effort of traversing new and difficult learning terrains throw their hands up saying "I'm done!" They sit down, take a deep breath, and vow that after a rest they'll get back on the learning trail having spent the day metaphorically (though sometimes literally, too!) napping or watching TV. After all, the brain is a muscle and needs rest and relaxation just like any other muscle. Once it's been rested and energy starts to flow, the trail doesn't look quite so steep any more, and learners decide to have one more go to see if they can just make it round the next bend. In effect, taking a temporary break from the struggle of learning something new and challenging allows students to regroup and recharge their batteries so that they themselves decide they'll make one more effort.

The key point here is that permitting, or even encouraging, learners to take a break from the struggle is what allows them to gird up their loins to engage with the next stage of the learning project. Were the teacher to jump in at the first sign of the learner flagging, saying "Come on, one more heave, you're almost there," the effect could well be to reinforce the learner's decision to quit. The last thing she needs when trying to recover energy for learning is the teacher buzzing round her like an annoying pedagogic mosquito reciting motivational clichés ("Good job! You can do it") intended to sting her into resuming learning. So what seems like a generic act of skillful teaching that holds true across all learning contexts (that it's always a good idea to encourage students you see struggling) now becomes seen as highly situational. If good teaching is what helps students learn, then sometimes good teaching is leaving the student without assistance until she has time to catch her breath and feels strong enough to resume the struggle. Of course, the only way we can judge the situational appropriateness of either moving in supportively or leaving the student alone is if we have an accurate sense of how the student concerned is experiencing learning. This is the whole point of the third assumption (the most important knowledge skillful teachers need to do good work is a constant awareness of how students are experiencing their learning and perceiving teachers' actions) that we will examine at the end of this chapter.

A final illustration of the assumption that skillful teaching is whatever helps students learn concerns a practice that is a particular favorite of mine, which is to walk out of the classroom during the first meeting of a course. I hasten to add that I have never pushed this commitment to the point where I have walked out and left the class without a teacher when I have been observed for promotion or tenure! But on occasion, particularly when I'm teaching a required course that many students do not wish to attend, walking out is one of the first things I do. Let me explain.

One of the most difficult things for me to face as a teacher is a group of students that is at best apathetic, at worst angry, hostile, and contemptuous regarding the prospect of learning. Yet in mandated courses this is sometimes exactly what I encounter. In such a situation telling students that the course will benefit them, that what they learn will be crucial for their further progress through school or for their career choice, is often a waste of breath. Learners will receive this message with skepticism or suspicion (if they hear it at all) saying to themselves "Of course he's going to say that, that's what he's paid to say." The only voices they will take seriously regarding the importance of new learning are those of former students who themselves were initially resistant or hostile to the learning concerned but who subsequently realized its value. When new and resistant learners hear formerly resistant learners testify to the value of learning (particularly when the former learners use language and examples that new students can identify with), this has far greater credibility in the new students' eyes than if the teacher gives the same testimony.

This is why one of the first things I try to do when teaching a class full of resistant students is organize an opening class alumni panel made up of three or four students who were in the course in previous years. The important thing is that these students should be ones who were initially highly resistant to learning and engaged in various kinds of sabotage and hostile behavior, but who subsequently told me (either personally or in end-of-course evaluations) that they actually found some value in the course. One of the most pleasing things for me is to run into a student by accident on campus, or in a local bar or store, and hear that student say to me something like the following: "I don't know if you remember me but I was in your class last year—I was the one who put on a walkman as soon as you started speaking—and I have to tell you that if I didn't learn what you taught me I never would have made it through my second year of coursework." Or to hear a student say, "If I didn't know how to do what you taught me in that class I would have done something at work last week that would have brought a lawsuit down on the company and probably got me fired."

Whenever these (all too rare) golden moments happen, I always grab the student's phone number or e-mail address and then, the next time I teach the course they are referring to, I contact them to ask if they would be willing to be part of a first class alumni panel. The panel consists of two or three formerly resistant students who each take three to four minutes to pass on whatever advice they choose about how to survive and flourish in the course. They also talk about how they felt the first day of class when they were new students in the course, and then they take questions from the new students. As soon as I have introduced the panel to the new class, I leave the room. I want the new students to know that I am not monitoring in any way what the alumni panel of learners is saying. So I walk out, close the classroom door, cross my fingers, and hope that the panel members won't trash the course. Occasionally this has happened; but panel members mostly talk about the benefits they got from the class, how their learning was useful for them, and their perceptions of my own expertise and trustworthiness. At least this is what the new students sometimes tell me a few weeks later.

Had I not taken seriously the assumption that skillful teaching is doing whatever helps students learn, I would never have dreamed of walking out of class the first night. In fact it would have been hard for me to imagine anything more unprofessional than leaving a class without teacher supervision early in a semester. But as long as I keep checking my classroom choices and decisions by asking myself "Will doing this help students learn?" I find I am freed up from an inhibiting sense of how I should, or should not, be behaving. In this case, leaving the class early clearly communicates to new students that what they are getting from the alumni panel is the unfiltered truth of what it's really like to be a student in this course. This makes it much more likely that they will take seriously whatever the former students say about the importance or utility of the learning to be undertaken in the course.

Assumption 2: Skillful Teachers Adopt a Critically Reflective Stance Towards Their Practice

I have devoted a whole book, *Becoming a Critically Reflective Teacher* (Brookfield, 1995), to fleshing out this second assumption, so if you are really intrigued by this idea you can consult that resource. The point of the first assumption we have just discussed, indeed the point of teaching generally, is to help students learn. Doing this well means we have to take informed pedagogic actions. However, many of our actions are uninformed in that they involve us teaching in certain ways simply because we have been told we ought to. Uninformed teaching happens when we simply mimic whatever teaching behaviors we endured as students (I suffered through it so now it's your turn!). When our teaching is determined by an unthinking subscription to professional norms, or an uncritical mimicking of the behaviors of teachers we encountered in our own lives, our chances of helping our own students learn are severely reduced. We are like scatterguns spraying pedagogic pellets in the hope that some of them actually hit the target (the students). Skillful teaching, on the other hand, is teaching that is contextually informed. And one of the best ways of ensuring that our teaching is so informed is to integrate the critically reflective habit into our practice.

At this point I need to define my terms a little more. What do I mean by informed actions? And exactly what is critical reflection? By informed actions I mean actions that are based on assumptions that have been carefully and critically investigated. An informed teaching action meets three conditions. First, it can be explained and justified to ourselves and others. If a student or colleague asks us why we're doing something, we can show how our action springs from certain assumptions we hold about teaching and learning. Second, it is researched. The rationale we provide for informed actions is grounded in our scrutinized experiences. We can lay out the evidence (experiential as well as theoretical) for our choices and make a convincing case for their accuracy. As we shall see in Chapter Four, a teacher's ability to provide a convincing rationale for her practice is one of the most important indicators students take into account when judging a teachers' credibility.

Thirdly, an informed action is one that has a good chance of achieving the consequences it intends, precisely because it has been researched. An informed action is an action taken against a backdrop of inquiry into how students perceive what we say and do. As teachers we make decisions and choices on the assumption that these will be understood in the way we intend. Frequently, however, students and colleagues read meanings into our actions that are very different from, and sometimes directly antithetical to, those we intend. In cultural theorist Stuart Hall's (1991) terms, the meanings a teacher encodes in a teaching action are quite separate from those interpreted or decoded by the learner. This is why it is so important to try and view our actions from as many different perspectives as possible. When we can see our practice through others' eyes, we are in a much better position to speak and behave in ways that are perceived in the ways we want them to be. This increases the likelihood that our actions have the effects we want; in other words, that they are informed.

Now, what do I mean by critical reflection? Critical reflection is the process by which we research the assumptions informing our practice by viewing these through four complementary lenses—the lenses of students' eyes, colleagues' perceptions, literature, and our own autobiography. We can access the first lens of students' eyes through various classroom research techniques (Anderson, 2002; Angelo, 1998; Brookhart, 2000; Butler and McMunn, 2006) that help us get inside students' heads and see the classroom as they do. Colleagues' perceptions (the second lens) are available to us when we team teach with colleagues who debrief the class with us (Bess and Associates, 2000; Buckley, 2000; Eisen and Tisdell, 2000), when we invite a colleague in to our class to observe and comment on what they see happening, and when we join faculty reflection and conversation groups to talk about common teaching dilemmas (Connelly and Clandinin, 1988; Frase and Conley, 1994; Miller, 1990). The third lens entails reading educational literature—from stories and narratives of teaching (Preskill and Jacobvitz, 2000) to theoretical analyses (Freire, 1993)—in the hope that this will suggest new interpretations of familiar dilemmas. Finally, we can review our personal autobiographies as learners so that we can make visceral connections to, and gain a better understanding of, the pleasures and terrors our own students are experiencing.

Why is a critically reflective stance central to skillful teaching? First, as I have already argued, viewing our classroom choices and decisions through the four lenses of critical reflection increases the chances that our actions will be based on assumptions that are accurate and valid. Actions taken on the basis of such assumptions are, by definition, informed. Second, when we act in critically reflective ways, we model critical thinking in front of our students. By showing learners how we are constantly trying to unearth and research our assumptions, we demonstrate the very skills and dispositions we are asking our students to engage with. Thinking critically is something that many teachers urge on students without providing much scaffolding for this process. When we show students how we apply critical thinking to our own teaching, and when we name for them that this is what we're doing, we also earn the moral right to ask them to engage in the same process. So not only does modeling critical thinking provide a public example of what this looks like, it also underscores our expectation that students will take the process seriously.

Third, a critically reflective stance can also reenergize our teaching. One of the problems many of us face as the years pass by is that our teaching can become stale. As we travel further and further from our first tension-filled days in class, and as we become more confident in our content knowledge and our ability to anticipate students' questions or reactions, it is easy to relax to the point where predictability and even boredom take over. Semesters come and go, we get older, gain promotion and sometimes tenure. In such circumstances we risk going on automatic pilot—teaching the same content, using the same proven exercises, assigning the same texts, and setting the same assignments. A certain emotional flatness sets in, followed by a disinterest in the dynamics of our practice.

When we practice critical reflection, this staleness quickly dissipates. We discover that things are happening in our classes we had no awareness of. Actions that we thought were transparent and unequivocal are perceived in multiple and sometimes contradictory ways by students and colleagues alike. Books give us new "takes" on familiar dilemmas that we thought were impenetrable, colleagues offer ways of dealing with problems we had not thought of before, and students constantly surprise us with their privately felt (but not publicly voiced) reactions to our practice. Teaching in a critically reflective key is teaching that keeps us awake and alert. It is mindful teaching practiced with an awareness that things are rarely what they seem. For faculty in mid- or late career, introducing the critically reflective habit into their lives can make the difference between marking time till retirement and a genuine engagement in the classroom.

Assumption 3: The Most Important Knowledge Skillful Teachers Need to Do Good Work Is a Constant Awareness of How Students Are Experiencing Their Learning and Perceiving Teachers' Actions

Having some insight into what students are thinking and feeling in our classes is the foundational, first-order teaching knowledge we need to do good work. Without this knowledge the choices we make as teachers risk being haphazard, closer to guesswork than to informed judgments. We may exhibit an admirable command of content, and possess a dazzling variety of pedagogic skills, but without knowing what's going on in our students' heads that knowledge may be presented and that skill exercised in a vacuum of misunderstanding. Skillful teachers realize that most of their procedural decisions (what content to teach next, what examples to use to illustrate a complex idea, who to call on in discussion, how to frame an assignment, the amount of time needed for small group break-outs, when to depart from the plan for the day, and so on) should be guided by an awareness of how students experience the classroom.

Getting inside students' heads is enormously tricky. First, we cannot just ask students how things are going and expect honest responses, at least not if students are asked to speak these responses publicly or put their name to written evaluations. The power we have over students will ensure that any identifiable responses we get from them will be filtered through students' desire not to offend us and thereby arouse our ire. Students are understandably reluctant to be too honest with us. They may have learned that giving honest commentary on a teacher's actions can backfire horribly. Teachers who say they welcome criticism of their actions vary widely in how they respond when it is actually expressed. Consequently, students may be circumspect in describing how they see the teacher's actions affecting adversely what happens in class. Even under the cloak of anonymity, it feels risky to point out oppressive aspects of a teacher's practice. Rarely will students publicly raise questions about how teachers have unwittingly stifled free discussion, broken promises, or treated certain kinds of students with more deference than others. Given the egomania and power wielded by some academics, student paranoia is sometimes justified.

So a cardinal principle of seeing ourselves through students' eyes is that of ensuring the anonymity of students' responses to any questions we ask regarding their classroom experiences. When students have decided that you have earned their trust, they may choose to speak out publicly about negative aspects of your actions. But early on in the history of your relationship with a class, you will only get honest criticism if the anonymity of this is guaranteed. You have to make students feel safe. After students have seen you, week in week out, inviting anonymous commentary on your actions and then discussing this publicly, they start to believe that you mean what you say about the value of critical reflection. But saying you welcome critical commentary from students, and having them actually believe you, are two quite distinct and separate events. Between them lies a period of time during which you model consistently a public, critical scrutiny of your actions. The Critical Incident Questionnaire (CIQ) described in the next chapter is a classroom assessment instrument that has helped me enormously in demonstrating to students what critical reflection looks like. It has also provided invaluable information about the submerged dynamics and tensions that are either inhibiting or enhancing learning in my classes.

Another alternative exists for teachers who are trying to experience how their students feel as they approach new, and potentially intimidating, learning. One of the hardest things for us to imagine is the fear that students feel as they try to learn what we teach. If we have been teaching in a particular discipline, content, or skill area for a long period of time, we have most likely forgotten what it feels like to come to this learning as an uncertain novice. Moreover, since most of us end up teaching what we like to learn, we probably never felt much anxiety about it in the first place. If we teach what we're good at and love, it is almost impossible for us to understand, much less empathize with, students who find our subject boring or intimidating. The more we teach something, and the farther we travel from our first experiences learning it, the easier it is to forget the fears and terrors new learning can provoke.

If, however, we find ourselves regularly in the situation of trying to learn something new and difficult, we can use this experience to gain an appreciation of what some of our own students are going through. We are provided with an experiential analog of the terrors and anxieties that new learning produces. As people used to orchestrating others' learning, we probably won't enjoy feeling frightened, embarrassed, and intimidated when we find ourselves in the role of learner. But if we care about helping our own students learn, the experience of struggling as learners ourselves is a kind of privilege. It gives us a gift of empathy that helps us adjust what we're doing to take account of students' blockages and anxieties.

When we try, and fail, to learn something as quickly and easily as we would like, we experience all the public and private humiliation, the excruciating embarrassment, the fear, anxiety, and pain that some of our own students are feeling. As we endure these feelings and emotions, we can reflect on what it is that our own teachers do that alleviates this pain for us, and what it is they do that exacerbates or sharpens it. This will almost certainly give us some valuable insights into actions we can take towards our own students who are struggling with these feelings. How does our teacher make it easier, or harder, for us to ask for help? Are there actions she takes that boost our confidence, and ones that kill us inside? We can also observe how we deal with the experience of struggle on a personal level. Do we try to keep our problems private? What supports and resources do we turn to? Where do our fellow students come into the picture and under what conditions are we more or less likely to ask them for help?

Noticing the kinds of teaching methods, classroom arrangements, and evaluative options that either make our struggles as learners easier to bear, or bring us to the point of quitting altogether, alerts us to the kinds of practices that should be a central feature of our own work. We may know, intellectually, that a kind word, a cutting remark, or a tension-breaking or inappropriate joke can make all the difference to fearful students. But it is one thing to know this rationally and quite another to feel we are the victims of a sarcastic aside or the beneficiaries of a respectful acknowledgment. Being on the receiving end of these utterances as learners reinforces our appreciation of their significance.

Treating Students As Adults

When we follow the assumption discussed above and start to put ourselves in students' heads, several themes emerge. In my own classroom research over the years, particularly in thousands of responses to the Critical Incident Questionnaire, it seems that students, whatever their age, wish to be treated as adults. They don't like to be talked down to or bossed around for no reason. They don't trust (at least not initially) teachers who tell them that they (the students) know as much as the teacher and that everyone is an equal colearner and co-teacher. To use Freire's terms (Horton and Freire, 1990) they want their teachers to be authoritative, not authoritarian. They say they wish to be treated with respect, though what that looks like varies enormously according to learners' class, race, and culture. One of the most important indicators they mention that convinces them they are being treated respectfully is the teacher attempting to discover, and address seriously, students' concerns and difficulties.

They also want to believe that teachers know what they're doing, that they have a plan guiding their actions, and that they're not new to the classroom. They want to be able to trust teachers to deal with them honestly, and they hate it when they feel the teacher is keeping an agenda or expectation concealed from them. They like to know their teachers have lives outside the classroom, but they dislike it when teachers step over that line and make inappropriate disclosures regarding their personal life. They also want to be sure that whatever it is they are being asked to know or do is important and necessary to their personal, intellectual, or occupational development. They may not be able to understand fully and completely why the learning they are pursuing is so crucial, but they need to pick up from the teacher the sense that this is indeed the case. One indicator of this that they look for is the teacher's willingness to model an initial engagement in the learning activity required. This is particularly appreciated where the learning involves a degree of risk and where failure entails (at least in the students' minds) public humiliation and embarrassment.

Finally, it's clear that students experience a vigorous emotional life as learners that is often concealed from teachers, and sometimes from peers. Students frequently feel like impostors, believing they don't deserve to be in the role of learner. They worry about committing cultural suicide as friends and family see them changing because of college. They often feel in limbo, that they are leaving old ideas and capacities behind as they learn new knowledge, skills, and perspectives. Sometimes it feels as if learning is calling on them to leave their own identities in the past. However, if they can find others with whom they can share these fears—a supportive peer-learning community—many of their anxieties apparently become much less corrosive.

I began this chapter by emphasizing the contextual, shifting nature of what we consider good practice. So perhaps it is appropriate to end it by acknowledging that, although the situational nature of teaching cannot be denied, there are some broad insights we can hold on to. First, there are some definite similarities across learners of different ages, races, cultures, genders, and personality types regarding their perceptions of teachers. Credibility, authenticity, modeling, full disclosure, and consistency are some of the characteristics universally appreciated in teachers. There also seem to be some distinctive tensions and emotional rhythms experienced by very different groups of learners. Impostorship, cultural suicide, lost innocence, incremental fluctuation, and a yearning for community are all mentioned as being at the heart of the student experience. These characteristics, tensions, and rhythms have a level of generality that make them worthy of the attention of teachers across disciplinary areas, and they will all be explored further in Chapters Four and Five.

3

Understanding Our Classrooms

In the previous chapter I proposed as a core tenet of skillful teaching that the most important knowledge we need to do good work as teachers is a consistent awareness of how students are experiencing their learning and perceiving our teaching. In the last twenty years an impressive body of work has emerged that fleshes out this assumption by providing examples of classroom research and assessment exercises that teachers can use to gain this awareness. Typical contributions are the work of Anderson (2002), Angelo (1998), Angelo and Cross (1993), Brookhart (2000), Butler and McMunn (2006), Cross and Steadman (1996), Hammersley (1993), and Hopkins (1993). These authors have suggested numerous exercises that yield extremely valuable information concerning student learning yet are quick and easy to administer. Some of the best-known ones are the one-minute paper and the muddiest point, both described in this chapter.

Classroom research (or classroom assessment—the two terms are often synonymous) describes the regular attempt by teachers to study their classrooms in order to find out what and how students are learning. This kind of research serves the twin functions of alerting us to learning and teaching dynamics we might be missing and of developing students' own reflective capacities. Regarding the first of these functions, classroom research provides a series of cross-sectional snapshots of where students are in their learning and what important dynamics exist in class that are escaping our attention. Are some students behaving in ways that work to block the learning of others? Are teachers doing things they believe are helpful that are actually confusing learners? Knowing these things helps us take more informed actions as teachers. When we start to see ourselves through students' eyes, we become aware of what Perry (1988) evocatively described as the different worlds in the same classroom. We learn that different students perceive the same actions, and experience the same activities, in vastly different ways.

When we know something about the symbolic meanings that our actions have for students, and the way their backgrounds, personalities, cultural traditions, and racial identities frame how they experience learning activities, then we're better placed to be able to judge how to behave in ways that have the effects we're seeking. For example, if we know that our silence is never meaningless or innocent to students (they think it either implies tacit approval or signifies condemnation), then we are reminded of the need constantly to say out loud what we're thinking. Without the insights provided by classroom research, it is hard to know how to develop exercises that will engage students, encourage them to take on responsibility for their learning, and help them see themselves as co-creators of knowledge. This is why Shor (1992) argues that "the first responsibility of critical teachers is to research what students know, speak, experience, and feel, as starting points from which an empowering curriculum is developed" (p. 202).

The second function of classroom research is to develop students' reflective capacities. When students complete the different exercises outlined in this chapter, they cannot help but become more aware of what and how they are learning. If you believe that it is important to develop a student's capacity to be reflective about her learning (to "learn how to learn" as it is often described), and if you hope that this habit will then be applied across the lifespan, then classroom research is a crucial element in this project. Undertaking classroom research exercises helps students develop the kind of epistemic cognition proposed by King and Kitchener (1994) as the chief objective of higher education. Epistemic cognition is students' ability to say not only what they know but also why they know it. It involves them providing the grounds for truth that demonstrate why they have confidence in a piece of knowledge. It also requires them to describe the procedures they have conducted that convince them of the accuracy of those grounds. This kind of cognition can only be developed through an intentional and consistent study of one's own learning processes and reactions. Developing such a focus is, of course, at the heart of classroom research. In this chapter I provide snapshots of four popular classroom research techniques—the one-minute paper, the muddiest point, the learning audit, and student learning journals—and then describe in more detail one instrument (the Critical Incident Questionnaire) that has been particularly helpful to me in finding out what is really going on in my classrooms.

The One-Minute Paper

The one-minute paper is one of the best-known classroom research techniques; in fact, Cross (1998, p. 7) reported that over four hundred courses at Harvard were using the exercise. Students are asked to spend one minute writing a quick response to a specific question asked about the subject matter covered in class that day. The one-minute paper can be used at the beginning of class to prep for discussion or to orient students towards the theme of the lecture. When used this way, students can be asked to write a response to questions such as "What is it most important to know about the topic of today's lecture?" or "Why do you think the topic of today's discussion is important?" An interesting variation on this second question is "Why do you think the teacher feels the topic of today's discussion to be important?" When asked at the beginning of class, students should be allowed time to share their responses with each other or with the teacher.

When used at the end of class (which is how I use it), the one-minute paper can be used to assess students' comprehension of ideas covered in the discussion or lecture. Here students are given one minute to write a brief reflection on a question posed by the teacher. When I use this device after a class, I typically ask "What was the most important idea or insight that you engaged with today?" It can also encourage students to start thinking about where they go next with their learning. After a discussion my one-minute paper question is usually "What issue was raised in the discussion today that most needs addressing next time we meet?" Themes that emerge from these papers can then be used to frame the lecture or begin the discussion the next time the class meets.

The Muddiest Point

In the Muddiest Point exercise, students are asked to jot down their response to the question "What was the muddiest point you encountered in the material covered in class today?" Variations on this question I have used are "What was the most confusing idea we addressed today?" or "What was the most poorly explained idea we covered today?" Both these latter questions are appropriate for lecture or discussion-based classes. In demonstration-based teaching (in labs or skills-building classes), I ask "What was the most poorly demonstrated process you observed today?" The muddiest point provides an indication of what needs to be reviewed next time the class meets. Depending on what the responses reveal, we can judge whether the level of confusion is roughly what we'd expect at this stage of the course, or whether we need to take a serious look at slowing down the pace of the class in order to revisit earlier concepts or skills.

The Learning Audit

In the learning audit students are asked to respond to three questions at the end of the last class of the week:

What do I know now that I didn't know this time last week?

What can I do now that I couldn't do this time last week?

What could I teach others to know or do that I couldn't teach them last week?

The origins of this instrument lie in students' complaints that they are learning nothing, making no progress, getting nowhere. It's pretty depressing to hear a student say this, particularly if you know it might indeed be true. However, another interpretation of these complaints is also possible. It could be the case that small incremental learning gains are being made without students noticing that this is happening. In completing the audit, learners sometimes realize that more is going on than they had assumed. Over several weeks students can review their audit responses and notice that by putting together the small things they are able to know and do at the end of each week some cumulative progress has occurred.

Student Learning Journals

Student learning journals are regular summaries of students' experiences of learning. In contrast to the three classroom research instruments outlined above, they require considerable time and energy to complete. They can be highly revealing, but writing them is arduous and sometimes difficult. There is nothing more intimidating than being asked to fill a blank page with reflections about learning, particularly if the teacher has not modeled this. In my view, asking students to write journal entries, but giving them no help as to how this might be done, is a mistake. If students are to take journal writing seriously, then they must be given some specific guidelines on what a learning journal should look like, they must be convinced that it's in their own best interests to keep such a journal, and their effort in doing this must in some way be publicly acknowledged and rewarded.

I have found it helpful in this regard if the teacher keeps and distributes to students her own learning journal. This modeling of self-disclosure serves two purposes: it provides an example of what a journal might look like, and it also earns for the teacher the right to ask students to engage in this activity. It is important to emphasize, however, that the teacher's journal should *not* be a catalog of stunning revelations documenting the transformative power of learning. Such a journal will only provide an intimidating template that will bias the students toward inventing transformative moments, whether or not these have actually occurred. The teacher's journal should contain plenty of entries that reveal that nothing particularly significant happened that week.

Some examples of questions you might include as prompts for completing learning journals are the following. I would not ask all of these, by the way, only two or three.

What have I learned this week about myself as a learner?

What have I learned this week about my emotional responses to learning?

What were the highest emotional moments in my learning activities this week?

What were the lowest emotional moments in my learning activities this week?

What learning tasks did I respond to most easily this week?

What learning tasks gave me the greatest difficulties this week?

What was the most significant thing that happened to me as a learner this week?

What learning activity or emotional response most took me by surprise this week?

What do I feel proudest about regarding my activities this week?

What do I feel most dissatisfied with regarding my learning activities this week?

I usually tell students not to worry if their answers to these questions overlap or if they feel one question has already been answered in their response to an earlier question. I do ask them to try and write something, however brief, in response to whatever questions are chosen as prompts. Even noting that nothing surprised them, or that there were no high or low emotional moments in their learning, tells them something about themselves as learners and the conditions under which they learn.

The Critical Incident Questionnaire

In this section I want to describe in detail one particular instrument for finding out how students are experiencing their learning and your teaching. This instrument—the Critical Incident Questionnaire— is the one that has most helped me see my practice through students' eyes. The Critical Incident Questionnaire helps us embed our teaching in accurate information about students' learning that is regularly solicited and anonymously given. It is a quick and revealing way to discover the effects your actions are having on students and to find out the emotional highs and lows of their learning. Using the Critical Incident Questionnaire gives you a running commentary on the emotional tenor of each class you deal with.

The Critical Incident Questionnaire (referred to from this point on as the CIQ) is a single-page form that is handed out to students once a week at the end of the last class you have with them that week. It comprises five questions, each of which asks students to write down some details about events or actions that happened in the class that week. Its purpose is not to ask students what they liked or didn't like about the class, though that information inevitably emerges. Instead students are requested to focus on specific events and actions that are engaging, distancing, confusing, or helpful. Having this highly concrete information about particular events and actions is much more useful than reading general statements of preferences.

The form that students receive has a top sheet and a bottom sheet divided by a piece of carbon paper. This allows the student to keep a carbon copy of whatever she has written. The reason I ask them to keep a copy is because at the end of the semester they are expected, as part of their assigned course work, to hand in a summary of their responses. This summary is part of the end-of-course participant learning portfolio that documents what and how students have learned during the semester. The portfolio item dealing with the CIQ asks for a content analysis of major themes that emerged in students' responses over the semester. It also asks for a discussion of the directions for future learning that these responses suggested. Consequently, students know it's in their own best interests to complete these questionnaires as fully as possible each week because they will gain credit for an analysis of them later in the term.

The CIQ takes about five minutes to complete, and students are told *not* to put their name on the form. If nothing comes to mind as a response to a particular question, they are told to leave the space blank. They are also told that at the next class I will share the group's responses with them.

The questions are:

At what moment in class this week did you feel most engaged with what was happening?

At what moment in class this week were you most distanced from what was happening?

What action that anyone (teacher or student) took this week did you find most affirming or helpful?

What action that anyone took this week did you find most puzzling or confusing?

What about the class this week surprised you the most? (This could be about your own reactions to what went on, something that someone did, or anything else that occurs.)

As they leave the room, I ask students to leave the top sheet of the critical incident form on a chair or table by the door, face downwards, and to take the bottom carbon copy with them. After I have collected the CIQ responses at the end of the last class each week, I read through them looking for common themes. For a class size of thirty to thirty-five students, this usually takes about twenty minutes. I look for comments that indicate problems or confusions, particularly if they are caused by my actions. Anything contentious is highlighted, as is anything that needs further clarification. Major differences in students' perceptions of the same activity are recorded as well as single comments that strike me as particularly profound or intriguing. These themes then become the basis for the questions and issues I address publicly the next time we're together.

At the start of the first class of the next week, I spend three to five minutes reporting back to students a summary of the chief themes that emerged in their responses. I tell them I've conducted an elementary frequency analysis and that anything that gets mentioned on three or more forms (which usually represents approximately 10 percent of the class) will be reported. I also let them know that I reserve the right to report a single comment if I find it to be particularly revealing or provocative. I also let them know that the only comments I will *not* report publicly are those in which students identify other students in a disparaging way. I inform students that if such comments are included on the form I will either reframe them as general observations or problems the group needs to address, or communicate them in a private, confidential conversation with the student concerned. Such conversations are usually with students who are reported on the CIQs to be dominating the class or generally throwing their weight around in an obnoxious manner.

If I have the time, I will type up a one- or two-page summary and leave copies of this on students' chairs for them to read as they come in. Most times the pressures of other work mean I give a verbal report. If students have made comments that have caused me to change how I teach, I acknowledge this and explain why the change seems worth making. I try also to clarify any actions, ideas, requirements, or exercises that seem to be causing confusion. Criticisms of my actions are reported and discussed. If contentious issues have emerged, we talk about how these can be negotiated so that everyone feels heard and respected. Quite often students write down comments expressing their dislike of something I am insisting they do. When this happens I know that I must take some time to reemphasize why I believe the activity is so important and to make the best case I can about how it contributes to students' long-term interests. Even if I have spoken this case before, and written it in the syllabus, the critical incident responses alert me to the need to make my rationale explicit once again.

Using the CIQ doesn't mean that I constantly change everything I'm doing because students tell me they don't like it. We all have nonnegotiable elements to our agendas that define who we are and what we stand for. To throw them away as a result of students' opinions would undercut our identities as teachers. For example, I won't give up my agenda to get students to think critically, even if they all tell me that they want me to stop doing this. I will be as flexible as I can in negotiating how this agenda is realized, but I won't abandon it. I'll ask students to suggest different ways they might show me that they're thinking critically. I'll also vary the pace at which I introduce certain activities and exercises to take account of students' hostility, inexperience, or unfamiliarity with this process. But for me to abandon the activity that defines who I am as a teacher would mean that I ceased to have the right to call myself a teacher. So if students use their CIQ responses to express a strong opinion that challenges what you're trying to do, or how you're trying to do it, you owe it to them to acknowledge this criticism. But you don't owe it to them to abandon entirely your rationale for teaching. What you need to do is make your own position known, justify it, and negotiate alternative ways of realizing your aims.

Advantages of Critical Incident Questionnaires

I am such a strong advocate of CIQs because of the clear benefits their use confers. Let me describe these briefly in turn.

1. They Alert Us to Problems Before They Are Disasters

I have always prided myself on my conscientious attempts to create a safe opportunity for students to make public anything that is troubling them. I regularly invite them to speak up during the class about anything they find problematic, unfair, ambiguous, confusing, or unethical about the course or my teaching. These invitations are frequently met with silence and serried ranks of benign smiling faces. Not surprisingly, I used to interpret this to mean that things were going along just fine. Indeed, it seemed at times that students were a little tired of this heavy-handed attempt by yours truly to appear fair and responsive. So you can imagine my surprise, hurt, and anger when I would receive end-of-course written evaluations from students that described how my course was of no real use to them, uninspiring, a waste of their time, too fast, or too slow. I had given them ample opportunity to say these things to me earlier and had assured them I wanted to know about any problems they had so we could work on fixing them. Why had no one spoken out?

This scenario of silent, smiling happy faces during troubleshooting periods followed by "take no prisoners" final evaluations happened enough times that I resolved to find a way to detect early on in a course any smoldering resentments students felt. If I knew about them soon enough, I could address them before they built up to volcanic proportions. Using CIQs has helped me do this very effectively. My teaching has certainly not been without its problems, some of them very serious ones, but I have stopped being taken by surprise when these emerged.

Using CIQs helps teachers detect early on in a course any serious problems that need addressing before they get out of hand. The CIQ provides a direct, unfiltered account of students' experiences that is free from the distortions usually caused by the unequal power dynamic between teacher and taught. CIQs are particularly helpful in providing teachers with accurate information about the extent and causes of resistance to learning. They also make us aware of situations in which our expectations about appropriate teaching methods and content are not meshing with those held by students. In my own teaching CIQs give me good information about students' readiness for a particular learning activity. This, in turn, helps me avoid pushing them too quickly or too slowly. They also help me curb my tendency to equate silence with mental inertia. Let me explain.

Many times in the middle of giving a lecture I have one of those "Beam me up Scotty" moments. This usually happens when I sense from students' body language that I've lost them. They're looking at the table, at the ceiling, out of the window—anywhere else but at me. Faced with this lack of eye contact, I feel a rising sense of panic. So I stop and ask students if there's anything I can clarify or if they have any questions about what I've just said. When my invitation is met with silence, I feel demoralized and glumly conclude that the session has been wasted. After all, didn't their blank expressions and muteness prove they had no idea what I was talking about? Yet many times after such occasions I have been relieved and heartened to read in students' critical incident responses how particular moments in the lecture were the most engaging moments of the class, or how comments I made during the presentation were particularly affirming. Moreover, my asking if there was anything I could clarify is often reported as the most puzzling or confusing section, or the most surprising aspect of the class. Clearly, then, gestures I interpret as student disinterest (particularly silence) some-times indicate a grappling with difficult material.

2. They Encourage Students to Be Reflective Learners

A second advantage of the CIQ lies in its encouragement of student reflection. When the instrument is first introduced into a class, students sometimes find the activity of completing the five questions on the form to be somewhat artificial, a going through of some not very convincing motions. Over time, however, they start to notice patterns emerging in their own emotional responses to learning. They tell me that as they go through a course they have pedagogic "out of body" experiences. By weeks five or six of the course, they are in the habit of hovering above themselves and studying the ways they react to different situations. Throughout each class meeting they start to jot down notes about critical events and their reactions to these as they occur. They tell me that they want to make sure they include these on their CIQ sheet when the class finishes an hour or so later. A real turning point is reached when students ask for the CIQ to be distributed early so they can complete them as the class is proceeding.

3. They Build a Case for Diversity in Teaching

Invariably, when teachers report back to students the spread of responses to the last week's classes, a predictable diversity emerges. One cluster of students writes that the most engaged moments for them were during the small-group activity. Typical comments are "I could recognize what others were saying," "I learned something important from a group member," "I felt my voice was being listened to," and "Group members helped me clarify my thinking." This group of people often reports that the most distancing moments were experienced during my presentation. They write that "I couldn't see the point of the lecture," "What you said didn't seem to make sense to me," and "I'd had a long day and was fighting to stay awake."

Another cluster of responses says exactly the opposite. To these students the most engaged moments in class were experienced during the instructor's presentation. Typical comments are "What you spoke about related directly to me," "I enjoy hearing what you think about this," and "I really benefit from having things laid out in front of me." This same group usually reports that for them the most distancing moments happened in the small-group exercise: "We got off task," "An egomaniac dominated our discussion," and "One man felt it was his duty to solve our problems though we hadn't asked him to." Again, in picking out affirming actions, one cluster of responses might summarize people's favorable reactions to a teacher's self-disclosure. Another cluster of responses might report this as too discomforting or irrelevant. One student wrote about a class of mine "Your willingness to be open with us is wonderful. It makes me feel like being open in return." Another wrote of the same class "Too much psychoanalysis, not enough content—90 percent of our class is personal disclosure and only 10 percent is critical rigor."

As I read out these responses at the beginning of each new week, students often comment on their diversity. They laugh as they hear how eight people picked out the small-group experience as the most engaged moment and how another eight reported the same activity as the most distancing or confusing episode in the class. They say to me that they didn't realize how different students experience the same things so differently. Then we talk about the concept of learning styles or situated cognition and about the ways that culture, race, class, history, and personality structure how events are experienced. Seeing a diversity of responses emerge every week is a dramatic way to teach students that different people learn differently.

Each week I emphasize that my recognition of this diversity lies behind my own efforts to use a range of teaching methods and materials. I tell students that I ground my use of different methods in students' reports of their own experiences as learners in my courses. If different people learn differently, then I need to use as many different approaches as possible to make sure that for some of the time in class each person feels they are learning in a style that feels comfortable, familiar, and helpful. I could write "conviction" in my syllabus, and explain it at the opening class, but this is often ignored by students who believe that everyone else learns the way they do. Without realizing it students often universalize their experience as learners, assuming that others exhibit the same reactions and responses as they do. But when they hear, week after week, how people sitting next to them have a completely different reaction to what goes on in class, the reason why I use a variety of approaches starts to make sense.

4. They Build Trust

The CIQ can play an important role in building trust between students and teachers. Students say that the experience of having their opinions, reactions, and feelings solicited regularly, and addressed publicly, is one crucial reason for their coming to trust a teacher. They tell me they are used to filling out evaluations at the end of courses but that they view this activity as artificial and meaningless since they never hear what use is made of their comments. They know that these might change what a teacher does with another group in the future, but this has little importance to them.

However, with the weekly CIQs students wait expectantly at the start of each new week for the report of the responses to last week's classes. They know that during this report, and in the discussion that follows it, the teacher will be talking about what she feels she needs to change or emphasize even more strongly in her own teaching as a result of what she's learned from these responses. Students say that hearing their anonymously given comments reported back to them as part of a commonly articulated class concern somehow legitimizes what had formerly been felt as a purely private and personal reaction. When they see teachers consistently making changes in their practice, and explicitly demonstrating that these are in response to students' CIQ responses, the feeling develops that these teachers are truly responsive, that they can be trusted.

Sometimes teachers quite legitimately feel that they can't change their practice to accommodate students' wishes as expressed in their CIQ responses. But the very fact that teachers acknowledge that they know what those wishes are, and the fact that they take the time and trouble to explain why they feel they can't, in good conscience, do what a group of students wants them to do, builds a sense that the class is one in which open and honest disclosure is encouraged.

5. They Suggest Possibilities for Our Development

CIQ responses can be a very effective way of forcing us to confront our own shortcomings and blind spots as teachers. For example, one of the first times I used the CIQ, I learned several important and discomforting things from the set of responses I received. I was alerted to an ethnic slur I'd made (I made a crack linking the Mafia to an article authored by someone with an Italian sounding name). I became aware of a methodological miscalculation (assuming that in an introductory course students would appreciate my lecturing a great deal and finding out that in fact they were far more engaged during small-group work and discussions). I was reminded of an action I needed to explain (why I didn't visit small groups while they were doing a task I'd set). And a distracting behavioral tic of which I was already aware was pointed out to me (looking at the floor while answering questions).

So from just one week's critical incident responses, I had four possible developmental projects suggested, each very different in kind: (1) becoming more aware of and monitoring my unacknowl-edged racism, (2) rethinking my assumptions about the pedagogi-cal dynamics of introductory courses, (3) making sure that I explain the reasons why I set up small-group activities they way I do, and (4) working to increase the frequency of my eye contacts with stu-dents. Of these four items the last two were familiar, but the others took me by surprise. The first—my racial slur—was a real shock. I had always assumed that my care with words, and my awareness of racist language, placed me beyond the kinds of conversational slips endemic to racist speech. Without the CIQ comment I would have continued to congratulate myself on being the embodiment of multicultural sensitivity.

6. *They Help Us Model Critical Thinking*

Teachers who, like me, think it's important to get students to think critically can use the CIQ to model their own commitment to that process. Each week as I report the form's responses back to the students, I make the point to them that in doing so I am applying critical thinking to my own actions as a teacher. This is because I am using students' perceptions to check the assumptions I am operating under as I set up and then teach the course. As I talk about their reactions to last week's class, I reflect publicly on the relative accuracy of the assumptions that informed the activities I arranged for them. I discuss the assumptions informing the assignments I designed and those underlying the specific decisions I made in the midst of the class. I keep telling them that I am trying to demonstrate critical thinking in action—publicly checking my assumptions as a teacher by reviewing them from the different perspectives represented by the students in the class.

If no surprises are evident in the CIQ responses, and it is clear that most people felt the class had gone well, I say that the CIQ responses are still valuable because they allow me to do confirmatory critical thinking. Confirmatory critical thinking is what happens when we research an assumption that we've held uncritically and trusted intuitively and discover that it is indeed a good one to follow. Classroom research can be confirmatory as well as challenging and will often illustrate to us the reasons why our habitual assumptions are so well grounded. It's reassuring for students to know that critical thinking can be confirmatory, that sometimes it can lead to us committing even more strongly to assumptions we already hold. If they think that critical thinking only happens when they are forced to change everything they believed up to that point, then it is unlikely that many will wish to engage in it.

Using CIQs with Large Classes

Teachers often raise the problem of how to use this method with large classes. The largest group with which I've used this method had about 250 students. Most of my classes have between thirty and thirty-five people enrolled. If you're teaching classes considerably larger than that, I would still advocate that the method be tried but that you read only a portion of the responses each time. It's not realistic to think that a teacher with a class of one hundred or so students can do a weekly analysis of a considerable amount of qualitative data. But asking a fifth of the class (a group of twenty or so students) to complete the CIQs at each meeting is much more manageable, and you still get some valuable insight into what's going on.

Another approach is to ask all students to complete the forms individually and then to put them in small groups where they read their responses out loud to each other. Or, the groups can take each question on the form in turn, and anyone who wants to respond to a particular question speaks up. One person from each group then fills in a summative CIQ that contains the main themes that emerged in the group's discussion. This summative CIQ is then handed to the teacher. In this way a class of a hundred students working in groups of five produces twenty CIQ forms for the teacher to read. Another option is to ask twenty students each to collect forms from four or five other students, to summarize the responses, and to hand their summaries in to me. Those twenty students then have part of the homework assignment for the week forfeited as a reward for their summarizing work. This means that instead of reading one hundred individual forms you end up reading twenty summaries that contain the full range of student opinions.

I use a variant on this approach when I'm working with very small classes or with groups that I have taught for a long period of time. Because it becomes easier in these situations for me to recognize handwriting, or to see the order in which students hand in their forms, there is a risk of students clamming up because they think I will be able to identify individual contributions. To prevent this happening I ask a student to collect the forms and summarize the responses. Again, this student is excused from part of that week's homework. Although I know the identity of the student who hands in the summary of group members' responses, that person is simply the reporter or conduit for group members' responses. I have no idea who made which of the comments that appear.

A Caution

Although I have argued forcefully for the use of Critical Incident Questionnaires as a central component of skillful teaching, I want to acknowledge that my use of these has been bedeviled by one constant problem. I have called this, at various times, the trap of conversional obsession, or the perfect-ten syndrome. Conversional obsession describes the process of becoming obsessed with converting all your students, even the most hostile, to becoming enthusiastic advocates of whatever learning process you are trying to encourage. This trap compels me to think that unless everyone leaves my class bubbling over with exultant expressions of unblemished self-actualized joy, I have wasted my time. The perfect-ten syndrome describes the unreasonable desire to want to collect a batch of critical incident forms at the end of every class that contains no negative comments and a surfeit of compliments. I find myself repeatedly frustrated by not achieving an unblemished record of expressed student satisfaction for every week of the course. Unless the CIQ sheets are returned with the sections on distancing moments and puzzling actions all left blank, or marked "Not applicable," and unless no negative comments are written in response to the question about surprising aspects of the class, I then feel as if somehow I've failed.

Knowing that this is a stupid, irrational reaction on my part doesn't seem to help me very much. Intellectually and viscerally I know all about the contextual, complex nature of learning, and I am well aware of the contradictions and ambiguities inherent in teaching. I know, too, that the phenomenology of classrooms means that the same event is perceived and interpreted by different students in a myriad of sometimes antithetical ways. But the voice of reason is not heard very loudly by whatever emotional demons are driving me to assume the mantle of consistent perfection.

Even after many years of collecting, analyzing, and reporting back students' critical incidents, I still die a hundred small deaths each semester as I read descriptions of distancing moments and unhelpful actions. So, if you're thinking of trying out something like the Critical Incident Questionnaire, try to learn from my mistakes. Remember that the point of doing this is not to score a perfect ten of student satisfaction week after week. The point is to situate your teaching in an understanding of the emotional, cognitive, and political ebbs and flows of group learning that help you realize why achieving such a score is impossible.

4

What Students Value in Teachers

In this chapter I want to explore the characteristics of helpful teachers that students say they particularly appreciate. In students' eyes an important component of successful learning is perceiving the teacher as both an ally and an authority. Students want to know their teachers stand for something and have something useful and important to offer, but they also want to be able to trust and rely on them. When describing teachers who have made a difference in their lives, or who are recalled as memorable and significant, students rarely talk the language of effectiveness. Instead they say they trust a particular teacher to be straight with them or that a teacher really helped them "get" something important.

A teacher is perceived as being effective because she combines the element of having something important to say or demonstrate with the element of being open and honest with students. Students do not measure a teacher's effectiveness solely in terms of a particular command of technique. Rather students want to feel confident they are learning something significant and that as they are doing so they are being treated as adults. Given the diverse nature of contemporary college classrooms, it is a mistake, in my view, to think we can generate the seven (or any other number) habits of effective teachers. Racial identity, learning style, personality, cultural formation, age, class location, gender, previous experience with the subject, readiness to learn, organizational values—all these factors and more render bland generalizations about effective teaching naïve and inaccurate.

Does this mean we are left with such a bewildering complexity of student identities, histories, and preferences that we simply throw up our hands and give up any hope of ever developing some broad guidelines to inform our teaching? Not necessarily. After reviewing thousands of Critical Incident Questionnaires completed by students in different disciplines and geographic locations who represent a considerable diversity in terms of the factors identified above, it is clear that two general clusters of preferred teacher characteristics emerge. Both clusters are subject to multiple interpretations, and recognized in multiple ways, but both have enough internal validity to be considered as useful guides to practice. These two clusters are credibility and authenticity.

Students define credibility as the perception that the teacher has something important to offer and that whatever this "something" is (skills, knowledge, insight, wisdom, information) learning it will benefit the student considerably. Credible teachers are seen as teachers who are worth sticking around because students might learn something valuable from them. They are seen as possessing a breadth of knowledge, depth of insight, sophistication of understanding, and length of experience that far exceeds the student's own. Authenticity, on the other hand, is defined as the perception that the teacher is being open and honest in her attempts to help students learn. Authentic teachers do not go behind students' backs, keep agendas private, or double-cross learners by dropping a new evaluative criterion or assignment into a course halfway through the semester. An authentic teacher is one that students trust to be honest and helpful. She is seen as a flesh and blood human being with passions, enthusiasms, frailties, and emotions, not as someone who hides behind a collection of learned role behaviors appropriate to the title "professor." From a student's viewpoint both credibility and authenticity need to be recognized in a teacher if that person is to be seen as an important enhancer of learning—as an authoritative ally, in other words.

Interestingly, it appears that an optimal learning environment is one where both these characteristics are kept in a state of congenial tension. A classroom where teacher credibility is clearly present but authenticity somewhat absent is one where students usually feel their time has been reasonably well spent (because necessary skills or knowledge have been learned) but also one that has been experienced as cold, unwelcoming, intimidating, or even threatening. Without authenticity the teacher is seen as potentially a loose cannon, liable to make major changes of direction without prior warning. Students often report a touch of arrogance or coldness about such a teacher that inhibits their learning. This creates a distance between teacher and learner that makes it hard for learners to ask for assistance, raise questions, seek clarification, and so on.

On the other hand, a classroom that is strong on teacher authenticity but weak on credibility is seen as a pleasant enough locale but not a place where much of consequence happens. Students often speak of such classrooms as locations to pick up easy grades and the teachers in charge as "soft touches." Authentic teachers are personally liked and often consulted concerning all manner of student problems. Students who feel they have been misunderstood or victimized by more hard-nosed teachers often turn to teachers they perceive as allies. The authentic teacher is seen as someone who will represent the student to the uncompromising teacher and convince unsympathetic colleagues that the student concerned has been misunderstood and is in fact a diligent learner. But being an advocate for a particular student is seen as something quite different from being an important learning resource. Students say that they like teachers they view only as authentic, but they don't usually stress how they learned something very important from them.

Personally, I find this analysis very disturbing. I have always placed a high premium on authenticity, believing, in Palmer's

(1997) terms, that we teach who we are. By inclination and formation I believe the presence or absence of my own authenticity in students' eyes is a crucial variable in whether or not they are learning. Authenticity is something I have always stressed as a component of teaching for critical thinking (Brookfield, 1987). As someone who self-identifies as a teacher of critical thinking, I need my students to trust (as far as this is possible) that they are in safe hands when they risk that intellectual and political journey; in other words, that they are guided by someone authentic. My mistake has been to assume that it is enough for me to be open and honest with students, or for me to model my own engagement in critical thinking before asking it of them. These things are certainly important and necessary. But what is equally important is that in my modeling of critical thinking I should demonstrate a facility with the process.

If I try to model a critical analysis of my own assumptions in front of students and they have no idea that's what I'm trying to do, or if I model this in an incompetent or unconvincing way, then my authenticity counts for little. What is crucial is that I model this engagement well, that students pick up the sense that I know what I'm doing, that in teaching critical thinking I've been around the block a few times so to speak. So while it is true that trust is derived partly from the sense that I'm being honest and open with students about my modeling of critical thinking, it is just as importantly derived from the sense that I can demonstrate some expertise in this area.

Common Indicators of Credibility

I have said that when teachers display credibility students perceive it as beneficial to stick around them. What is it that such teachers do that convinces students this is the case? How is a teacher's credibility recognized? Four important and very specific indicators are commonly mentioned in this regard: expertise, experience, rationale, and conviction.

Expertise

Expertise is recognized in a teacher being able to demonstrate a high level of command of the skills or knowledge she is seeking to communicate to students. It is not enough just to possess these; what is crucial is that they are publicly displayed and recognized by students. Students say it is reassuring to know that the person in charge of their learning clearly knows, and can do, a lot. They stress how important it is for them to be able to see the teacher displaying a facility with the subject being taught that qualifies her to be regarded as an expert. The specific demonstration of this expertise obviously varies according to the nature of the subject. Expertise in teaching auto maintenance will be demonstrated differently from expertise in analytic philosophy. But whatever the subject, students apparently need to have confidence that teachers know what they're doing.

How is such expertise displayed? Partly it comes from the student witnessing a relatively unconscious display of a high-level command of content or skill to the extent that the teacher appears almost to be unaware of this. When demonstrating a clear command of a subject appears to come easily and quickly to a teacher, this is usually construed as a solid indicator of expertise. Of course, student opinion is not necessarily a reliable judge of this since novices can be dazzled by a superficial glibness that masks an underlying incompetence. Just because a group of new students pick up the sense that a teacher knows what she's talking about does not necessarily mean that person actually is as talented as she appears. To neophytes even a rudimentary but flawed grasp of content can appear impressive.

Students also mention two more reliable indicators of expertise. The first concerns how teachers deal with questions. Teachers who welcome questions are seen as confident enough in their own abilities to open themselves up to being challenged. Of course, being open to questions is not in and of itself a sign of credibility. Teachers can make any number of munificent declarations about how they love to take questions and welcome challenges, but if their response to these is stumbling incoherence or clear avoidance, this actively destroys credibility. Where questions are concerned credibility comes from being able to respond clearly, quickly, and knowledgeably to requests for clarification or further information that seem to come out of the blue. Although it personally scares me to read students' comments to this effect, I have to acknowledge that a large measure of my credibility (if I have any) comes from my ability to answer questions as I have described.

An ability to deal with unexpected classroom events is a second indicator of expertise that students often mention. Questions are certainly one category of unexpected event. Students love it when they see teachers momentarily pause, clearly caught off guard by an unanticipated or complex question. As indicated above, a facility with responding to these quickly builds credibility. But other unexpected events frequently happen in teaching, and the response to these is crucial. Sometimes the audiovisual equipment fails and the PowerPoint presentation is reduced to a frozen screen that repeated clicking of the mouse fails to dislodge. Alternatively, one of your partners in a team-taught course does something that clearly has not been planned for and that, students can see, has taken you by surprise. Maybe in the middle of a skill demonstration you make a mistake a novice would make. Perhaps in a lecture you attempt an impromptu analogy that ties you in knots, and you have to find a way out. Or, in a discussion, a student starts off on a rant or tangent that the majority of group members can see is clearly uninformed, and you have to find some way to make a convincing connection between that student's interjection and the ideas the discussion is focused on.

How teachers respond to such unexpected events can make the crucial difference between students perceiving them either as highly competent or as occupying their role under false pretenses. Indeed, these events are so important to a teacher's developing credibility that it is almost tempting for teachers to stage these and then to respond in ways that appear superbly spontaneous but that have actually been carefully rehearsed beforehand! This might work once (though I wouldn't advocate it), but people will soon see through this. However, a capacity to respond capably to unexpected events does underscore the importance of developing the kind of practical, clinical reasoning outlined in Chapter One in which, faced with unanticipated situations, the processes of scanning, appraisal, and action are compressed into a relatively short period of time.

Experience

A second indicator of teacher credibility often mentioned by students is the perception that the teacher has considerable experience in the field being taught (if it is an example of vocational teaching) or in the activity of teaching itself. Regarding this latter item students recognize pedagogic experience when the teacher not only knows the subject back to front but also is able to draw on a substantial history as the course instructor so that it allows her to teach it in a way that clearly helps students learn. In students' eyes having a backlog of experience helps a teacher make good decisions about learning activities. Students say they appreciate it when the teacher explains that her decisions are grounded in her previous experiences teaching the subject. They interpret the creation of interesting assignments, well-paced classroom activities, different teaching methods, and the use of appropriate evaluative criteria as linked to the number of times the teacher has taught that particular course. Referring to earlier strategies that did, or did not, work in previous courses, or providing plenty of appropriate examples, metaphors, or analogies that have proved in the past to help students understand complex ideas, are also important indicators of valuable teaching experience to students. The point is that students recognize this experience only if the teacher states her reasoning process out loud as she makes classroom decisions, uses particular examples, or introduces new activities. This underscores the importance (discussed below) of making explicit to learners one's rationale for teaching decisions.

The problem with students viewing teaching experience as an important indicator of credibility is that every course we teach is at some point taught for the first time, so at various points in our career we will find ourselves in the role of novice where a particular course is concerned. If you already have teaching experience under your belt, this is not such a problem since you can refer to the way teaching decisions made in other courses inform your decisions in the new course. But if it is your first time teaching, the lack of experience can be a serious mark against your credibility.

Sometimes there is nothing else you can do but suffer through this situation, endure the skepticism of students, and by learning from each of the courses you teach gain enough experience so that your credibility is strengthened. However, another alternative is possible. If, for the first few class meetings of a new course, you are paired with a senior faculty member whose longevity of experience or status brings with it considerable credibility, and if that colleague is seen by students publicly to defer to you and to follow your decisions enthusiastically, then your credibility is considerably enhanced. This is why I advocate that for the first few classes of a new faculty member's career she be accompanied in the classroom by an experienced colleague who makes it clear she is not there to supervise but rather to learn from the novice instructor.

Creating this dynamic is particularly important for faculty who do not possess White privilege. Faculty of color and junior women faculty have a much tougher time establishing credibility than do White males. This reflects a broadly held (though often unarticulated) ideological assumption that if scholars of color, or women, are faculty members they are there only because of affirmative action requirements. White males like myself, however, tend to enjoy a considerably longer experiential probationary period when people are liable to give them the benefit of the doubt and to write off early mistakes as a necessary part of learning on the job. One of the useful contributions senior White males can make, therefore, is to show up in the classrooms of junior faculty and to make it very plain to students exactly how much they are deferring to, learning from, and being stimulated by the teaching of junior faculty of color and junior women faculty.

Rationale

The indicator of "rationale" refers to teachers' ability to talk out loud the reasons for their classroom decisions, course design, and evaluative criteria. Students say that it inspires confidence when they see that teachers clearly have a plan, a set of reasons, informing their actions. Speaking out loud about why you are introducing a particular classroom activity, changing learning modalities, choosing certain readings, demonstrating skills in a particular way, putting students in certain groups, or moving into a mini-lecture—all these conversations with yourself demonstrate to students that you are a thoughtful teacher. Knowing that they are in the hands of such a teacher builds students' confidence. No one likes to think that the person leading them in an activity is making it up as she goes along with no forethought, reasoning, or previous experience. This is particularly the case when the teacher is asking students to engage in a particularly risky learning activity, as would be the case with learning critical thinking.

So an important element in building credibility is to make explicit the implicit assumptions about teaching and learning that guide a teacher's actions. We need to create a window into our heads so students can see the reasoning behind our decisions.

When students can see our thought processes, they are often reassured to realize that our decisions are not mindless but grounded in previous experience and researched assumptions. I would venture to say that it is almost impossible to do this activity of talking your practice out loud too much. In hundreds of Critical Incident Questionnaires collected over the years, students' appreciation of this behavior is an amazingly consistent theme. Comments are made concerning how learners really appreciate knowing why the teacher is doing what she is doing. They say that not only does this help them learn whatever is being taught but that it also gives them the sense that they are in the hands of a trusted guide. To know why doctors wish us to take particular medications is an important element in our trusting that the doctor has our best interests at heart and that she knows what she is doing. To know the reasons why an auto mechanic is suggesting that a certain part needs to be replaced is crucial to our trusting that we are not being conned. The same holds true for teachers. If students are to have confidence in our abilities, they need to know, and trust, that there is a rationale behind our actions and choices.

One helpful aid to communicating our rationale, by the way, is the Critical Incident Questionnaire. If students are unclear about why we are doing something, this uncertainty will be recorded on the CIQ. When our students express puzzlement over the way the class is organized, the reporting back and discussion session regarding that week's CIQ data allows us to explain, or reexplain, why we organized things the way we did. This is another way we can talk out loud our rationale for practice in a way that responds directly to student concerns.

Conviction

Conviction is the sense students pick up from us that we consider it vitally important that they "get" whatever it is we are trying to teach them. It is communicated in a variety of ways, many of which are relatively low key. There is a tendency sometimes to think of holding a conviction as something that is recognized by the ferocity with which an idea is advanced. But conviction is not the same as charismatic passion; it is not to be confused with evangelical fervor. A teacher does not necessarily show conviction by making ardent, theatrical declarations in a lecture or seminar of how powerful or transformative it will be to learn a particular skill or grasp a particular idea. Rather, conviction is recognized by students when teachers make it plain that they feel the subject matter, content, or skills being taught are so crucial that they want to explore every way they can to make sure students have learned them properly.

The most common indicator of teacher conviction mentioned by students is the receipt of individual feedback or attention. When a teacher takes the time to write detailed comments on a student's paper, particularly concerning a misunderstanding or misapplication of an idea, the student knows immediately that the teacher places great importance on the student's understanding it correctly. Similarly, when a teacher catches a student in the hall after class to have a quick follow-up conversation—perhaps because a question the student asked in class has led the teacher to check whether or not the student truly understood what she was saying—then a conviction concerning the importance of correct understanding is communicated. In a graduate program I worked in at Columbia University Teachers College (in New York City), one of the program policies was that all essays would be regarded as first drafts and returned to students for further work. Much of the second, third, or (on occasions) fourth draft work was focused on students rewriting certain parts of their papers until it was clear that they had learned a particular theoretical position and were able to communicate it accurately to others.

Unfortunately, when dealing with large classes this level of individual feedback is hard to sustain. One way round this difficulty is to spend part of class time talking about your responses to students' work that draws on individual assignments or comments to underscore your commitment to ensuring they understand concepts or information correctly. For example, when commenting on CIQ responses that document individual students' difficulties with particular learning tasks, you have the chance to reiterate why these tasks are so important and how they might be tackled. Again, starting a new week's class by doing a meta-analysis of common difficulties apparent in last week's homework assignment allows you to emphasize just how important it is to understand certain things correctly. Debriefing one-minute papers or muddiest point papers also provides an opportunity to hone in on particularly problematic aspects of the course, repeat how important it is that students grasp difficult knowledge, concepts, and skills, and demonstrate your conviction about this by revisiting and reviewing those items that students are having a hard time understanding.

A Final Comment on Credibility

Being made aware of the importance of credibility nearly twenty years ago made me quickly stop my sincere, but misconstrued, attempts at self-deprecation with which I used to begin all my classes. Apparently, judged by CIQ responses, when students are new to a subject matter or new to a teacher, it does not build confidence for them to hear the instructor say that students have as much to contribute to the class as does the teacher or that all in the classroom (teachers as much as learners) are equal co-learners. Philosophically, I believe this to be true; but consistent CIQ evidence has forced me to tone down such declarations at the outset of a course if I know that the learners involved are novices in the field or if this is the first course they have taken with me. I have often displayed a tendency to attempt to dignify students' experiences by belittling my own. Saying to students "Look, my own experiences have no more innate validity than yours—you'll teach me as much as I teach you" does not necessarily signify that you are recognizing and affirming students' experiences. In fact the opposite might be true. Such protestations ring false from teachers who are demonstrably more knowledgeable, skilled, and experienced than their learners. Also, if students do actually believe what such teachers say, then they may well conclude that they should go to the registrar's office and register quickly to take the class from a different instructor who knows what they're doing and has something valuable to offer them!

When learners have grasped the fundamental concepts of a subject area and can appreciate the criteria of good and bad skill performance, and when they have come to trust in a teacher's basic credibility, then her declarations that learners have valuable knowledge and experience that she can learn from are much more likely to have the effect she intends. But until students believe you have expertise and experience, are teaching according to a thought-through rationale, and can see how important it is to you that they learn the knowledge and skills you deem central to the subject, then saying that your voice has no more merit in the class than anyone else's will be perceived as dishonest, false, and disingenuous.

Common Indicators of Authenticity

Students recognize that teachers are authentic when those teachers are perceived to be allies in learning who are trustworthy, open, and honest in their dealings with students. They are viewed as allies in learning because they clearly have the students' interests at heart and wish to see them succeed. In Grimmet and Neufeld's (1994) words, authentic teachers strive to do "what is good and important for learners in any given context and set of circumstances" (p. 4) and are perceived this way by learners. This is echoed by the teachers interviewed by Cranton and Carusetta (2004) in their study of authenticity who spoke about the importance of being helpful to learners more than any other factor. However, students see authenticity as more than just being helpful. It is also being viewed as trustworthy. Colloquially students often say that such teachers "walk the talk," "practice what they preach," have no "hidden agendas," and that with such teachers "what you see is what you get." Cranton (2001) views this dimension of authenticity as "the expression of one's genuine Self in the community and society" (p. vii). In Palmer's (1997) terms, this is teaching who you are. It is interesting that none of these formulations necessarily implies that students personally like such teachers (though they often do). The most important thing is that such teachers can be trusted. How is such trust developed? Four specific indicators are typically mentioned: congruence, full disclosure, responsiveness, and personhood.

Congruence

The congruence here is congruence between words and actions, between what you say you will do and what you actually do. This congruence is paramount. Nothing destroys students' trust in teachers more quickly than seeing teachers espouse one set of principles or commitments (for example, to democracy, active participatory learning, critical thinking, or responsiveness to students' concerns) and then behave in ways that contradict these. Students usually come to know pretty quickly when they are being manipulated. You may be able to get away with breaking a promise to them once, but that's pretty much it.

Students commonly mention the different ways that teachers break the four commitments mentioned above as examples of the teacher acting in bad faith. Spuriously democratic teachers tell students that the curriculum, methods, and evaluative criteria are up for genuine negotiation and in large measure are in students' hands. As the course proceeds, however, it becomes clear that the democratically negotiated curricula to be studied, methods to be used, and evaluative criteria to be applied just happen to match the teacher's own preferences. Falsely participatory teachers tell students that they don't want to lecture too much, that they value students' contributions, and that they will use a mixture of teaching approaches (role plays, case studies, simulations, small-group discussions, peer-learning triads) that require students' active participation. They then proceed to lecture most of the time (each week protesting that this is a temporary necessity because the class is falling behind), not allow time for questions or not really answer those questions that are raised, and prematurely close case studies or small-group discussions because of pressures of time.

Teachers who are counterfeit critical thinkers say they welcome a questioning of all viewpoints and assertions, but then bristle when this is applied to the teacher's own ideas. Such teachers also make it clear that certain viewpoints (often those the teacher dislikes) are out of bounds. Practicing phony responsiveness happens when teachers collect CIQs and then either edit out inconveniently critical comments or refuse to negotiate around any concerns students raise. In all these instances students quickly conclude that your word is worthless, that any promise you make cannot be taken seriously, and that you are not to be trusted. They may still think they can learn something from you, but they will not experience that happening in a congenial environment.

The problem is that sometimes we do not realize how incongruent our words and actions appear to students. We may genuinely believe we are living out commitments we made earlier in the course and, in the absence of vocal student criticisms, be completely unaware of how much we're shooting ourselves in the foot. But, realistically speaking, few students will have the nerve to call you out on your lack of authenticity. Mostly they'll decide it's simpler not to risk offending you and safer to keep their head down and not make a fuss. So we may be entirely unaware of the impression we're creating.

How can teachers avoid unwittingly falling foul of the "do as I say not as I do" trap? Two responses suggest themselves. The first is to use the CIQ data to check for perceived inconsistencies in your words and actions. My experience is that these are mentioned widely as soon as they are perceived to occur. I have sometimes made off-the-cuff statements that were expressions of mild personal preference only to discover subsequently that these were taken by students as iron-clad declarations of classroom policy. As soon as I am seen to be contradicting any promises I have made, students bring this to my attention using a route in which their anonymity is guaranteed— the CIQ. I can then address this apparent inconsistency in class. The second response is to be explicit about your commitments and convictions in the course syllabus and then find some way of assessing once or twice a semester as to how consistently you are living these out. For example, every now and again one of the muddiest point papers, or one-minute papers, might be devoted to this theme.

Full Disclosure

This refers to the teacher's regularly making public the criteria, expectations, agendas, and assumptions that guide her practice. Students know and expect us to have such agendas and are usually skeptical of statements to the contrary. After all, if we don't have criteria, expectations, agendas, and assumptions, what do we stand for and why do we bother to show up for work? In Myles Horton's words, "There's no such thing as being a coordinator or facilitator, as if you don't know anything. What the hell are you around for, if you don't know anything. Just get out of the way and let somebody have the space that knows something, believes something" (Horton and Freire, 1990, p. 154). Unless you make your expectations, purposes, and criteria explicit you will be perceived as holding these close to your chest in a secretive way and therefore not to be trusted. The fear students have is that you have these expectations anyway, and they will reveal themselves at some point in the course in a way that is likely to trip students up, catch them off guard, and cause them problems.

It is interesting that even if students dislike teachers' expectations and agendas, knowing clearly what these are because the teacher consistently makes them explicit builds trust in students' eyes. Students would much prefer to know what you stand for— even if they disagree with or dislike this—than to like you personally but be in the dark as to what it is you're expecting. So an important part of skillful teaching is to find ways to communicate regularly your criteria, assumptions, and purposes and then to keep checking in to make sure students understand these. At a minimum your syllabus should contain a summary of your expectations and assumptions as well as an unequivocal statement of the criteria you are applying to judge students' work. This should then be underscored in two ways: first by your speaking to these at the first class meeting and second by the first homework assignment being a points-bearing test on the syllabus. Nothing will drive home to students the importance of paying attention to the expectations you set out in the syllabus more powerfully than having the first meaningful assignment be a test of their knowledge of the syllabus.

Responsiveness

Responsiveness is the dimension of authenticity stressed earlier by Grimmet and Neufeld (1994) that focuses on demonstrating clearly to students that you teach to help them learn in the way that is likely to be most helpful to them. Such clear student-centeredness is recognized in two ways. One is the teacher's constant attempt to show that she wants to know how and what students are learning, what inhibitors and enhancers to learning are present in her teaching, and what concerns students have about the course. The other is her public discussion with learners of how this knowledge affects her own teaching, including the extent to which some elements of the course can be negotiated. As I have already observed in Chapter Three, responsiveness is not the same as capitulation, as always bowing to majority wishes. But it does involve teachers taking those majority wishes seriously enough to be ready to discuss with students why they cannot always be met and to be ready to negotiate how particular learning tasks might be accomplished. In my own case I will not negotiate the teaching of critical thinking—that's why I'm in the classroom. But I will negotiate how students demonstrate such thinking if the assignments I have set are dissonant with their learning styles, personalities, or cultural formation.

Adopting some of the classroom assessment techniques discussed in Chapter Three is one important way to demonstrate responsiveness. In my own teaching the CIQ has been crucial in this regard. Each week it provides a running commentary on how students are experiencing their learning and my teaching using words and examples that spring from students' own experiences. In class, or online, I can talk out loud my reactions to these publicly disseminated student comments, say how they've challenged or confirmed my assumptions about the best ways to teach the class, discuss any discrepancies that seem to be emerging between what I expect of learners and what they think I expect of them, and generally show that I take their opinions seriously enough to solicit them in the first place and then respond publicly to them.

Personhood

Personhood is the perception students have that their teachers are flesh and blood human beings with lives and identities outside the classroom. Students recognize personhood in teachers when those teachers move out from behind their formal identities and role descriptions to allow aspects of themselves to be revealed in the classroom. Instead of being thought of as relatively faceless institutional functionaries, teachers are now seen as people moved by enthusiasms or dislikes. This is not to say, though, that teachers should indiscriminately turn their classrooms into zones of personal confession. Coming in and talking about how your partner doesn't really understand you, or disclosing highly personal details of your private life or anxieties, hardly creates an atmosphere in which students feel they can focus on learning. Personhood is more appropriately evident when teachers use autobiographical examples to illustrate concepts and theories they are trying to explain, when they talk about ways they apply specific skills and insights taught in the classroom to their work outside, and when they share stories of how they dealt with the same fears and struggles that their students are currently facing as they struggle with what to them is new learning.

When I first learned of the importance of personhood to students, I was reluctant to follow its tenets (I am English, after all). But because its presence seems to support students learning, I have tried to pay attention to this dynamic, particularly when teaching difficult material. One of my teaching preoccupations has been to introduce students to the body of work broadly known as critical social theory (Brookfield, 2005). My main concerns are to explain some of its central concepts in ways that are accessible but not overly simplistic, and to show how these concepts (such as alienation, hegemony, or commodification) might illuminate students' lives. As I do this I draw explicitly on how these ideas help me understand better what I have personally witnessed in workplace relationships and teaching practices over the years. I show how dominant ideology shapes my decisions as a teacher, how I unwittingly engage in self-surveillance and self-censorship, how hegemony causes me to conclude that I've only been a good teacher on those days when I come home completely exhausted, how repressive tolerance manifests itself in my attempts to open up a discussion or broaden the curriculum, or how automaton conformity frames my response to new practices or ideas. I am using autobiographical examples but only to help students understand core concepts in the course—not to tell entertaining stories for the sake of storytelling.

I also talk frequently about my own struggles engaging with this tradition. I talk about how much time it takes me to read its texts, how I study the same sentence over and over again and still have no idea what it means, and how I frequently feel like an idiot compared to colleagues who seem very comfortable with Gramsci, Althusser, Foucault, or Marcuse. Students consistently tell me what a shocking, though very welcome, revelation this is. They automatically assume (as I probably would in their place) that as the designated professor for the course I have got critical theory "down." Interestingly, this admission does not seem to weaken my credibility, or if it does, that perception is not recorded on anonymous weekly student evaluations. Instead, students seem relieved that someone who has studied this work for some time, and who has credibility in their eyes, still feels like a novice. Again, my interest is that this autobiographical disclosure be done in the cause of supporting student learning and that such disclosure increases my sense of personhood in learners' eyes.

A Final Thought

Although it is reasonable for us to strive to be credible and authentic in equal measure, it is unreasonable for us to expect ourselves ever to attain some sort of perfect balance between these two features. In stressing credibility we will likely reassure some students with our expertise, experience, rationale, and conviction and intimidate others who find these qualities initially overwhelming. In stressing authenticity we will probably decrease the anxieties of students who are fearful of teachers' arbitrary exercise of authority but raise concerns amongst those who feel they are not going to learn anything worthwhile. So, while it is important to pay attention to these two clusters of characteristics, you have to realize that you will never be a perfect embodiment of them for all the students with whom you deal. Using various classroom research instruments, such as those discussed in the previous chapter, will help you chart your course in this regard and stop you from veering too wildly in one direction or the other. As with so many matters in my own teaching, it is the Critical Incident Questionnaire that I depend on to provide me with the information I need to check out the degree to which students see me as embodying aspects of these two characteristics. Without regular anonymous data from students, it is extremely difficult to judge how far they see these two important elements as present in your teaching.

5

Understanding and Responding to the Emotions of Learning

I n this chapter I shift the focus from teaching to learning, as I explore students' emotional responses to the experience of being in college. In Critical Incident Questionnaires, and in research on how students experience college (Astin, 1997; Baxter Magolda, 1992; Evans, Forney, and Guido-Di Brito, 1998; King and Kitchener, 1994; Marton, Hounsell, and Entwistle, 1997; Pascarella and Terenzini, 1991; Perry, 1999; Weinstein, Palmer, and Hanson, 1995), learning is rarely spoken of in an emotionally denuded way. Developing understanding, assimilating knowledge, acquiring skills, exploring new perspectives, and thinking critically are activities that prompt strong feelings. This holds true across racial and gender differences as is evident in studies of African American, Hispanic, and Asian students (Treisman, 1992; Steele, 1995; Cross, Strauss, and Fhagen-Smith, 1999; Gardella, Candales, and Ricardo-Rivera, 2005), as well as work done on women's ways of knowing (Belenkey, Clinchy, Goldberger, and Tarule, 1986; Goldberger, Tarule, Clinchy, and Belenky, 1996). Students talk about the exhilaration of intellectual stimulation, the anxiety of personal change, the pleasurable rush of self-confidence that comes from successful learning and the shame of public humiliation that accompanies what they see as failure.

When students use the jargon of intellectual development to describe their learning journey, they nearly always imbue it with emotional, even visceral, overtones. Physiological terms are invoked to describe moments of intellectual discovery or major break-throughs in skill development. Learners talk of getting chills as they stumble across a piece of knowledge that puts everything into per-spective or of painful knots of anxiety forming in their stomachs as they fall short of self-imposed or teacher-prescribed standards. Some of the most emotionally laden themes are those concerned with self-doubts that are universally felt but rarely articulated. Students talk of feeling like an impostor, of committing cultural suicide, of losing the innocent belief that teachers have all the answers, and of regu-larly falling into demoralizing troughs of lost momentum. It is cru-cial for teachers to know how the emotional rhythms of these periods of self-doubts are experienced because left untreated they may well end with the learner deciding she can no longer continue her journey. These emotions are silent killers of student engage-ment, a kind of pedagogic hypertension. On the surface students appear fine, yet internally they are experiencing emotions that can end their careers as learners. This chapter explores these emotions and considers how teachers might respond to them.

Impostorship

Impostorship is the sense learners report that at some deeply embed-ded level they possess neither the talent nor the right to become college students. Students who feel like impostors imagine that they are constantly on the verge of being found out, of being revealed as being too dumb or unprepared for college-level learning. The secret they carry around inside them is that they don't deserve to be stu-dents because they lack the intelligence or confidence to succeed. They imagine that once this secret is discovered they will be asked to leave whatever program they're enrolled in, covered in a cloud of public shame, humiliation, and embarrassment. Each week that passes without this event happening only serves to increase the sense that a dramatic unmasking lies just around the corner.

"Surely," the student asks herself, "sooner or later someone, somewhere is going to realize that letting me onto this campus was a big mistake. I'm not smart enough to succeed."

Not all share this feeling, it is true, but it does seem to cross lines of gender, class, and ethnicity. It is also felt at all levels, from developmental, remedial learners to participants in doctoral seminars. For example, Simon (1992) writes that when his doctoral students (who are mostly working teachers) read theoretical literature in education and its allied fields it often induces in them feelings of impostorship. The student decides "that one does not belong in this class; that one does not belong in graduate school; that one is not as smart as others think; that one is not really an 'intellectual'; that one is not as well read as one should be" (p. 85). When I spent a semester as a visiting professor at Harvard Graduate School of Education, it was striking to me how much like an impostor I felt. Me, a Harvard professor? They must have confused this Stephen Brookfield with some other Stephen Brookfield who actually deserved the position. What was even more striking was how strongly so many of the students (all master's and doctoral candidates at a premier Ivy League school) acknowledged their own feelings of impostorship once I had introduced this concept to them. Whenever I face a class full of seemingly confident new students, I have to keep telling myself that many of them are probably smitten with impostorship.

The psychological and cultural roots framing impostorship are hard to disentangle, but most who speak about it view it as having been produced by their awareness of the distance between the idealized images of omniscient intellectuals they attach to anyone occupying the role of "student" and their own daily sense of themselves as stumbling and struggling survivors. This distance between the idealized image of a student and the actuality of their own lives is so great that they believe it can never be bridged. With older students this feeling is compounded by their believing that their intellectual muscles have atrophied for lack of use. Not having written an essay for years, they feel they have lost the ability to do this ever again. Taking a closed book exam fills them with blinding panic.

The triggers that induce impostorship are remarkably predictable. One is the moment of being publicly defined as a student. Gardella, Candales, and Ricardo-Rivera (2005) are typical when they write of the Latino/Latina adults they studied that "deciding to go to college was itself a developmental crisis that challenged assumptions, expectations, and beliefs" (p. 43). The news that one has been admitted into an educational program is greeted by many applicants with a sense of disbelief, not entirely pleasurable. Perhaps the admissions letter was a fraud, a trick played by an enemy determined to find new ways to humiliate us. Perhaps there has been a bureaucratic error in the admissions office whereby someone with the same last name as ours but a different middle initial has received the letter of rejection that was really intended for us. When students finally get to their first classes, their sense of impostorship is compounded by teachers asking all the participants to introduce themselves at the opening session and to talk about their previous experiences, current interests, and deepest enthusiasms. Teachers do this as a way of relieving students' anxieties and making them feel welcome. But this practice often seems to have the converse effect of heightening anxieties for many students. Rather than affirming and honoring their prior experiences, this roundtable recitation of past activities, current responsibilities, and future dreams serves only to convince such learners that everyone else in the class will make it while she'll be the one person who just won't get it.

College teachers then ratchet up these feelings of impostorship to an almost unbearable level by telling students that they have to think critically about the subject matter they are studying. Many students feel a reverence for what they define as "expert" knowledge enshrined in professors' heads and academic publications. Being asked to undertake a critical analysis of ideas propounded by people seen as experts smacks of temerity and impertinence to them. They report that their own experience is so limited that it gives them no starting point from which to build an academic critique of major figures in their fields of study. There is a kind of steamroller effect in which the status of "theorist" or "major figure" flattens these students' fledgling critical antennae. This flattening is perhaps most evident when the figures being critiqued are heroic in their eyes, but it is also evident when students are faced with a piece of work in which the bibliographic scholarship is seen as impressive. Engaging in critical analysis seems a rather unconvincing form of role taking, even playacting, to them. They assume that sooner or later any critique they produce will be revealed to be the product of an unqualified and unfit mind.

It is not just students who feel like impostors: teachers often feel this way too. They feel that they don't really deserve to be taken seriously as competent professionals because they know that they're doing their best to muddle through the day, week, or semester without falling flat on their faces. The one thing they're certain of is that unless they're very careful they will be found out to be teaching under false pretenses. Sometimes teachers' feelings of impostorship are communicated to students, inducing in them an unnecessary anxiety and level of mistrust or doubt. For example, Brems, Baldwin, Davis, and Namyniuk (1994) reported that teachers without self-reported feelings of impostorship were viewed more favorably by students.

Teachers smitten by impostorship have the conviction that they don't really merit any professional recognition or acclaim that comes their way. Kets de Vries (1993, p. 129) summarizes their feelings as follows:

> These people have an abiding feeling that they have fooled everyone and are not as competent and intelligent as others think they are. They attribute their success to good luck, compensatory hard work, or superficial factors such as physical attractiveness and likeability. Some are incredibly hardworking, always over-prepared. However, they are unable to accept that they have intellectual gifts

and ability. They live in constant fear that their impos-
turous existence will be exposed—that they will not
be able to measure up to others' expectations and that
catastrophe will follow.

The presentation of the false face of confidence that impostorship entails is usually done for reasons of survival. We believe that
if we appear incompetent then our students, colleagues, and administrative superiors will eat us alive. We think too that admitting
frailty will be interpreted as a sign of failure. As Clark (1992) comments, "Asking for help makes us feel vulnerable—vulnerable
to being discovered as imposters who don't know as much as we
pretend to know" (p. 82). After all, we know that colleges don't generally reward those who appear unable to control what's going on in
their classes. How many "Teacher of the Year" awards go to teachers
who admit to struggling—sometimes unsuccessfully—to make sense
of, and respond to, the chaos they encounter in their practice?

Impostorship means that many of us go through our teaching
lives fearing that at some unspecified point in the future we will
undergo a humiliating public unveiling. We wear an external mask of
control, but beneath it we know that really we are frail figures, struggling not to appear totally incompetent to those around us. There is
the sense that around the corner is an unforeseen but cataclysmic
event that will reveal us as frauds. When this event happens we
imagine that our colleagues' jaws will drop in synchronization. With
their collective mouths agape, they will wonder out loud "How could
we possibly have been so stupid as to hire this obvious incompetent
in the first place?" We anticipate the pedagogic equivalent of a military court-martial in which our epaulettes of rank are ceremoniously
and publicly ripped from our shoulders. Perhaps our mortarboards
or diplomas will be taken away. Or, horror of horrors, our overheads or
CD PowerPoint presentations will be removed, never to be returned.

Following this book's admonition constantly to examine how
students experience our classrooms also heightens considerably the

chances of our feeling like impostors. Asking our students what they think of us carries with it the risk that they will tell us what we already think but have hidden from others—that we're incompetent. Anyone who reacts to students' evaluations of their teaching by ascribing great significance to negative comments and discounting positive ratings is displaying impostorship. For example, if ninety-eight out of one hundred students give me terrific evaluations, I usually infer that the people who praised me are operating at a lower level of critical discrimination and insight than the two who said I stank. I decide that these two are the most sophisticated in the class and have caught my pedagogical soul. They've seen through my facade and realized I don't really know what I'm doing.

Feelings of impostorship also accompany most attempts at pedagogic experimentation that spring from reflecting on students' CIQ data. Any time we depart from comfortable ways of acting or thinking to experiment with a new way of teaching, we are almost bound to be taken by surprise. The further we travel from our habitual practices, the more we run the risk of looking foolish. The moments of failure that inevitably accompany change and experimentation increase the sense of impostorship by emphasizing how little we can predict and control the consequences of our actions. In the midst of experimentation gone wrong, it is not uncommon for teachers to resolve never again to put themselves through the experience of looking foolish in front of students while trying desperately to conceal the fact that they don't really know what they're doing.

Dealing with Impostorship

How can this feeling of impostorship be kept under control for students and teachers? The response for both groups is the same— make the phenomenon public. Once impostorship is named as an everyday experience, it loses much of its power. It becomes commonplace and quotidian rather than a shameful, malevolent secret. To hear someone you admire talking graphically and convincingly about their own regular moments of impostorship is enormously reassuring. If they feel exactly they way you do, you conclude, then perhaps you're not so bad after all. In public forums and private conversations, teachers who are acclaimed as successful can do a great deal to defuse the worst effects of impostorship by admitting to its reality in their lives.

Students who feel like impostors usually don't realize that this feeling is universal rather than idiosyncratic. However, once one student talks about her own sense of impostorship, there is a domino-like effect, as, one by one, many of the other learners in the class admit to this feeling. This is why it's so important for teachers to name impostorship early on in a course. A teacher can talk about her own feelings of impostorship both as student and teacher. In line with the advice concerning personhood given in the previous chapter, teachers can share stories of how they dealt with their own impostorship as they faced the struggle to learn for the first time what they are asking their own students to learn. Even more dramatically, perhaps, a teacher can start the course off by arranging for a panel of former students to visit the class and pass on their best advice on how to succeed in the course. Almost inevitably the former students will speak about the feelings of impostorship they felt on the first day of class. Each of them will likely say they felt that they would be the only one who wouldn't make it to the end of the semester, that everyone else in the class was much smarter than they, that they felt they didn't really deserve to be there, and so on. As the new students hear the former students say these things, you can see smiles of recognition break out and feel a palpable release of tension as the new students recognize their own anxieties and perceptions in these words.

As far as teachers are concerned, being involved in team or peer teaching makes us less prone to being smitten by impostorship. When you teach a class with one or two colleagues, you have built-in reflective mirrors available to you. As you walk across campus after what you think is a bad session and you start to engage in your usual enthusiastic bout of self-flagellation, your colleagues are likely to point out to you the things that went well. They will tell you about the situations you handled confidently and how impressed they were with your abilities. They will provide you with immediate multiple perspectives on events that you have only seen one way and suggest readings of students' actions that would never have occurred to you.

Impostorship can, however, ruin students' and teachers' lives. Taken to extreme levels it is crippling. The worst way to live as a student or teacher is to believe that you are the only one who is falling far short of the perfection that you suspect is exemplified by your fellow learners or colleagues. Few of us are strong enough to continue learning or working if we are burdened with the sense that those around us are paragons of virtue while we are incompetent amateurs struggling to keep intact a false mask of command. The sense of aloneness this induces is almost impossible to bear.

For teachers, however, a degree of impostorship is not totally negative. Indeed, properly controlled it can be productively troubling. It stops us from becoming complacent and ensures that we see our practice as being in constant flux and evolution. Teachers who remain completely free of all and any feelings of impostorship may well be teachers who have an unrealistically developed sense of confidence in their own perfectibility. Never to feel humbled in the presence of students or colleagues can betoken an unhealthy streak of arrogance or a well-developed capacity for denial. Additionally, any teacher who steps into a faculty or staff development role needs the humility born of an awareness of her own impostorship. If teachers pick up a whiff of presumed superiority in a staff developer, that person may as well pack up and go home. For students, however, impostorship is disastrous, a strong but unacknowledged cause of student attrition. It is vital that they know early in their studies that this feeling is normal, universal, and predictable. Once it is named this feeling does not disappear, but it loses some of its power to torpedo learner confidence. Left unnamed it is the elephant in the room, the silent assassin of student engagement and motivation.

Cultural Suicide

Cultural suicide describes the process whereby students are punished by their families, peers, and communities for what appears to be an act of betrayal; that is, to be seen to be changing as a result of participating in learning. This risk forces itself onto the consciousness of students of color in high school, as taking education seriously is condemned as "acting White" (Bergin and Cooks, 2002). It is felt particularly keenly by students of all racial backgrounds who are first in their family to go to college and also by many adult learners. Cultural suicide is something that also affects working-class students who "often become alienated from their families in direct proportion to their procurement of new ideas and attitudes" (Casey, 2005, p. 35). As a result they "feel their identities shattered, and find themselves psychologically adrift" (p. 35). Students intuitively sense from their intimates and work colleagues that if college prompts them to begin a critical questioning of conventional assumptions and beliefs shared by their peers, they (the students) will risk being excluded from the culture that has defined and sustained them up to that point in their lives. Just showing how much they are learning, growing, and changing, even if this involves no criticism of partners, friends, and colleagues, can be risky, leading eventually to cultural suicide. The perception of this danger, and experience of its actuality, is a common theme in working-class students' autobiographies (see, for example, Dews and Law, 1995; Welsch, 2004) and was even the topic of a successful commercial feature film *Educating Rita*. Students who take critical thinking seriously and start to question shared assumptions, or students who clearly believe themselves to be changing for the better as a result of their learning, report that those around them start to view them with fear and loathing, with a hostility born of incomprehension.

When a student who was formerly seen by friends and intimates as "one of us" engages in purposeful learning, she risks being seen in one of two negative ways. On the one hand, she may be viewed as putting on airs and pretensions, as growing "too big for her boots." She is seen as aspiring to the status of an intellectual in contrast to her friends, family members, or work colleagues who feel that they are now somehow regarded as less developed creatures grubbing around in the gritty gutters of daily life outside academe. The learner who is clearly engaged in exploring new vistas of skill and knowledge can pose a real threat to those who are not on a similar journey of self-discovery. In the eyes of those left behind, the student is perceived as having betrayed her origins to embrace the values, behaviors, and allegiances of an alien academic culture.

On the other hand, learners in critical process are sometimes seen as turning into subversive troublemakers whose raison d'être now seems to be to make life as difficult and uncomfortable as possible for those around them. A common experience reported by first-generation college students is of their rapidly being marginalized as a result of their slipping into a more critical mode in their daily lives. They find that raising critical questions regarding commonly held cultural assumptions engenders resentment and suspicion. Those around them feel that the students concerned have betrayed the group culture and somehow become pink-tinged revolutionaries. Many students complain that displaying their honest engagement with learning only serves to make them disliked by their colleagues, harms their careers, loses them fledgling friends and professionally useful acquaintances, threatens their livelihoods, and turns them into institutional pariahs.

Cultural suicide is not only the preserve of learners. Teachers also unwittingly commit cultural suicide when their peers and intimates see them as committing ethnic or class betrayal. Students from ethnic minorities with a history of oppression who enter college and become teachers can be seen as selling out to the host culture and joining the oppressor. Venturing into what is seen as the White supremacist mainstream of Anglo culture, they run a real risk of being regarded as traitors to their race. Academics from working-class backgrounds find themselves, as aptly described in Ryan and

Sackey's (1984) evocatively titled book, *Strangers in Paradise*. Their parents, siblings, and friends are nonplussed and threatened by the incomprehensible path into academe that they have taken.

Teachers who are seen to be constantly experimenting with their teaching can commit cultural suicide without even being aware that this is happening. As they speak to colleagues about how they're questioning and reevaluating their practice, or how they're doing things differently, they run a real risk that those colleagues will see them as engaged in an act of betrayal. They are whistle-blowers on the culture of stasis—the collective agreement not to rock the boat by asking awkward questions or doing things differently. As one teacher-reflection group member puts it, "I guess a lot of people want things to remain as they are. They don't like it when I start asking questions or posing alternatives" (Miller, 1990, p. 140).

One common scenario for committing cultural suicide concerns teachers who reenter their institutions after a provocative period of reflection. This reflection might have been occasioned by attending a professional conference or by a faculty development workshop, by informal conversations with colleagues, or a private period of sustained reading and introspection. One result of the reflection is a newly realized conviction of the importance of getting colleagues to ask a few more questions about why they work in the ways that they do. Surfing on a wave of unbridled enthusiasm for critical questioning (and unaware of the possibility that others might not share this zeal), teachers report how their wave collapses in on them as colleagues seem at best bemused, and at worst angry, at being confronted with new and challenging ideas or practices.

As newly energized teachers begin talking enthusiastically about the need to question and challenge taken-for-granted assumptions, they can easily, and unwittingly, alienate their colleagues. Teachers who start to distribute xeroxed articles on how college curricula mask racism, sexism, and classism can force otherwise liberal teachers into a defensive, overly reactionary posture. When teachers return from graduate classes talking about new concepts, theoretical constructs, and fifty-seven brands of hermeneutic postmodernism, they can easily be perceived as having "gone native" and turned into a fully fledged participant in the tribal culture of academe. This feeling may be completely unjustified, but the sense of betrayal remains.

Avoiding Cultural Suicide

How can we minimize the risk of committing cultural suicide? To help students keep this danger to a minimum, I have run role plays in class that explore what happens when students go back after class to their dorms, homes, and communities on fire with the joys of learning. In the role plays students usually reenter their home space talking enthusiastically of their new friends, the new ideas or skills they are learning in the subject, how they are developing a real sense of confidence about their abilities, and the new vistas and possibilities opened up by their studies. The friend, partner, or colleague in the role play who is hearing this can barely get a word in edgewise. Not surprisingly, when this happens in real life those who occupy the home space and who see former friends changing in front of their eyes feel intimidated and betrayed.

During the debriefing of these role plays the students involved have proposed some simple rules for avoiding cultural suicide:

----

1. If you've just come back from class, the first thing you should do is ask your friend, partner, family member, or roommate what happened to them while you were away.

2. If your time away has involved this person covering for you in any way, find some way of acknowledging that and returning the favor.

3. Never talk about what happened in class until you're asked directly to do so.

4. If you absolutely cannot follow rule 3, and you feel you really have to share what happened in class, you should make sure that you begin your sharing by talking about moments of anxiety or insecurity. Instead of celebrating the marvelous things happening to you as a student, talk about how you feel like a fraud, how

difficult you find studying, how you fear you won't make it to the end of the semester, and so on. Then, and only then, should you talk about your triumphs and the changes happening to you. This way of disclosing the details of your learning journey heartens rather than threatens.

5. Try to find a small group of peers—just one person is better than no one—who is also going through the experience of being a first-generation college student. Meet with them regularly to do some informal strategizing and to give each other support as you run into problems with hostile friends and family members.

The same logic that informs the avoidance of student cultural suicide applies also to teachers who reenter work spaces determined to share a new idea or practice they have learned in graduate school or at a professional conference. The newly energized teacher often speaks evangelically about her raised awareness, probably using language that is unfamiliar. She is so concerned to share her good news with peers that she ends up almost haranguing them. Very soon after introducing her insight, she starts to sketch out how her colleagues can act on it to change what they do. The combined effect is to make colleagues feel like the victims of an arrogant onslaught unleashed by an egomaniac. Not surprisingly, they beat a retreat.

Adapting the rules for students' survival outlined earlier suggests the following protocol for faculty:

---

1. If you've just come back from an event (for example, a conference) that triggered some important reflection, but that your colleagues did not attend, the first thing you should do is ask them what happened to them while you were away.

2. If your time away has involved colleagues covering for you, find some way of acknowledging that sacrifice and offer to return the favor.

3. Before talking about the event, person, or book that triggered a reflective insight, affirm your colleagues' experience and abilities. Tell them that attending the conference made you realize how much expertise your colleagues have or how any one of them could have been a presenter there. If you have been reading an edited collection, let them know that you feel that they had just as much to say as did the contributors to the volume. This sets an important tone by affirming the experience of the people to whom you are speaking.

4. Introduce information about the new idea or technique that has engaged you by saying how it helped you deal with some feature of your teaching about which you feel embarrassed or worried. Grounding your disclosure in a description of the shortcomings of your own practice does not threaten fragile egos to the point where people feel they have no option but to turn away from you. It prompts colleagues to look critically at their own practice in a way that is invitational and affirming rather than confrontational. If the problem you have been helped with is graphically described in concrete terms, the chances are high that your colleagues will recognize their own dilemmas in the story. Consequently, they will be likely to come to you asking for further details about what you have learned.

5. If possible, use language that you know is familiar and congenial to your colleagues when describing the new technique or idea and its application.

6. At all costs hold back from telling colleagues what they should do. Wait till they start knocking on your door asking for information and advice.

7. Try to find a small group of peers—just one person is better than no one—who share your convictions about the need to work differently. Meet with them regularly to do some informal strategizing and to give each other support as you run into problems with hostile colleagues.

Lost Innocence

Students often come to campus with high hopes. They think that college will turn their lives around, that now they are going to get "truth," and that finally they'll understand how the world really works and who they really are. Going to college is viewed as a transformative marker event that's going to change their lives dramatically for the better by opening up career possibilities and helping them to self-knowledge. However, this sense of confidence is sometimes eroded almost from the first week as these students hear how their teachers describe learning. Many professors stress that there are no right answers and that students will have to discover their own meanings for themselves. When students ask teachers for the correct response to a dilemma or question, teachers often reply "It depends." These same teachers then go on to say that knowledge and ideas cannot be understood in starkly dualistic terms, as either right or wrong. Instead, the world of intellectual inquiry is painted with the grey shades of ambiguity. Students are told that the purpose of a college education is to get them to ask the right questions, not to find the right answers.

As students hear all this they sometimes feel cheated, lost, and confused. Or they just don't believe it. To them the professor is playing a sophisticated and evasive guessing game, pretending not to have the answer and testing the students to see if they have the wherewithal to push him to own up to the truth. When the penny drops and students realize their teachers mean what they say about there being no easy answers, universally correct views, or unequivocally right ways to think, they panic.

This intellectual anxiety attack is a crucial one in students' autobiographies as learners. If they can live through it, they experience an epistemological transformation. Knowledge and truth become seen as contextual and open, as constantly created and recreated in a community of knowers. Students realize their lives as learners will be marked by continual inquiry, questioning of assumptions, and reframing of perspectives, just as their teachers say. However, if students can't face this epistemological reframing, they are at a high risk of dropping out of the whole college experience. Epistemological panic has been neglected in studies of student attrition which focus almost exclusively on the exterior details of students' lives—their financial difficulties, problems with meeting college schedules, lack of preparedness for taking responsibility for their own learning, and so on. These factors are crucial, and their importance should never be underestimated, but the interior factor of lost innocence should also not be forgotten.

Roadrunning

As learners speak about how they experience learning new skills, knowledge, and concepts, they describe a rhythm that might be called incremental fluctuation. Put colloquially, this learning rhythm can be understood as one where the learner takes two steps forward, one step back, followed by four steps forward, one step back, followed by one step forward, three steps back, and so on in a series of irregular fluctuations marked by overall progress. It is a rhythm of learning that is distinguished by a gradually increased ability to learn new skills and knowledge juxtaposed with regular interruptions and dissonances when it seems progress is impossible. When these apparent regressions to earlier ways of thinking and acting take place, they are felt as devastatingly final. Instead of being viewed as the inconvenient interludes they really are, they seem like the end point of the process. Learners believe they will never "get it," that the learning concerned is "beyond them." They are tempted to return to tried and trusted ways of thinking on the grounds that even if these didn't always work or make sense at least they were familiar and comfortable.

The way this halting, jagged, incrementally fluctuating rhythm of learning is spoken of reminds me of the long-running Warner Brothers *Road Runner* cartoon. In the cartoon the same scene is repeated endlessly. The Road Runner is hurtling along the highway, his "beep beep" cry raising Wile E. Coyote's frustration to ever higher levels. The Road Runner comes to the edge of a canyon and, because he's possessed of supernatural powers, he leaves solid ground to go into mid-air. Suspended several hundred feet above the canyon floor, he turns around and makes a face at the coyote who is himself coming to the rim of the canyon.

The coyote's adrenaline is already pumping through his veins with the thrill of the chase, and he becomes even more incensed by the Road Runner's evident temerity. The coyote picks up his speed and hurtles off the edge of the canyon into thin air in frantic pursuit of the Road Runner, his legs pedaling in space. After about three seconds, however, the coyote realizes his situation. He freezes, looks down at the canyon floor several hundred feet below, and then looks back at the camera with a goofy, quizzical, deflated expression. Realizing the nature of his situation causes an immediate existential crisis. Until he realizes where he is, he's safe. But at the moment of awareness of his situation hundreds of feet in mid-air, physics and perception cohere and the law of gravity takes effect. He plunges to the canyon floor, and the screen is a mess of limbs and disconnected but bloodless body parts. In the next frame, of course, we see that the coyote has been magically reassembled off camera and that the chase has begun anew.

The moment when Wile E. Coyote realizes his predicament and crashes to the canyon floor has the same emotional quality as a particular moment in the incremental rhythm of student learning. It is the moment when students realize that the old ways of thinking and acting no longer make sense for them, but that new ones have not yet formed to take their place. This state of limbo—similar to the coyote's suspension several hundred feet above the canyon floor—is frighteningly uncertain.

Like the coyote, students experience the beginnings of college with boundless energy and an optimistic sense of how it will make their lives better. Entranced by the prospect of transformation—of learning new skills and knowledge that will open new employment opportunities, bring self-knowledge, or help them develop self-confidence—they embrace the changes they know college entails. As they begin struggling to discard or reformulate assumptions and understandings that now seem not to explain the world adequately, there is a sense of forward movement, of progress toward true clarity of perception. The struggle to learn, with its attendant aspects of impostorship, cultural suicide, and lost innocence, is seen as worthwhile because of the transformative fruits it will bear.

But as students leave behind the solid ground of their old ways of thinking and acting, their enthusiasm sometimes turns to terror. They realize that they have nothing that supports them. Their previously solid and stable assumptive clusters and skill sets have evaporated, but no substitutes have solidified to take their place. This is the moment when their confidence drains away. They crash to the floor of their emotional canyons resolving never to go through this experience again.

However, in the same way that the coyote is reassembled off camera to begin the chase anew in the next frame, so the quest for learning is not put off so easily. Sooner or later, students are confronted by whatever hopes and dreams, or niggling anomalies or discrepancies, that spurred them to enroll in college in the first place. Learning begins anew, but this time students know that at some point they will find themselves perched precariously above the canyon floor. Out of such knowledge comes the ability to stay dangling for a few seconds longer than was formerly the case and the forethought to bring along a parachute in the form of a supportive learning community.

Surviving the Rhythms of Roadrunning

Time and time again, as students speak about their crashing to the canyon floor, it becomes clear that the people who pick them up, dust them off, and set them back on track are their peers. The importance in college of belonging to an emotionally sustaining peer learning community cannot be overstated. "Community" might seem a rather grandiose word to describe the clusters of four or five good friends that students say they value so highly. But the emphasis the members of these groups place on the emotional warmth and psychological security they provide makes the term "community" more appropriate than, say, "network."

The important thing about these small communities is that they reassure their members that their private anxieties are commonly experienced. Through talking about their individual experiences of learning, students come to know that crashing to the canyon floor is a predictable moment, not an idiosyncratic event. Learners lucky enough to be members of emotionally sustaining peer learning communities speak of them as "a second family" or "the only people who really know what I'm going through." These communities provide a safe haven, an emotional buttress against the lowest moments in their autobiographies as learners.

Teachers who know the rhythms of their semester well can also help, particularly if they can predict when a substantial number of learners will be crashing to the canyon floor. They can let students know that this will happen and prepare them for it by giving time and space in class to describe this process and to assure students that to feel this way is normal. They can also bring former students into class for a brief period to say how they felt when they were at this stage of their learning, and how they survived the crash to the canyon floor. Teachers can also foster the development of conversations by providing lists of students' phone numbers, e-mail, and home addresses to course members.

When I taught on a commuter campus in New York, I would compile a list of subway routes that students took to get to and from class. Since many students were concerned about personal safety when riding the subway, I suggested they form traveling parties based on shared routes. My intuition was that as they were walking to and from the subway the topic of conversation that would come easiest to them would be the one experience they all shared—being students in my course. Such conversations would be relatively relaxed environments in which students could disclose their anxieties about the learning involved in the course. In online teaching I also make sure students have a student-only listserv or chat room to which they have access so that they can talk about their emotional responses out of the direct gaze of the teacher.

A Final Comment

As should be clear from this chapter, emotions are rampant in the college classroom. Even if students appear calm, you can't assume from their demeanor that learning is being experienced by them in bloodless, wholly rational, or exclusively cognitive ways. If you regularly collect CIQ forms from students, it will soon be apparent which learning activities are emotionally laden. In reporting back CIQ responses, students' emotional reactions and rhythms can be named and presented as normal and predictable. Through this reporting back process, students can be helped to realize that what they thought were private anxieties are shared by those sitting next to them. Even if no advice on how to deal with these anxieties is given, just knowing that others share these is reassuring and calming.

Never to feel pain, or only to feel pleasure in the classroom, is a wholly unrealistic expectation that experience is bound quickly to upset. hooks (1994) has written about the bourgeois decorum that many of us view as the emotional template for college classrooms, and our fear that when emotions are displayed it is a sign that things are, by definition, out of control. This chapter has argued that the opposite is true—that teaching and learning are highly emotional activities that bring forth strong responses and that to feel such emotions is predictable and normal, a sign that you are alive and alert in the classroom. Indeed, it is no exaggeration to say that if classrooms are experienced as emotion-free zones of practice, then something essential to the process of learning and teaching is missing.

6

Lecturing Creatively

As the twenty-first century dawned, prognosticators in higher education predicted confidently that the digital era would see a massive diminution of face-to-face teaching. It was assumed that something as mundane as lecturing would be consigned to the graveyard of pedagogic history and replaced by online teaching formats geared to student convenience. The Internet was expected to be the final nail in the coffin of uninterrupted, mind-numbing teacher-talk delivered in a sleep-inducing monotone. Yet, for having been declared dead, the corpse of lecture-based teaching shows remarkable signs of life. Those who periodically read the last rites on the method usually find themselves resuscitating it, much to their surprise.

Lecturing can certainly be done abominably. But just because something is done badly by some teachers in some classrooms does not mean the method as a whole is inherently flawed. To think that all lecturing is bad and that all attempts at discussion-based learning are good is to exercise a myopic dualism as simplistic as the "Four Legs Good, Two Legs Bad" mantra in Orwell's *Animal Farm*. Lecturing can certainly be abused and discussion can certainly be engaging and enlightening, but in and of themselves neither are innately good nor bad ways to teach. One of the traps that advocates of discussion methods often fall into is that of setting up a false dichotomy between lecturing and discussion. They give the impression that anyone who lectures combines the moral sensitivity of Caligula with the democratic impulses of Joseph Stalin. If you lecture, so their argument goes, you only serve to confirm your authoritarian, demagogic tendencies. This is a disservice to well-intentioned colleagues and a gross misunderstanding of pedagogic dynamics. Exhorting colleagues to stop lecturing altogether and only use discussion methods forces teachers to make a choice between two apparently mutually exclusive options.

This simplistic pedagogic bifurcation is wrong. Lectures are not by definition oppressive and authoritarian. And lecturers are not, by definition, demagogues. Similarly, discussions are not, by definition, liberating and spontaneous. And discussion leaders are not, by definition, democratic. You have probably been a participant in discussions where the leader manipulated the group to reach certain predefined conclusions, what Paterson (1970) described as counterfeit discussions. Through their power to control the flow of talk, to summarize and reframe students' comments, and to respond favorably to some contributions and unfavorably to others, discussion leaders can act in extremely authoritarian ways. To borrow a term from Foucault (1980), discussion leaders act as judges of normality. So instead of reducing questions of pedagogic method to a simplistic dichotomy—discussion good, lecture bad—these two methods should be seen as symbiotic.

The critique of lecturing as inducing passivity and turning students into objects is often associated with Paulo Freire. In his classic *Pedagogy of the Oppressed* (1993), Freire explored the concept of "banking education" in which lecturers assumed learners' minds were like empty vaults waiting for knowledge to be deposited in them. His view was that banking education cast students as passive recipients of knowledge rather than active constructors of learning. However, it is often forgotten that Freire later clarified his position to observe "We have to recognize that not all kinds of lecturing is banking education. You can still be very critical lecturing. . . . The question is not banking lectures or no lectures, because traditional teachers will make reality opaque whether they lecture or lead discussions. A liberating teacher will illuminate reality even if he or she lectures. The question is the content and dynamism of the lecture, the approach to the object to be known. Does it critically re-orient students to society? Does it animate their critical thinking or not?" (Shor and Freire, 1987, p. 40). So, as Freire reminds us, an abused method calls into question the expertise of those abusing it, not the validity of the method itself. The challenge is to make our lectures as helpful, enlivening, and critically stimulating as possible.

We should also remember that the lecture is not a unitary method. In fact its only unifying characteristic is that it involves sustained periods of teacher talk. Such talk can, however, be conducted in a variety of forms. At times it is highly sequential, an intellectual road map that guides students past the trail markers along the way to an eventual destination. It can also take quite the opposite form, beginning with the expression of a position or explanation of a concept and then tracing its intellectual adherents in terms of previous understandings or evidence. At other times it resembles an extemporaneous improvisation in which teachers explore associations that occur to them as they speak or that are prompted by their response to student questions. Occasionally it is deliberately theatrical, a way of piquing interest. It can also take the form of a spiraling critical debate, with the lecturer presenting one position supported by convincing evidence, then vigorously articulating the opposite view supported by equally persuasive data, then responding to that opposite position, then critiquing that view, and so on. It also frequently begins with the lecturer posing a problem of the day and then exploring different ways of responding to this.

Be Clear About Why We Lecture

When we use any teaching approach, we need to be clear exactly what it's intended to achieve. This clarity should not be apparent just to us, it should also be apparent to students. As Farrah (2004) points out, lectures are a good way to create windows into the instructor's mind, something Chapter Four described as central to building both teacher credibility and authenticity. So a lecture should begin with a statement to students as to why it is being used and what it is intended to accomplish. Its relevance to course goals, its connection to some part of the syllabus, and its relevance to earlier lectures, discussions, or assignments can all be clarified for students at the outset of the session.

In his classic review of research into lecturing, Bligh (2000) argues that its primary function is to introduce information to learners, not to prompt or develop skills of critical analysis, synthesis, or integration. In fact, as an advocate of lecturing Bligh argues that it should be used relatively sparingly and that "it behooves lecturers to lecture less . . . and create opportunities, in lessons and outside, in which thinking can flourish" (p. 182). He also cites research, supported by others such as Race (2000, 2001) and Brown and Race (2002) that no lecture should entail more than twenty-minute blocks of uninterrupted teacher talk.

So why should we consider using lectures as an element of our teaching? Some of the most frequently proposed reasons are as follows:

To establish the broad outline of a body of material. Here the lecture is positioned at the outset of a course, or module within a course, to survey the intellectual terrain that students will be traversing in the next few weeks or months. This kind of lecture presents students with contrasting schools of thought, groups a confusing variety of positions into general interpretive categories, and makes the case for focusing on some of these over others. Such a lecture is particularly important if students are being asked to make choices about future independent study projects. It functions as a sort of intellectual relief map outlining the territory and topography waiting to be traversed in the weeks ahead.

To explain, with frequent examples, concepts that are hard for learners to understand. This can be done prior to students' own struggles with such concepts or after their initial engagement with them through individual study.

To introduce alternative perspectives and interpretations. This kind of lecture can review the different positions in a debate prior to a more detailed analysis of these or to advance a view that is critical of material that has been studied previously.

To model intellectual attitudes and behaviors you wish to encourage in students. Here the lecture is used to model critical thinking through the lecturer regularly critiquing her own position, playing devil's advocate against her previously articulated comments, or demonstrating to students how she deconstructs the prevailing groupthink in an area of study. If you want students to be critical of their own ideas, to be ready to cite the evidence that supports their arguments, and to be open to exploring alternative perspectives that are inconvenient to their positions, then you must be ready to model these actions in your lectures and to explain to students that this is what you're doing. Also, by publicly grappling with complex ideas and talking of your difficulties understanding these, you can show learners that encountering problems in the struggle for under- standing is neither a sign of failure nor source of shame.

To encourage learners' interest in a topic. A lecture can be an inspir- ing, galvanizing event that conveys your personal animation and pas- sion for a topic. As Bligh (2000) writes, in a lecture "there's only one thing more contagious than enthusiasm, and that's the lack of it" (p. 59). The lecture can also be used to demonstrate to learners the rel- evance of an area of study by connecting the new knowledge to stu- dents' current or previous experiences or by showing its centrality to the chief purposes of a class. The lecturer can also use the lecture to make clear her own conviction that the topic is so important that she wishes students to understand it thoroughly—a crucial indicator of credibility as demonstrated in Chapter Four.

Characteristics of Helpful Lectures

To understand how lectures can be helpful to students' learning, we need to consult those students and find out from their point of view the features that are most conducive to learning. Research on this topic (Bligh, 2000; Race, 2000, 2001; Brown and Race, 2002; Farrah, 2004) indicates that students believe helpful lectures exhibit the following characteristics:

- They use a variety of teaching and communication processes.

- They are clearly organized so students can follow the thread of the lecturer's thought.

- The lecturer clearly models learning behaviors expected in the course.

Using a Mix of Teaching and Communication Approaches

Given that students clearly have different learning styles, varying communication styles and modalities in a lecture has long been argued as an essential component of good practice. In any lecture I would advocate that at least three different approaches or modalities be used. Any more than this and the lecture is experienced as too fractured, any less and interest declines. Some simple ways to introduce variety are to use plenty of visual aids (such as overhead graphics, PowerPoint mini-presentations, cartoons, and brief film clips), to introduce occasional guest speakers, to play audio extracts from tapes, radio, or web broadcasts or other lectures, to use Internet video-streaming clips, and to provide frequent pauses for student responses and questions. Four particularly useful options are discussed below.

Deliberately Introduce Periods of Silence

One barrier to learning in lectures is teachers' belief that learning results from continuous teacher talk. For more reflective or introverted learners, or for those who process new information best by having plenty of time to mull it over and connect it to their existing experience and stock of knowledge, periods of reflective silence are crucial. For such learners too much teacher talk mystifies and confuses rather than clarifies. Teachers need to learn the very hard lesson that silence does not represent a vacuum in learning or indicate complete disengagement. It signifies a different but often a significant and intense engagement with the topic of the lecture. Many students prefer a "chunked" approach that divides the lecture into a series of ten- to fifteen-minute blocks with a brief silent interlude following each expository "chunk."

There are various ways we can introduce helpful silence into our lectures. We can tell students they need a minute to think about how to answer a question we have just asked them, and then we take that full minute before asking for responses from the floor. After every twenty minutes or so of uninterrupted lecture, we can call for two or three minutes of silent reflective speculation. During this time students are asked to think about the preceding twenty minutes and write down the most important point they felt was made, or the most puzzling assertion that was expressed, or the question they most would like to ask. At the end of these few minutes of silent reflection, students can either spend a couple of minutes sharing their ideas in pairs or triads, or they can volunteer to speak these to the whole class, or they can write them down and pass them to the lecturer and have her read out a random selection. The next section of the lecture would then have these responses incorporated into its content.

Introduce Buzz Groups into Lectures

The pairs or triads mentioned above are often referred to as buzz groups—small groups that buzz with purposeful conversation at various times during a lecture. Buzz groups can be used at different points in a lecture. At the outset they can generate questions students hope will be answered in the lecture, perhaps based on assigned prereading. At the end they can be used as the vehicle for

sharing individual responses to the Muddiest Point exercise discussed in Chapter Three. Buzz groups interspersed throughout the
lecture usually ask students to make some judgments regarding the
relative merits, relevance, or usefulness of the constituent elements
of the lecture. Examples of such questions are:

- What's the most contentious statement you've heard so
  far in the lecture today?

- What's the most unsupported assertion you've heard in
  the lecture so far?

- What assumptions do you see as underlying the arguments made so far?

Other buzz groups can focus on deepening students' understanding by asking group members to propose some examples that
illustrate a particular concept that has been addressed in the previous twenty minutes of lecture. Sometimes I deliberately insert an
assertion into my lecture chunk that I know to be empirically
wrong, ethically dubious, or contradictory to the rest of the lecture,
and then I ask students to discuss in buzz groups what the deliberate error in that chunk might be.

In buzz groups students usually take turns giving a brief response
to the question asked or task demanded and then note if one
response draws particular agreement or produces significant conflict.
When the two- to three-minute buzz group period is up, the lecturer
asks for random responses to the questions asked or task set. She
then faces the challenge of integrating these responses into the body
of her comments that comprise the next chunk of the lecture.

Lecture from Siberia

In his book *When Students Have Power* (1996), Ira Shor describes
the Siberia zone that exists in every college classroom. This is the

part of the classroom furthest away from the teacher's body, usually the last row of the auditorium or the seat in class by the door at the back of the room. If the teacher's body or desk represents Moscow, the center of Party authority, then the seat by the door represents Siberia, the territorial area furthest from central authority. Unlike the case of the old Soviet Union, however, students are not exiled to Siberia as punishment for their thought crimes. Instead they choose to locate themselves there so as to be as far away from teacher surveillance as possible. Their assumption is that it will be harder for them to be noticed, or called on, if they exile themselves to this zone. The student micro-sleeps that Bligh (2000) describes as occurring regularly in every lecture are taken much more easily in Siberia.

Shor describes how he deals with Siberia by moving there and speaking from that zone. Doing this is a dramatic, powerful gesture, one that breaks with the thousands of hours students have experienced listening to, or ignoring, the teacher standing or sitting at the front of the room by the chalkboard. Energy, and often panic, immediately rise when the lecturer works from Siberia, and micro-sleeps are much harder to take. Moving your position around the room can be a very effective way of engaging student attention.

Break Lectures into Ten- to Fifteen-Minute "Chunks"

In his meta-analysis of attention spans in lectures, Bligh (2000) proposes approximately twelve minutes as the optimum period of time in which students can be expected to focus on one idea or subtheme. In terms of planning our time, then, it might be useful to think about ways of "chunking" lectures into a series of fifteen-minute expositions interspersed with a number of linking or bridging activities. Some of these linking interludes might be buzz groups, periods for audience questions, reflective silences, the use of a visual illustration, the lecturer moving to another part of the room to make a new point, and so on. Here's a plan for such a sixty-minute lecture.

Minutes 1–5: Audience Research. Give a pop quiz that asks students to choose the correct answer to a factual or interpretive problem you pose based on the lecture's theme or some assigned prereading, and then give the real answers; or talk about the way an element of last week's Critical Incident Questionnaire responses connects to the theme of today's lecture.

Minutes 5–20: First Formal Presentation. Explore the lecture's major theme with one or two illustrative examples.

Minutes 20–25: Audience Questions. This can be preceded by one or two minutes of silent student reflection.

Minutes 25–40: Second Formal Presentation. Explore the second major theme.

Minutes 40–45: Buzz Groups. Students discuss the most important or muddiest point covered so far or the assumptions underlying the first two major themes.

Minutes 45–50: Respond to Buzz Groups' Comments.

Minutes 50–55: Recap of Major Points. This is followed by the lecturer's raising questions about her lecture, pointing out omissions, and acknowledging unaddressed ethical dilemmas.

Minutes 55–60: CIQ.

Organizing Lectures So Students Can Follow the Lecturer's Train of Thought

One of the most frequently mentioned features of good lectures is the clarity of their organization. There is nothing students hate more than sitting in a lecture feeling like they have lost the plot, that they are being swamped by masses of meaningless material in which they can discern no pattern. Two ways to deal with this difficulty are to provide handouts that supply the scaffolding for the lecture and to provide plenty of verbal signals when new points, changes in direction, or important caveats are being made.

Scaffolding Notes

Scaffolding notes are skeletal notes that summarize the contours of a lecture for students. They are provided beforehand either electronically or in paper form and give enough information so that students can follow the lecture's progress but not so much as to make actually showing up a duplication of effort. Often the notes are a summary of the main headings and subheadings of a lecture with space provided for students to write in their own examples, illustrations, and questions. Below is an example of scaffolding notes for a lecture on critical thinking.

Exhibit 1.   Scaffolding Notes for a Lecture on Critical Thinking

SECTION A: Understanding Critical Thinking

How Do People Define Critical Thinking?
The process of identifying and checking the assumptions underlying our ideas, beliefs, and actions, and those of others.
Example:

What Are Assumptions?
Paradigmatic (structuring, taken for granted)
Example:

Prescriptive (assumptions about what ought to be)
Example:

Causal (assumptions about cause and effect)
Example:

Why Is Critical Thinking Important?
For our intellectual development

To make sure our actions are informed

To hold authority accountable—"speaking truth to power"

To create democracy

(continued)

Exhibit 1.   Scaffolding Notes for a Lecture on Critical Thinking (continued)

SECTION B: Traditions of Criticality

What Intellectual Traditions Inform Criticality?
  a. Critical Theory—being critical is challenging dominant ideology that helps maintain an iniquitous, unjust system

  b. Psychoanalysis—being critical is understanding how adult development is stifled by inhibitions learned in childhood

  c. Analytic Philosophy—being critical is knowing when arguments are well structured and recognizing logical fallacies

  d. Pragmatism—being critical is constantly reexamining assumptions in light of new experience and being ready to experiment continually with new ways of creating beautiful social forms

In what ways do these traditions contradict each other?

SECTION C: How Is Critical Thinking Experienced?

Incremental Fluctuation—two steps forward, one step back
Example:

Context-Specific—can be critical in one domain and uncritical in another
Example:

Unsettling—ambiguous and continuous
Example:

SECTION D: Questions About Critical Thinking

  1. Ethical dimensions—should we push this on people who resist it?

  2. Eurocentric—a European intellectual construct?

  3. Freeze—does it lead to a relativistic freeze on action?

  4. Language—alienating, confusing, obfuscating?

Give Clear Verbal Signals

The kinds of signals I am talking about here are indications that an important point is being made or that a major change of direction is now being initiated. Bligh (2000) distinguishes between global signals (those that inform students a new section or change of direction is now being broached), key point signals (those that emphasize that one of the main points of the lecture is now being made), and local signals (those that refer to subpoints or more detailed elaborations of key points). Other signals are aside signals (those that alert students that you are branching off into a point that you find intriguing but that is not central to the main themes being covered), example signals (that tell students you are going to illustrate an idea with one or two specific examples), and meta-review signals (a form of global signal that quickly summarizes where we are in our plan for the day's lecture).

Model Learning Behaviors

One of the mantras of skillful teaching is that teachers must model publicly their own commitment to, and engagement in, the learning activities they are seeking to encourage in their students. Lectures can be used transparently and intentionally to draw students' attention to the kinds of behaviors you are expecting of them in subsequent discussions, team presentations, and homework assignments. It is important to remember, though, that you must regularly explain to learners when you are seeking to model the behaviors you regard as important. This means interjecting phrases such as "Now I'm going to try to lay bare the assumptions my position is based on," "Now I'm going to discuss the piece of evidence I find the most convincing for this point of view," "Now I want to look at this issue from a completely different viewpoint that calls into question a lot of what I've been saying up to now," and so on. We can't expect learners to see into our minds unless we open up a window for them by telling them what we're doing. Four opportunities to model desired learning behaviors are given below.

Begin Every Lecture with a Question or Questions That You're Trying to Answer

This allows you to position the lecture as an example of active intellectual inquiry as much as a passive transfer of information. Posing two or three central questions that the lecture will address at the outset of your talk means you frame your comments as part of your continuous effort to make sense of a subject. This tells students that you see education as a never-ending process of inquiry in which you're constantly trying to come to a point of greater understanding, all the while acknowledging that whatever truths you claim are provisional and temporary. Moreover, if students are used to seeing you open all your lectures by raising a series of framing questions, they'll be very open to this tactic when you begin discussions by posing a question or questions to be explored.

End Every Lecture with a Series of Questions That Your Lecture Has Raised or Left Unanswered

Lecturers are often told that the golden rule of effective lecturing is to "tell 'em what you're going to tell 'em, tell 'em, then tell 'em what you've just told 'em." The problem with this rule is that it commodifies knowledge as a neatly bounded package of facts or concepts. Doing this is inimical to intellectual inquiry, particularly to the student's ability to make connections across subject areas and disciplines. Even more worryingly, ending with a summary of what's already been said establishes a sense of definitive closure, of the last word having been spoken on the subject.

I argue that good lecturers end their presentations not only by recapping the territory that has been crossed but also by pointing out all the new routes that have been opened by the content of the lecture, and also by pointing out which of the questions posed at the start of the lecture have been left unanswered or been reframed in a more provocative or contentious way. This prepares students for the same practice in discussion where conversation sessions can be ended by asking students to volunteer the questions the discussion has raised for them (rather than by giving a summary of "what we've learned today in our discussion"). If possible, lecturers should spend the last ten minutes of a lecture asking students to write down the questions the lecture has raised for them, and then find a way to make some of these public. Students can be asked to speak their questions to the whole class, they can be asked to share them with each other in small buzz groups of two or three, or they can write them down, pass them to the lecturer, and have the lecturer read out a random selection.

But even if none of these things are possible, your own behavior of finishing a lecture with a list of new questions the lecture raises for you, or ending with an acknowledgment of the omissions, ethical dilemmas, and contradictions that challenge what you've just articulated, is a powerful piece of modeling. You should be warned, though, that initially students will probably be very critical of this behavior. On CIQs they will record their frustration that the lecture didn't end with a clear recap of the main points. They will see your behavior of ending with questions or raising problems as unnecessarily confusing, as pulling the rug out from under their feet. Over time, as you consistently explain how doing these things is your best attempt to model the spirit of critical inquiry you are trying to encourage in learners, students' frustration will often diminish (though it will never disappear).

Deliberately Introduce Alternative Perspectives

Lectures can be used to model a willingness to consider different viewpoints or explore alternative perspectives seriously and nondefensively. One way to do this is to present as part of your lecture any arguments that counter our own assertions. A dramatic and theatrical approach is to state your opening position while you stand in one part of the room, and then to move to another part of the room, look back at where you were standing, and then direct a second set of comments back at that spot. This second set of comments should be the articulation of a different perspective on what you've just said that places an alternative interpretation on it or opens up questions about it. You say things like "However, if we look at this idea from another point of view we see that . . ." or "A whole other interpretation of this argument is possible that calls many of its central assumptions into question." You can also use this as an opportunity to model critical analysis by presenting counterarguments or rebuttals. When you do this you address your imaginary other self by name and say things like "Stephen, what you're omitting to mention is . . . " or "Of course Stephen, you could pursue a very different line of reasoning if you argue that . . . "

Another approach is to bring a colleague (or colleagues) into your lecture who disagrees with your presentation and give them some air time to speak their views. By listening respectfully and then following their presentations with a brief period of discussion in which you acknowledge and explore your differences, you model the kind of respectful attention to diverse perspectives that you hope will be paralleled in subsequent student discussions.

Introduce Periods of Assumption Hunting

One of the most frequently articulated purposes of higher education is to encourage critical thinking by students. A central part of this process involves students identifying and scrutinizing the assumptions that inform their ideas and actions. We can show students what this looks like by first introducing periods of assumption hunting into our lectures. These are times when we stop professing what we believe and spend a few minutes in a "time out" compiling the assumptions on which our beliefs rest, and musing out loud in front of our students on how we might investigate these. When students see us identifying our assumptions and subjecting them to critical scrutiny, it gets them used to the idea that doing this is a regular part of discussion seminars and written assignments.

Assessing Your Lecturing

Probably the best way to improve your lecturing is to see yourself lecture. There are several ways you can do this. One is to use the Critical Incident Questionnaires your students complete to explore what it is you are doing that students find helpful or hindering. A second is to invite a colleague you trust into your classroom to observe you lecturing. You should instruct that colleague as to how she can be most helpful by letting her know the things you would most like feedback on (such as the clarity of your explanations, your ability to project to the back of the lecture hall, your appropriate use of examples, your pacing, your ability to encourage student questions, your use of eye contact, or your variety of vocal modulation) as well as anything else she feels you should know. Peer observers should be careful to let you know what you did well as well as what needs to be improved.

But probably the most useful approach is to arrange to have yourself videotaped as you deliver a lecture. It is relatively easy to arrange this and, as long as you don't roam too much, need not even involve someone else to operate the camera. Videotaping yourself allows you to become aware of your visual and verbal tics that you may be unaware of but that students find annoying. If videotaping is not feasible, you can make an audiotape of your lecture and listen for ways to improve your pacing, pitch, and delivery. In my experience there is nothing more dramatic or revealing than seeing yourself give a lecture on tape. Sometimes it is embarrassing but it is never less than instructive.

In my own case videotaping made me aware of lifelong habits I have struggled to break: looking at the floor or in middle distance while explaining a particularly difficult point, and answering questions with mini-lectures that are often far too long and meandering. On the other hand videotaping has also underscored my determination to include plenty of practices that seem to play well on tape. These include providing frequent autobiographical examples, programming time for student questions by deliberately allowing silent, reflective interludes, and finishing my lectures by raising questions about, and pointing out omissions in, the comments I have just made.

7

Preparing Students for Discussion

For teachers who prize participatory learning, discussion is the jewel in the crown of the engaged classroom. It appears to equalize student-teacher power relationships, to affirm the validity of students' opinions, to get learners used to grappling with diverse (and sometimes contradictory) perspectives, and to encourage students to take responsibility for the development of their own judgments. For some of its advocates, classroom discussion has an even wider political resonance as constituting a democratic learning laboratory. Indeed, the subtitle of a book I co-authored—*Discussion as a Way of Teaching: Tools and Techniques for Democratic Classrooms* (Brookfield and Preskill, 2005)—illustrates my own belief that discussion-based classrooms can help prepare learners for the process of participatory democracy. Social philosophers such as Jürgen Habermas (1992) argue that the same basic rules of full, free, and equal discourse that govern good classroom discussion constitute an ideal speech situation that can also be applied to judging whether or not the wider community is reaching its economic, social, and political decisions in a fair and morally defensible way. For him good discussion, and therefore good democratic process, depends on everyone contributing, on everyone having the fullest possible knowledge of different perspectives, and on everyone being ready to give up their position if a better argument is presented to them. The adult educator Eduard Lindeman ([1945], 1988) anticipated Habermas, claiming that learning to participate in discussion was integral to the maintenance of democracy and, hence, to world peace.

When I read the words of Habermas and Lindeman, and then I look at the discussions that occur in my own courses, the chasm between their rhetorically uplifting vision and the reality of my own classroom sometimes seems unbridgeable. Many times I have been in nominal charge of classrooms where the students in my discussions appeared distracted, bored, even actively hostile. In such classrooms uncomfortable silence was far more common than engaged conversation. My brilliantly framed, teasingly provocative questions were usually met with a complete lack of response. When this happened I would usually panic (after carefully and silently counting off my wait time of fifteen or twenty seconds, which seemed like an eternity) and then answer questions myself by producing a series of elegant disquisitions on the topic of the day. In situations like these the students quickly learned they needn't bother actually answering my questions since I did such a good job of it myself!

This dark side of discussion is laid out in Michel Foucault's analysis of the microdynamics of power. Foucault (1980) argues that in modern society people learn to internalize norms (including norms governing discussion participation) that serve to keep existing structures intact. In higher education the norm of good discussion equates participation with extraversion and intelligence with an articulate command of academic jargon. It holds that discussion is distinguished by garrulous and confident speakers who talk cogently about ideas and concepts covered in lectures and assigned reading, and who then testify as to how these illustrate central themes of the content studied. If this norm is unchallenged by teachers, it quickly establishes an unequal pecking order of contributions in the group and creates a negative conversational dynamic. Students who want a good grade will do their best to exemplify this norm by taking up as much of the available airtime as they can. They will monitor themselves, and others, to gauge how they are doing in the discussion performance stakes, turning the conversation into a competitive intellectual game. In effect, they will exercise what Foucault calls disciplinary power on themselves; that is, they will watch themselves to make sure they are behaving in the way they feel the discussion leader (the judge of what constitutes good participation) desires.

If teachers assign part of a grade for discussion "participation," without defining what participation looks like, this will immediately activate the norm that defines participation as speaking frequently and confidently. Learners invariably interpret the teacher's injunction to participate as meaning that they (the students) should do their best to exemplify this norm of loquacity. So they carefully rehearse stunningly insightful contributions that will make them sound profound and informed. Discussion teachers then often deploy a range of subtle, nonverbal behaviors to signify approval or disapproval of participants' efforts to conform to the norm. Through nods, frowns, eye contact (or the lack of it), sighs of frustration or pity, grunts of agreement, disbelieving intakes of breath at the obvious stupidity of a particular comment, and a wide range of other gestures, discussion leaders communicate to group members when they are close to, or moving away from, the norm.

Unless discussion leaders redefine criteria for discussion participation to challenge this norm, learners will work assiduously to gear their behavior towards its realization. Discussion groups always contain potentially powerful psychodynamics and can easily become competitive emotional battlegrounds, gladiatorial arenas in which participants verbally slug it out to gain recognition and affirmation from the teacher. Sometimes the frequency of a student's verbal contributions—almost regardless of their lucidity or relevance—becomes the criterion for judging participation. Furthermore, unless the pattern of participation is deliberately disrupted in the first couple of meetings of the course, the pecking order is firmly established by the third meeting. This pecking order is powerfully self-fulfilling; the longer a student remains silent, the more intimidating becomes the prospect of speaking.

These problematic elements of discussion are not just elements of Foucault's analysis, they are also my life! As a student I was so unconfident and shy in discussions, and so aware of the norm prescribing that good group members only made profound comments, that I never wanted to say anything unless I could guarantee that my contribution would be met with universal acclaim and admiration. Consequently, I would find out the topic of the discussion beforehand, carefully rehearse some stunningly insightful contribution, and then arrive at the discussion site ready to be the first person in the group to blurt out my comments. That way I knew I would register a check mark on the teacher's sociometric mental map as having participated in the requisite manner the norm implied. Also, if I could be the first to speak, my comments would not suffer by comparison with previous contributions. Unfortunately, my wishfully penetrating and sophisticated interjections often had little to do with the way the leader opened the discussion on any particular day, and I was left looking and feeling foolish. So much energy expended on such a meaningless performance! In this situation learning was the last thing I had in mind where discussions were concerned. Performing, not learning, was the point. In this chapter and the next, I lay out some ideas to stop students' channeling their energies into the kinds of pointless performances I engaged in during my own college discussions.

When to Use Discussion

Discussion is not suitable for all pedagogic ends. If you wish to introduce students to a highly detailed body of new knowledge, or to teach them complex instrumental skills, there are much better ways to accomplish these things than through a discussion. Neither is initiating students into a predefined body of truths, facts, or ideas a good use of discussion. The reasons to use discussion can be grouped into three categories—intellectual, emotional, and sociopolitical.

Intellectual Purposes

To Engage Students in Exploring a Diversity of Perspectives

Discussion is one of the most effective ways to make students aware of the range of interpretations that are possible in an area of intellectual inquiry. Teachers can introduce these diverse perspectives themselves through lecturing or prereading, but there is nothing like students hearing from each others' lips the diversity of interpretations that can be made of the same, apparently objective, facts, or the same, apparently obvious, meanings. It's much harder for learners to ignore views that are contrary to their own if they're expressed by their peers, rather than being discovered between the pages of a text or mediated through a lecturer's comments. The physical presence of equals with inconvenient opinions is a powerful force. We cannot skip or skim contrary views that are expressed in discussion by peers in the same way we can skip a few paragraphs in a book or tune out parts of a lecture.

To Increase Students' Awareness of, and Tolerance for, Ambiguity and Complexity

A good discussion is one that leaves issues open for further inquiry and in which as many questions are raised as are answered. If participants begin a discussion with definitive views, they should conclude it with a productively disturbing sense of equivocation. They should learn that the topics explored are complex and that our understanding of them is contingent, always requiring further study and reflection. Through repeatedly illuminating how judgments and arguments are constantly evolving, discussions help students learn to tolerate the ambiguities inherent in so much intellectual inquiry.

To Help Students Recognize and Investigate Their Assumptions

In discussion we enjoy multiple opportunities to clarify and scrutinize each others' assumptions. Students can serve as critical mirrors for each other reflecting back the assumptions they see in each other's positions. As students question each other about the reasons, evidence, and experiences that lie behind the comments each makes, they start to realize that seemingly random viewpoints are always grounded in assumptive clusters. They learn that what different people consider obvious, factually true, or common sense, depends very much on the different assumptions they hold.

To Increase Intellectual Agility and Openness

Engaging in discussion requires a certain intellectual agility—an ability to think on your feet and to react to unanticipated comments. Students know this, and it's one of the reasons why some of them fear discussion so much. They realize that they can't anticipate the range of responses and questions that their comments will bring forth. Since it's almost impossible to frame a contribution so perfectly that everyone will agree with every aspect of it, students know that what they say will sometimes be challenged, contradicted, even negated. This means they'll have to think quickly to formulate a counterresponse or to mount a defense against arguments that are new to them.

Of course, it's quite permissible in a discussion to ask for time to formulate an informed and useful response. We can say to someone, "Before I reply to you I need some time to think about what you've said, so I'd like to deal with your comments later." Students should not feel they have to have an immediate, intelligent, and articulate reaction to every disputable point that their comments provoke. Discussion is not a performance in which we're all expected to win intellectual Oscars for the brilliance of our speech or the speed of our thought.

To Develop the Capacity for the Clear Communication of Ideas and Meaning

Through discussion we can help students grapple with the difficulties of trying to communicate ideas and meanings not immediately clear to others. Students learn the importance of giving examples to illustrate complex propositions, to think and speak metaphorically, and to use analogical reasoning. They can become more adept at entering into other participants' frames of reference and seeing the world through the multiple lenses these represent. As they respond to questions asked by their peers, they can learn to recognize what aspects of their own communicative styles are either helping or creating difficulties for others.

To Develop Skills of Synthesis and Integration

In discussions students can learn the importance of linking apparently unconnected insights, of drawing the group's attention to emerging themes, and of pointing out similarities of reasoning or evidence embedded in multiple contributions. Students who are skilled in discussion strive to discover commonalities and previously unnoticed connections. Over time they learn to keep in mind several apparently disparate strands of analysis. Occasionally this leads to a creative and exciting synthesis. More usually, it helps students become comfortable with ambiguity. They accept that discussions are open and not always supposed to lead to some form of definitive conclusion.

Emotional Purposes

To Help Students Become Connected to a Topic

When you introduce students to a new discussion topic, it's usually a mistake to assume that any inherent emotional connection exists between the topic and students' concerns or enthusiasms. However, it is possible to work at creating such a connection by asking students to play certain predefined conversational roles as they discuss the topic. Some can be provocateurs, arguing in the strongest and most controversial terms a certain line of analysis. Others can be devil's advocates, with a charge to counter every element in a particular line of argument. Still others can be intellectual detectives concerned to point out certain biases that keep recurring in the discussion, or to bring the group's attention to areas of inquiry it keeps approaching and then steering away from. As students begin to adopt these roles, there is often a sense of playfulness, a feeling that this is just a game of artful pretense (which, of course, it is). However, after a while this sense of artificiality starts to diminish, and students find they actually care about what others think and say about the topic being discussed.

To Show Respect for Students' Experiences

An important element of good discussion is encouraging students to analyze their experience and to help them understand that individual experience is socially formed. Discussion shows students that while formal knowledge and theoretical understanding are necessary it is also important to dignify (in a critical way) participants' experiences. Yet, students often dismiss their own experiences as anecdotal and idiosyncratic. They denigrate personal experience in contrast to "book" knowledge that is codified, legitimate, and seen as existing above and beyond individual stories. Good discussions affirm that personal experience is an important object of study, and they take the analysis of experience beyond individual storytelling to an analysis of the generic, recognizable elements that are embedded in particular tales. In discussion we often realize that our individual stories have shared elements and are shaped by common economic and political forces existing in the larger society.

Sociopolitical Purposes

To Encourage Attentive, Respectful Listening

Listening attentively is not easy. In fact, it is probably much more tiring to do this seriously than it is to make a contribution oneself. Given the complex multiplicity of expressive styles students display, the nuances of race, class, and gender, and the variety of idiosyncratic speech forms, it is sometimes amazing to think that anyone ever understands anything another person has said! Race, class, gender, learning style, personality—all these things complicate our efforts to understand one another in discussion without the added difficulties posed by the complexities of intellectual inquiry. Concrete thinkers in a group become frustrated with those who speak only in abstract or holistic terms. Those who express themselves in rambling, disconnected sentence fragments infuriate more task-oriented learners anxious to get to the point. What to one person is a permissible question according to standards of critical inquiry is rude, bigoted, and hurtful to another.

Grappling with these different patterns of communication is enormously challenging. But showing another person that you are striving to understand as closely as is humanly possible the exact meaning of what she's saying is wonderfully respectful and affirming. It is also crucial to the building of democratic trust.

To Help Students Learn the Processes and Habits of Democratic Discourse

Learning democratic discourse is difficult. In the immediate aftermath of World War II, the adult educator Eduard Lindeman (1947) proposed several democratic disciplines that, taken together, formed the natural code of behavior for a citizen living under democratic conditions. These disciplines included learning to live with diversity, learning to accept the partial functioning of democratic ideals, learning to avoid false antitheses (such as that an argument is either wholly right or wholly wrong, an action wholly good or wholly bad), learning to ensure that means and ends are as congruent as possible, learning to value humor, and learning to live with contrary decisions and perspectives.

If discussions are created and conducted with careful attention to these disciplines, they can become laboratories through which students learn democratic habits. A discussion group can constitute a safe space in which the democratic experiment can be tried, adapted, and reframed with a minimum of serious consequences for participants. Discussion in which participants are given opportunities to voice concerns, work collaboratively, formulate ideas, express disagreement, and solve problems collectively is both a foundation for democracy and a sign that democracy is taking hold. Without this kind of constant experience of democratic process, it is hard to see how people can become citizens in any but the most nominal, legalistic sense.

To Affirm Students as Co-creators of Knowledge

When students feel themselves to be respected and treated as equal creators of knowledge, they are much more likely to take the discussion process seriously. Having your views attended to carefully, and witnessing people grant your ideas public credibility, is a powerful experience for students who have learned to think of themselves as failures or impostors. In the best discussions, students should feel that their contributions are indispensable. The feeling should prevail that to lose anyone's participation would be a loss to the group as a whole.

Getting Discussions Started

The foundation of productive discussion is the generation of ground rules. Such rules typically ensure that minority opinions are respected, that no one is allowed to dominate the group, that divergent views are allowed full and free expression, and that time limits are set on members' contributions. Teachers can impose such rules themselves but a more participatory approach, and one that will likely ensure that students take any rules proposed seriously, is to involve students in setting these. This can be done by encouraging students to reflect on their own experiences as discussion participants and then helping them extrapolate dialogic rules from this reflection.

Creating Ground Rules: A Critical Incident Approach

Here are the instructions students follow for evolving ground rules that are embedded in their own experiences.

---

1. Think of the best group discussions you've ever been involved in. What things happened that made these conversations so satisfying? Make a few notes on this by yourself.

2. Think of the worst group discussions you've ever been involved in. What things happened that made these conversations so unsatisfactory? Make a few notes on this by yourself.

3. Now form a group with three other people. Take turns in talking about what made discussion groups work so well for you. Listen for common themes, shared experiences, and features of conversation that a majority of you would like to see in the course.

4. Take turns in talking about what made discussion group work so awful for you. Listen for common themes, shared experiences, and features of group conversation that a majority of you would like to see avoided in this course.

5. For each of the characteristics of good discussion you agree on, try to suggest three things a group could do to ensure that these characteristics are present. Be as specific and concrete as you can. For example, if you feel good conversation is developmental, with later themes building on and referring back to earlier ones, then you could propose a rule that every new comment made by a participant is prefaced with an explanation as to how it relates to an earlier comment.

6. For each of the characteristics of bad discussion you agree on, try to suggest three things a group could do to ensure that these characteristics are avoided. Be as specific and concrete as you can. For example, if you feel that bad conversation happens when one person's voice dominates, then you could propose a rule whereby once someone has spoken they are not allowed to make a second comment until at least three other people have spoken (unless another group member explicitly invites the participant to say something else).

7. Try to finish this exercise by drafting a charter for discussion that comprises the specific ground rules you agree on. We will make each group's rules public and see if we can develop a charter for discussion to guide us in the coming weeks.

Your role as the teacher in this process is not to suggest images of how you think good discussants behave. That's the business of group members. However, when it comes to translating these images into specific rules of conduct, students sometimes do need some help. If the class agrees that good discussions involve lots of people talking, then you can work with them to suggest specific ways to make this more likely to happen. You could suggest putting a time limit on individual contributions or regularly calling for a circle of voices where each person in turn is given the floor. If a common desire is expressed for people to listen carefully to what each person is saying, this can be accomplished by suggesting a weekly circular response discussion period in which students take turns to listen carefully, paraphrase, and then respond to each others' contributions.

Opening Declaration of Speech Policy

In Chapter One I outline an opening declaration I make to students in discussion-based courses that you might consider adapting in your own class for the reasons described in the chapter.

Sentence Completion Exercise

One way to focus students on the topic at hand, and to ensure that what gets talked about is in some way connected to their own concerns, is to start the discussion session with a sentence completion exercise. Students are asked to complete on their own whichever of the following sentences seem appropriate.

What most struck me about the text we read to prepare for the discussion today is . . .

The question that I'd most like to ask the author(s) of the text is . . .

The idea I most take issue with in the text is . . .

The most crucial point in last week's lecture was . . .

The part of the lecture/text that I felt made most sense to me was . . .

The part of the lecture/text that I felt was most confusing was . . .

Students then form into small groups and read out the full sentences to each other. As students hear each other's responses, they jot down whichever of their colleagues' responses they would most like to hear more about. After everyone has read out all their responses, students can ask other students why they wrote what they did. Finally, the small group members choose one or two responses to report out to the whole class when the teacher calls the small groups back together.

Generating Truth Statements

One task that Frederick (1986) and Van Ments (1990) suggest for the start of a discussion is to ask students to generate what they call "truth statements" (Frederick, p. 144) or "statements worth making" (Van Ments, p. 38) based on their preparatory reading. Students are split into small groups, and each group is asked to generate three or four statements that they believe to be true on the basis of their reading. The point of this exercise is not so much to produce undeniable facts or theories but to generate, and then prioritize, questions and issues around which further discussion and research should be undertaken. The exercise helps participants develop an agenda of items for discussion and suggests directions for future research they need to conduct if they are to be informed discussants.

Responding to Contentious Opening Statements

Sometimes a strongly worded statement—spoken or written—is a good way to get the blood flowing and conversation going. This statement can be one that's already in the public domain or one that a teacher writes for this purpose. The statement should be one that's deliberately provocative, even inflammatory, and one that will likely produce strong emotional responses in students. Certainly it should be one that challenges at a fundamental level some of the assumptions that students take for granted or hold on to most fiercely. It's important to state in this exercise that no one assumes that the teacher articulating the opinion agrees with its sentiments. The teacher bringing the contentious statement to the group is doing so only to generate conversation.

After the statement has been made, the conversation opens with group members trying to understand the reasoning and circumstances that frame such a statement. Why would someone hold these views? What in the author's experience led her to write or utter such ideas? What possible grounds could we advance to support the making of such an argument? For a while students are asked to be devil's advocates, coming up with evidence and rationales that are completely outside their usual frames of reference. This kind of perspective taking is a cognitive warm-up. It serves the same function in discussion as stretching does at the start of an aerobic workout. By examining the grounds for a view that is contrary to their own, students engage in a form of intellectual muscle flexing. Moreover, being forced to take seriously opinions that they strongly disagree with helps draw students into the discussion at an emotional level.

Guided Discussion

I have often heard teachers say that they run guided discussions and am always made very uncomfortable by that term. If it is used to describe the way a teacher leads the discussion towards a predefined end point, the term is, in my view, an oxymoron. Discussion is, by definition, a free and open conversation in which no end point is specified. It entails the emergence of unpredictable avenues of inquiry and people changing their minds as they consider new evidence or alternative interpretations of existing evidence. At the heart of discussion is the open and unpredictable creation of meanings through collaborative inquiry. It is intellectually dishonest for a discussion leader to have decided in advance what these meanings should be and to call the resulting conversation a discussion.

This does not mean that the deliberate initiation of students into previously determined meanings or understandings through a Socratic dialogue is somehow invalid. On the contrary, it is a crucial element in introducing students to new concepts, bodies of knowledge, or areas of inquiry and is a strategy I use myself. In teaching critical theory I take full responsibility for introducing difficult concepts such as ideology, hegemony, liberation, and praxis in as clear a way as I can by talking with students about the different ways they understand those terms. But when I do this, I am *not* teaching through discussion. I have a very clear purpose in mind which is to make sure learners are "inside" the concept. To use a term borrowed from R. S. Peters (1967), I want to be sure that students command the "grammar" of the subject; that is, that they understand fully the criteria by which good and bad examples of intellectual work in the subject are determined and that they grasp correctly the essential conceptual building blocks of a particular body of knowledge.

Just because teachers and students are talking does not mean they are engaged in discussion. The intent and manner of the talk are crucial. For example, if I question students to make sure they have understood Marcuse's (1965) concept of repressive tolerance in the way he intended it to be understood, I do use classroom talk, but I am definitely *not* using discussion. My approach is more like the structured Socratic dialogue referred to earlier. However, when I ask the group to talk about the meaning this concept has for students' own experiences, the extent to which it explains things they have seen in their lives, the degree to which it raises the specter of censorship for them, or contains an implicit arrogance—then I *am* using discussion. I have no idea where the conversation will turn and no predetermined objectives that must be met before the day's class has finished.

A guided discussion is not only a contradiction in terms, it is also a profoundly inauthentic process. If you are asking students to enter into a collaborative inquiry to explore and create multiple meanings, it is basically dishonest to have worked out in advance what those meanings will be. In a classic article Paterson (1970) describes such conversations as counterfeit discussions led by a teacher "who unobtrusively and skillfully synthesizes the various discussion contributions of his students, by judicious selection and emphasis, into a neatly structured and rounded proposition or body of propositions, which are then presented as the 'conclusions' of the 'class discussion'" (p. 47). In my experience I know very quickly when I'm in such a discussion, and my immediate impulse is to get out of it as soon as possible.

I have often found myself a participant in a discussion where the leader is nudging the conversation along to a predetermined conclusion with which he agrees. I see this happen when the leader ignores questions or ideas raised by students that are inconvenient or awkward for his position. It also occurs when a teacher reframes what a student has said in a way that distorts the student's meaning so that it supports the leader's views. If something is forcing me to stay in the room during such a discussion, then I mount a consciousness strike. I withdraw my mental labor and start turning over in my mind some work or research problems that have no connection to what we're talking about. So in my view guided discussion is a self-negating concept if it means guiding talk towards a particular position or point of consensus. Whenever this happens it means that certain perspectives and information have been excluded at the outset.

It does make sense, however, to describe a discussion as guided if what is being guided are the processes by which students are helped to listen respectfully, seek clarification and understanding of each others' ideas, and create opportunities for all voices to be heard. In guided discussions we can guide students in learning the habits of democratic discourse but not in learning predetermined conclusions or prechosen meanings. Guiding the process of discussion is legitimate if it makes sure everyone gets a chance to participate, means that no one person dominates unfairly, and ensures that individuals cannot hijack the topic for their own ideological conversion of other participants without themselves being open to listening to others' points of view. Indeed, unless the teacher deliberately intervenes to guide the process of discussion to prevent these things happening, the patterns of conversational dominance that exist outside the classroom will immediately reproduce themselves inside. Those learners with intellectual capital, cultural prestige, and command of the dominant linguistic discourse will be listened to seriously, while those who are quiet, marginalized, unconfident, or whose first language is not English will remain on the conversational periphery. In the next chapter I provide several examples of how teachers can deliberately intervene to guide the creation of processes that ensure participatory discussions.

8

Getting Students to Participate in Discussion

For the social and cognitive reasons mentioned in Chapter Seven, most teachers who use discussion put a premium on student participation. As that chapter argued, however, participation should not be equated with frequent speech. The performance anxiety induced by thinking that good participation requires one to be a continuous and brilliant conversationalist can kill, rather than enhance, learning through discussion. For this reason, the criteria that teachers use to assess students' participation should include silent, or at least less verbal, measures. Students should know that participation includes posting discussion reflections online, bringing helpful materials to class that are not mentioned in the course syllabus, calling for quiet reflective interludes during discussion, and making useful observations on anonymous CIQs regarding discussion dynamics. Good participation can also be recognized when students perform the assigned roles mentioned later in this chapter, some of which require very little speech. Before addressing how to get students to participate in discussion, however, it might be useful to understand what stops them from speaking in the first place.

What Stops Students from Participating in Discussion?

Why won't students say anything even when they have ideas to express or when the teacher has done her best to create a safe climate for conversation? Generally the problem can be traced to one or more of the following factors.

Crippling Personal Introversion

Some students are so shy and introverted that nothing short of therapeutic intervention will embolden them to speak. There's probably not much that teachers can do about this, since a class that meets for one or two hours a week over three or four months hardly provides much scope for substantial developmental change. However, two small steps are possible. One thing you can do is make clear at the outset of the course that talking is not the only way students contribute to discussion and that if students choose to stay silent they will not be penalized or viewed as mentally negligent. An example of this is the speech policy mentioned in Chapter One. The relief induced on hearing this announcement sometimes emboldens very shy students to speak. If students still feel too shy to speak after such a declaration, at least they don't feel so inadequate and ashamed about their silence.

The other possibility is to make sure that some sort of electronic discussion is part of the course. Students who are too shy to speak up in groups may find it much easier to make their point on a class listserv or in a course chat room. The Internet allows students the time and privacy (though not always the anonymity) to say what they want to say in the way, and at the pace, they want to say it. Broadening discussion to include e-mail discourse can bring highly introverted students into the conversation.

Fear of Looking Stupid

Some students won't talk because they're afraid of making a mistake by saying something that's considered daft, unintelligent, or poorly expressed. This is particularly the case where the invisible norm of discussion participation implies that students and teachers should be models of confident loquacity. Four specific steps can help allay this fear.

- Make sure you begin each discussion with the reminder that in your class there are no stupid questions. Publish your speech policy in the course syllabus and repeat it regularly in class.

- If faculty conduct a discussion in front of students, make sure a debriefing is included so that any of the faculty who felt the fear of looking ignorant or unintelligent in the discussion can talk about this. If students see that the faculty "experts" (who are supposed to know everything and to be supremely self-confident) also suffer from this fear, then it loses some of its power to stifle speech.

- Begin a discussion-based course by convening a panel of former students. The panel members are asked to pass on to the new students the best advice they can give on how to survive and flourish in discussions. Chances are that the theme of fearing to appear sufficiently intelligent will emerge strongly. Panel members can describe this feeling and talk about how they dealt with it. The new students will see that the fear they feel is universal, not unique. Knowing that others who have shared this feeling have managed to pass the course will ease their anxieties on this matter.

- Make sure that before holding a discussion students are assigned specific tasks or roles that they are to perform in the discussion. Knowing that one has a specific task to perform in the discussion, and being able to prepare properly for it beforehand, provides a sense of security. It helps reduce the fear that one will be surprised by being asked to speak in an impromptu manner in the middle of a discussion.

Feeling Unprepared

Students often report that they feel they are being asked to talk about ideas or topics about which they know very little. In their eyes they're expected to speak intelligently on a subject for which they have no information and for which they have had no time or opportunity for thoughtful reflection or research that might lead to some informed opinions. In addition, many students have not had much sustained engagement in discussion during their precollege years and are unaware of how they should conduct themselves. Later in this chapter I provide some introductory exercises to get students talking that address this problem.

We Don't Trust You

If students sense that in a discussion the teacher is lying in wait for them, waiting to trip them up for saying something stupid, then they will keep their mouths shut. They will also stay silent if the teacher is asking students to give their opinions on contentious or difficult topics without the teacher ever having spoken from her own heart on these same matters. The student might sense that this is a "counterfeit" discussion that seems open but that actually has its end point already predetermined.

This mistrust can only be countered by the students seeing a teacher, week in, week out, earn their trust. One way this process can be foreshortened is by regularly reporting CIQ comments that criticize your actions as the teacher in discussion and then addressing these in a nondefensive way. You can thank students for expressing their criticisms and say how these have made you think about the way your contributions are perceived. Also, if you are asking students to discuss something that involves them in any kind of self-disclosure or personal revelation, make sure you go first. Let them know that by modeling your own willingness to do this you're earning the moral right to invite them into this process.

We're Not Welcome Here

Many students feel like aliens in a new cultural landscape. The speech patterns and behaviors of academics, or of other students, are seen as strange, intimidating, deliberately hostile. In this situation, to contribute to discussion means you have sold out to the host culture, joined the enemy. If you feel this way, then staying silent in class is an act of honorable resistance, a guarding of one's cultural identity. This is particularly the case with students who have grown up in a culture where silence is valued over speech or in one where giving one's personal opinion is seen as an arrogant act of self-indulgence. What is lauded by Euro-Americans as "speaking in your own voice" is seen by other students as an inappropriate challenge to the venerated authority of the teacher or as a betrayal of the collective wisdom of the group. If this is the case, then speaking out is a denial of one's loyalties and identity.

One response to this is to make clear in your own expectations of discussion participation that you will monitor, and act against, any speech that is hostile to those who are not part of the dominant culture. If you are a member of the dominant culture (as many college teachers are), acknowledge your position of privilege. But don't do this in a guilt-induced display of self-abasement. You shouldn't feel ashamed of your class or ethnicity.

Also, if you open your course with an alumni panel of previous students, make sure you choose as participants some who will act as cultural brokers. These are students from the minority groups represented who are trusted by members of those groups. Such students communicate minority students' concerns to the teacher, they interpret the teacher's behaviors and requests to other students in comprehensible ways, they keep the teacher informed about how her actions are being perceived, and they vouchsafe the teacher's honesty and sincerity to students who are skeptical or hostile.

We've Been Burned

Some students may have learned from past experience that speaking out in discussions triggers attacks on them by other students or by teachers. They know that the rhetoric of everyone's voice counting equally is contradicted by the reality of having to voice ideologically correct opinions. If a student's challenging of groupthink, or of professorial authority, has led them to be mocked, defamed, or just put in their "proper" place, then they will think long and hard before ever speaking out again.

Several of the responses already mentioned in the previous chapter address this feeling. For example, if you start a course with an alumni panel of former students and (when you're out of the room) these former students assure new students that you won't penalize them for dissenting or critical views, this goes a long way to emboldening new students to risk speaking out. Again, responding nondefensively and openly to CIQ criticisms will gradually convince some students that you mean what you say about welcoming challenges to your ideas.

Anytime a student makes a comment that's critical of you, you can also acknowledge how difficult this must have been and thank them for the comment. If other students jump in to save you by pointing out to the critical student how he or she's really just misunderstood you, or if they start to try to shut this student down, intervene immediately. Say that a commitment to open discourse is indivisible and that you are trying to preserve the critical student's right to voice an alternate view. Point out that without critical voices groups fall victim to groupthink. Ask the critical student to say more about their criticisms, and let other students know that you are trying to guard minority viewpoints.

If you spend some time at the outset of a course helping to develop ground rules for respectful discourse, and if these rules include a deliberate and regular effort to stop and make sure that dissenting views and critical comments are heard, enforce this. Call a time out every twenty to thirty minutes and ask for students to do some structured devil's advocacy where they argue against the prevailing tenor of opinion in the discussion. If students are unwilling to express alternative or challenging perspectives, make sure that you do this yourself. In lectures, and in the discussion itself, regularly argue against your own ideas or against an emerging consensus in the group. Point out ideas and information that you have omitted, ethical and moral dilemmas you have glossed over, contradictions in your position you have ignored, and questions you were tempted to avoid because you didn't have good answers to them.

Talking Isn't Cool

In some student groups the culture of cool is so strong that breaking it by speaking seriously in a discussion means losing friends and status. Students who belong to such groups sense that the price of talking authentically is an irretrievable loss of face in front of peers. This culture can be so ingrained in some students that there is often little a teacher can do to overcome it. However, three steps are worth considering. First, allowing students to make their comments through e-mail may persuade them that the privacy this affords allows them to contribute to the conversation without destroying their image. Uncool behavior is behavior that leaves you looking like a teacher's favorite in front of your peers. If the physical presence of peers is replaced by an electronic presence, the group norms regarding what is cool may be less influential. Second, you can try to include on the alumni panel of former students that are brought in at the start of a course some members who are, by general consensus, cool. This presumes, of course, that you are so plugged into campus culture that you know who these people are. The presence of these students does a lot to assure new students that talking doesn't blow one's cool.

Third, teachers can make clear that the ultimate price students might pay for their coolness is failing. If you truly believe that students who never speak are in some way in dereliction of their responsibilities as discussion group members, then you need to make that fact clear early in the course and repeat that message regularly.

You can provide a midterm review of students' performance or some interim evaluations of their progress that make clear to them the consequences of not contributing. By telling students early in a course that if this were the end of the term they would fail because they have never spoken in discussion, you bring home to them the consequences of their silence. Of course, students may choose to continue to stay out of discussions. But at least they can't turn round at the end of the course and complain that they didn't know you meant it when you said that participating in discussions was necessary for a passing grade.

The Teacher's Doing All the Talking

Students won't bother to say anything if they know you're going to do the job for them. If you always answer your own questions, if you interrupt students all the time, if you're the first to fill silence with your voice, then students will soon learn that they don't need to speak. Your conversation with yourself is quite sufficient to fill up the class time.

The answer to this problem is deceptively simple—stop talking so much! Enforce a decent wait time on yourself (try twenty seconds initially) after you have raised a question for consideration. Or, when assigning group conversational roles, make sure you play one of the less loquacious ones. Alternatively, tell the group at the outset of the discussion that you will function only as a facilitator who will make sure ground rules are observed and that everyone has a chance to talk, but that you will not interject any substantive opinions into the conversation.

Talking Isn't Rewarded

It may be that a teacher's desire for conversation is not matched by the reward system. If you say you value discussion, but you award grades based only on students' performance on midterms or final exams, then students will put all their available energy into working to pass those tests. The time and energy spent preparing for, and engaging in, classroom discussion will not be seen as worth the effort. So make sure that the criteria for assessing student work include participation in discussion and be as specific as possible as to what this looks like. Finally, establish an incremental reward system so that students can see from week to week that their participation is building points towards their final grade.

Grading for Participation

As mentioned above, establishing clear criteria for effective participation is crucial if students are to take discussion seriously. These criteria should be published in the syllabus, should be the focus of a pop quiz on the syllabus in the second week, should be underscored by members of the alumni panel, and should be modeled by faculty in any discussions they hold in front of students and also in their own facilitation. An example of criteria for class participation taken from a syllabus of mine is given below.

Class Participation

Twenty percent of your grade for this class is based on your participation in discussion. Participating in discussion does not necessarily mean talking a lot or showing everyone else what you know or that you have studied a lot. Good discussion participation involves people trying to build on and synthesize comments from others and on showing appreciation for others' contributions. It also involves inviting others to say more about what they are thinking. Some of the most helpful things you can do are call for a quiet interlude, bring a new resource to the classroom, or post an observation online. So there are multiple ways quieter learners can participate in discussion.

Below are some specific behavioral examples of good participation in discussion on which you will be assessed in this course. You will have been judged to have participated well in discussion in any given week if you:

Ask a question or make a comment that shows you are interested in what another person says.

Ask a question or make a comment that encourages another person to elaborate on something they have already said.

Bring in a resource (a reading, web link, video) that is not covered in the syllabus but adds new information or perspectives to our learning.

Make a comment that underscores the link between two people's contributions and make this link explicit in your comment (this can be done online).

Use body language (in only a slightly exaggerated way) to show interest in what different speakers are saying.

Post a comment in the course chat room that summarizes our conversations so far and/or suggests new directions and questions to be explored in the future.

Make a comment (online if this is appropriate) indicating that you found another person's ideas interesting or useful. Be specific as to why this was the case.

Contribute something that builds on or springs from what someone else has said. Be explicit about the way you are building on the other person's thoughts (this can be done online).

Make a comment on your CIQ that prompts us to examine discussion dynamics.

When you think it's appropriate, ask the group for a moment's silence to slow the pace of conversation to give you, and others, time to think.

Make a comment that at least partly paraphrases a point someone has already made.

Make a summary observation that takes into account several people's contributions and that touches on a recurring theme in the discussion (online if you like).

Ask a cause-and-effect question—for example, "Can you explain why you think it's true that if these things are in place such and such a thing will occur?"

Find a way to express appreciation for the enlightenment you have gained from the discussion. Try to be specific about what it was that helped you understand something better. Again this can be done online if this suits you better.

Scaffolding Discussion Participation Through Structured Conversation

Early on in a discussion-based course, it is a good idea to introduce students to a number of exercises designed to equalize participation and to teach students that listening, appreciating, and synthesizing are just as crucial to good discussion as is making brilliant original contributions. For students unused to discussion, or for those introverts who find talking in public an excruciating ordeal, an orientation or induction period is particularly appreciated. Such a period comprises a scaffolding experience, a time when students learn a series of protocols where the ground rules for participation are clear and the intimidating need to come up with impromptu contributions is removed.

Circle of Voices

The circle of voices is a protocol that students can learn on the first day of class. Participants form into circles of about five to discuss a topic assigned by the teacher. They are allowed a minute or so of silent time to think about what they want to say on the topic of discussion once the circle of voices begins. After this silent period the discussion opens with each person having a period of uninterrupted airtime of no more than a minute. During this time each speaker can say whatever she wishes about the topic at hand. While each person is speaking no one else is allowed to interrupt. People take their turns to speak by going round the circle in order, which removes from participants the stress of having to decide whether or not they will try to jump in after another student has finished speaking.

After the initial circle of voices has been completed, and everyone has had the uninterrupted chance to make their opening comments, then the discussion opens up into a more free-flowing format. As this happens a second ground rule comes into effect. Participants are only allowed to talk about another person's ideas that have already been shared in the opening circle of voices. Participants cannot jump into the conversation by expanding on their own ideas; they can only talk about their reactions to what someone else has said in the opening round. The only exception to this ground rule is if someone asks a group member directly to expand on her ideas. This second ground rule prevents the tendency toward grandstanding that sometimes afflicts a few articulate, confident individuals.

Circular Response

The circular response exercise is a way to democratize discussion participation, to promote continuity of conversation, and to give people some experience of the effort required in respectful listening. It was developed by Eduard Lindeman (Brookfield, 1988) as part of his efforts to democratize conversation amongst community groups and to help community groups focus on two or three shared concerns instead of trying to pursue multiple agendas.

As with the circle of voices, the exercise begins with participants having a minute or so to think about their response to a discussion question or topic assigned to them. Participants form into circles of six to eight, and the conversation begins with a volunteer who takes up to a minute to say whatever she thinks about the topic concerned. After the minute is up, the first discussant yields the floor, and the person sitting to the discussant's left speaks for a minute or so. The second speaker is not free, however, to say anything she wants. She must incorporate into her remarks some reference to the preceding speaker's message and then use this as a springboard for her own comments. This doesn't have to be an agreement—it can be an expression of dissent from the previous opinion. It can also be an expression of confusion where the second discussant identifies some aspect of the first speaker's remarks that she finds difficult to understand. The second speaker could also talk about how the first speaker's comments cover such unfamiliar ground that she is left with no conversational opening.

After a minute or so, the second discussant stops speaking, and the person to her left becomes the third discussant who follows the same ground rule to refer to some aspect of the preceding speaker's message as the springboard for her own comments. Following this pattern the discussion moves all the way around the circle. Each discussant must ground her comments in reference to something the previous speaker has said. After everyone has had a turn to speak, the floor is opened for general conversation, and the previous ground rules are no longer in force.

The interesting thing about this exercise is that the seventh or eighth person to speak has no inherent advantage over the first or second contributor. This is because the eighth person cannot sit in reflective luxury rehearsing a perfect contribution because she has no idea what the seventh person is going to say until that person speaks. Indeed, the first person to speak has the easiest task of all because she does not have to use a previous speaker's comments as the springboard for her remarks.

Conversational Roles

Students often find it helpful to know at the outset of a discussion the sort of conversational role they are required to play. Knowing that they have a particular task to fulfill seems to remove some of the performance anxiety created by the invisible norm. Practice in playing different conversational roles helps create opportunities for the more tentative students to speak, thereby building their confidence. Any roles assigned must, of course, be alternated so that everyone takes their turn. It is an abuse of this exercise to assign the quietest role to the most vociferous student each week. A number of commonly used conversational roles are given below.

- *Problem, Dilemma, or Theme Poser.* This participant has the task of introducing the topic of conversation. She draws on her own ideas and experiences as a way of helping others into conversation about the theme.

- *Reflective Analyst.* This member keeps a record of the conversation's development. Every twenty minutes or so she gives a summary that focuses on shared concerns, issues skirted, and emerging common themes.

- *Scrounger.* The scrounger listens for helpful resources, suggestions, and tips that participants have voiced as they discuss how to work through a problem or situation. She keeps a record of these ideas that is read aloud before the session ends.

- *Devil's Advocate.* This person listens carefully for any emerging consensus. When she hears this she formulates and expresses a contrary view. This keeps groupthink in check and helps participants explore a range of alternative interpretations.

- *Detective.* The detective listens carefully for unacknowledged, unchecked, and unchallenged biases that seem to be emerging in the conversation. As she hears these she brings them to the group's attention. She assumes particular responsibility for alerting group members to concerns of race, class, and gender. She listens for cultural blindness, gender insensitivity, and comments that ignore variables of power and class.

- *Theme Spotter*. This participant identifies themes that arise during the discussion that are left unexplored and that might form a focus for the next session.

- *Umpire*. This person listens for judgmental comments that sound offensive, insulting, and demeaning, and that contradict ground rules for discussion generated by group members.

- *Textual Focuser*. Whenever assertions are made that seem unconnected to the text being discussed, this person asks the speaker to let the group know where in the text the point being made occurs.

- *Evidential Assessor*. This student asks speakers to give the evidence for empirical generalizations that are stated as self-evident fact but that actually seem more like opinion.

- *Synthesizer*. This person attempts to underscore links between different contributions.

Conversational Moves

An alternative to assigning conversational roles is to use the conversational moves exercise. Here the teacher pastes a number of conversational moves (speaking directions) on 3 x 5 cards and then randomly distributes these among participants at the beginning of a discussion session. These moves should roughly parallel the criteria for good discussion participation published in the course syllabus.

Students privately read the move on their card and are asked to practice their move at some point during the discussion that follows. When the discussion is over the entire list of moves is distributed so people can see the wide variety of ways that discussion participation can be recognized. If they wish to, participants can recap how they tried to make the moves they were allocated.

Specific Moves

Ask a question or make a comment that shows you are interested in what another person says.

Ask a question or make a comment that encourages another person to elaborate on something they have already said.

Make a comment that underscores the link between two people's contributions.

Use body language to show interest in what different speakers are saying.

Make a specific comment indicating how you found another person's ideas interesting or useful.

Contribute something that builds on or springs from what someone else has said.

Be explicit about the way you are building on the other person's thoughts.

Make a comment that at least partly paraphrases a point someone has already made.

Make a summary observation that takes into account several people's contributions and that touches on a recurring theme in the discussion.

Ask a cause-and-effect question—for example, "Can you explain why you think it's true that if these things are in place such and such a thing will occur?"

When you think it's appropriate, ask the group for a moment's silence to slow the pace of conversation and give you, and others, time to think.

Find a way to express appreciation for the enlightenment you have gained from the discussion. Be specific about what it was that helped you understand something better.

Disagree with someone in a respectful and constructive way.

Create space for someone who has not yet spoken to contribute to the conversation.

Quotes to Affirm and Challenge

This exercise is designed to make it easier to begin discussions that are grounded in students' prereading of an assigned text. Students are asked to bring to class two quotes they have chosen from a text they have read to prepare for the class. One quote is chosen because the student wishes to affirm it. The other is one the student wishes to challenge. Students form small groups, and each member takes a turn to propose the quote they wish to affirm and the reasons for doing this. The quote does not have to be defended as empirically true. Sometimes a participant will propose a quote because it confirms a point of view she holds or because it supports what her intuition or experience tells her is accurate. Sometimes she feels the quote states the most important point in the text, or she chooses a quote because it contains a crucial new piece of information or different perspective. At other times the quote is affirmed because it is rhetorically rousing or expresses an idea so lyrically. When everyone in the small group has proposed a quote to affirm, the group then chooses one to report back to the larger class. During this whole class discussion, each group explains why it was that they chose the particular quote they did.

The quote to challenge activity follows the same procedure only this time students choose a quote that they disagree with, find contradictory, believe to be inaccurate, or consider reprehensible and immoral. The quote to challenge is then reported back to the class along with the rationale for its choice.

Hatful of Quotes

The Hatful of Quotes exercise aims to make the mandated act of contributing to discussion as stress free as possible. Prior to the discussion of a text, the leader types onto separate slips of paper multiple copies of five or six different sentences or passages from the text to be discussed. In class she puts these into a hat, and asks students to draw one of these slips out of a hat. Students are given a few minutes to think about the quote they have picked and then asked to read it out loud and make some comment on it. The order of contribution is up to the students. Those who feel more fearful about speaking usually go last and take more time to think about what they want to say. Because the same five or six quotes are used, students who go later will have heard their quote read and commented on by those who spoke earlier. So even if they have little to say about their own interpretation of the quote, they can affirm, build on, or contradict a comment a peer has already made on that quote. This exercise is a good way to create a safe opportunity for everyone to speak. Those who are diffident get to say something, thus building confidence for subsequent contributions.

Snowballing

Students uncomfortable with even small-group participation can be drawn into this, and then into whole class discussion, through the process known as Snowballing. This exercise starts with individual solitary reflection and proceeds gradually and incrementally (if numbers allow) until the discussion involves the whole class. The process begins by students individually and silently spending a couple of minutes jotting down their thoughts about an assigned discussion question. After this reflective beginning students then form into pairs and spend about five minutes discussing each other's ideas. When the five minutes are up, each pair then joins another pair to form a quartet. The quartet conversation opens with each pair sharing a question they raised, a difference they noted in their conversation, or a new insight that suggested itself. After ten minutes the quartets join another quartet to form octets. Again, the octets begin their conversation with each quartet sharing a question they raised, a difference they noted, or an insight that suggested itself in their conversation. After twenty minutes the octets join other octets to form groups of sixteen and again, share a question, difference, or insight. In a class of around thirty-two, the class ends by each group of sixteen joining the other for a final conversation. Through snowballing, a class of thirty-two students that began with private, silent reflection ends up in a whole class discussion.

The ideas presented in this chapter, and the one preceding it, should decrease the chances that your attempts to start a discussion are met with a resounding silence. But no matter how carefully you plan against this eventuality, at some time it will happen. When it does, try to remember that silence is not always indicative of hostility, confusion, or apathy. It could just as easily signal students' need to collect their thoughts on a complicated topic before venturing into speech. It could also represent a culturally induced preference for silence, or an unwillingness to be disrespectful to peers or teachers by speaking out of turn or against a prevailing view. If after several classes conversation remains desultory or nonexistent, then a wider structural problem is probably manifesting itself. Perhaps the institutional culture and reward systems are working against your commitment to discussion. Perhaps differences of race, class, and gender between you and the group, or between different group members, are generating a silence born of mutual suspicion. Perhaps students' past experiences have taught them that participating in discussion is a waste of time, a chance for a teacher or peer to catch them off guard, trip them up, and put them down.

In such situations a number of different courses of action suggest themselves. One is to confront the group with the problem (which will emerge anyway on the anonymous classrooms CIQs) and to seek their reactions and advice. Another is to rethink the dynamics of your pedagogy and how you use discussion. Maybe you will take a step back and insert a number of structured conversation exercises that can provide scaffolding, an initiation, for students new to classroom discussion. Still another is to ask your colleagues (perhaps by getting them to sit in on a discussion session) for their perceptions of and advice on the situation. After you have done these things, it is always possible that you may decide that discussion has been introduced too prematurely and that you need to explore other alternative means of instruction. What some of these alternatives might be is considered in the next chapter.

9

Teaching in Diverse Classrooms

In contemporary American higher education, diversity is not just a trendy buzzword but a perplexing reality. In some states a high school diploma is all you need to get into a state college, with the result that many schools operate virtually an open admissions policy. For many college teachers a student body that represents a wide range of academic diversity is now the norm, not the exception. Learners who are barely literate sit next to those who already show a talent for writing. Those skilled in time-management, self-organization, and linear thought mingle with highly lateral thinkers or those with little patience for detail. Self-directed learners co-exist with those who are highly teacher dependent and who lose focus once tight structure is removed. Levels of motivation run the gamut from practically nonexistent to dogged determination.

Personalities also range from extrovert to introvert, intuitive to logical. For some, identity is integrally linked to sexual orientation. For others, ideological or spiritual commitments define who they are. Those with disabilities—learning, physical, auditory, visual— need to be accommodated alongside those who have no awareness of how these might structure learning. Some people process information best through active experimentation; others are more comfortable with reflective observation. Some show a preference for learning grounded in concrete experience; others prefer abstract conceptualization. One group of students is field independent, liking to be left alone to plan and conduct necessary learning; another is field dependent, needing a lot of teacher direction and externally imposed structure. Syllabus-bound and syllabus-free learners, convergers and divergers, those who apply either deep or surface approaches to learning—the list of learning styles and personality orientations seems endless.

But variations in academic readiness, learning style, and personality orientations are only the beginning of diversity. Contemporary teachers now work in truly multicultural classrooms. Newly arrived immigrant groups, communities of color that have been part of this country for centuries but rarely seen as college-level material, Indigenous peoples that traditionally have been excluded from higher education, students for whom English is a second or third foreign language—all are now present in college classrooms in ever greater numbers. Sometimes students born and raised here may not speak what many teachers consider standard English. For example, in California the Oakland School Board claimed Ebonics—"the language of West African, Caribbean, and U.S. slave descendants of Niger-Congo African origin" (Smith, 1998)— as the home language of inner-city African American students. In college classrooms in my own twin cities of Minneapolis-St. Paul, Hmong students sit next to Somalis, who sit next to Ukrainian students, who sit next to the children of Mexican migrant workers, who sit next to African American learners, who intermingle with Tribal and Indigenous people, who learn alongside working-class White Minnesotans—and all these students are the first in their families to go to college. Sometimes tribal and ethnic conflicts present in the homelands of learners reemerge in college classrooms. And, of course, class differences also become apparent among all students, including those of color. For example, Guy (2004) notes how a class-based conflict develops amongst African American students attending GED programs "between students who see themselves as members of the hip hop culture and those who do not" (p. 52).

As we can see, then, the twin impulses of democracy and capitalism—of trying to widen student access while simultaneously attracting as many paying customers as possible in an era of brutal budget cuts—have combined to present contemporary college teachers with incredible challenges. Not only are we having to teach ever larger classes that contain ever greater diversities, we are also required to do this in a system that assumes the essential homogeneity of teaching and learning. Colleges are run on predetermined timetables, with curricula neatly sequenced and a certain amount of time deemed appropriate to cover the required content or skill sets. Woe betide the teacher who tries to buck this trend by slowing down, allowing more individualized instruction, or taking the time to develop her own teaching materials that are grounded in students' experiences, rather than using those prescribed by licensing boards or superiors.

Gauging Diversity

One understandable response to encountering diversity is to throw your hands up in frustration and conclude that since it is impossible to address this fully, one may as well teach as if your classrooms contain the same homogeneous mix as would have been the case thirty years ago. Most of us are not capable of such massive denial, however, so we must find some way of dealing with this reality. A useful starting point is to find some way of gauging the breadth and intensity of the diversity you encounter. This can be accomplished in a number of ways. Various instruments exist that purport to assess personality types and learning styles, many of them based either on the Myers-Briggs Personality Type Inventory or on Kolb's (1984) cycle of experiential learning. Others often used are the Learning Combination Inventory (Johnston and Dainton, 1997), the Learning and Study Skills Inventory (Weinstein, Schulte, and Palmer, 1987), and the Two Factor Study Process Questionnaire (Biggs, Kember, and Leung, 2001).

I have observed several classes where completing a learning style assessment is one of the first activities students are presented with. For students used to the paraphernalia of test-taking this can be an interesting task from which they can gain some self-knowledge. However, for many of the students that diversity initiatives are created to address, particularly those for whom English is a second or third language, for English speakers who operate at a low level of functional literacy, or for those who associate form-filling with surveillance and the arbitrary, even punitive, exercise of officialdom, this can be a highly intimidating task.

Another approach is for teachers to develop their own more informal measures of students' diversity. Diagnostic tests that ask students to demonstrate their familiarity with, or knowledge of, certain key skills or concepts usually give an early reading of the different levels of ability in the class. Some of these tests can be written in the form of multiple choice questions about course content, or the teacher can spend some time talking with students about their previous learning. Even a series of questions asking for a show of hands in response to certain questions about students' prior learning can tell you something. An interesting kinetic variant on the show of hands approach is to have learners stand in a large circle around the room and then have people who answer "yes" to a particular question move into a smaller circle within the larger circle. Although these approaches are highly informal and supposedly unscientific, they can yield some useful information. At the very least having people who have taken previous courses in the area move into the inner circle, or seeing who is taking the course as an elective as against those for whom the course is required, tells you something about the likely levels of motivation that exist.

Of course the means you use to find out about your students' backgrounds, inclinations, and abilities as learners needs to take account of their racial and ethnic identities. Asking First Nation or Indigenous students to go straight into voluble disclosure of their histories as learners won't get a White European teacher very far. Again, Laotian, Vietnamese, or Korean students typically will find it uncomfortable to speak about their individual experiences as learners. African American students may respond much better to a call-and-response rhythm of questioning than to a linear attempt to address a number of items in turn. One common exercise is to ask students to name themselves by describing the racial or ethnic groups they see themselves belonging to and to announce how they wish to be addressed. Another (common in elementary school classrooms) is the circle of objects exercise in which each student brings in an object she feels says something about her culture and family history and then talks about its meaning in her life. In both these exercises it is important that the teacher model her own commitment by going first with any disclosure. Cultural brokers—members of the minority groups represented in the classroom who agree to assist the teacher and can move between academic and minority culture—can also play an important role. Such brokers interpret students' behaviors and responses to the teacher whilst simultaneously vouching to minority students for the teacher's integrity.

As you move into teaching a course containing a diverse group of students, the Critical Incident Questionnaire will give you a weekly reading of how the diversity of the student body reveals itself in learners' responses to specific classroom activities. This data is important because it represents a longitudinal balance to the cross-sectional nature of information derived from assessment instruments that are administered at the first class meeting. As the semester proceeds and people become more used to a range of different teaching approaches, they may find their culturally induced resistance to particular learning activities weakening (though sometimes the opposite happens). They also come to know their peers better, a process that can reduce or increase student-student hostility. Only by conducting some form of continuous classroom research such as the CIQ will you be able to know how diversity is manifesting itself and how successful are your efforts to address it.

In the rest of this chapter, I outline a number of responses teachers can make when they encounter the kinds of diversity outlined above. Before exploring them, however, it is important to state that any comments I make must exhibit a necessarily restricted level of generality. Local, contextual factors always distort any global pedagogic strategies, and that is never truer than when teaching to address difference. So the following analysis only comprises a series of possible starting points for responding to all forms of diversity. How they might play themselves out depends very much on your own reading of your own students and classroom environments.

Team Teaching

One of the most predictable realities in American college classrooms is that solo teaching reigns supreme. A classroom full of diverse students is confronted by one person in the role of instructor who, no matter how much she might strive to empathize with different learning needs, racial traditions, and personality types, is inevitably limited by the boundaries of her own personality, racial group membership, talents, and experience. However, when two or three people with different racial identities, experiences, talents, and personalities form a teaching team, the possibilities for connecting to a wider range of students expand exponentially. In a team-taught course the likelihood is substantially increased that at some point in the class most students will be taught by someone whose learning style, personality, cultural background, and communicative preferences match their own. This is particularly the case when multiracial teaching teams work in multiracial classrooms.

As teachers we all bring different gifts and handicaps to the table. A team that works well is aware of the different talents of its members and attempts to mix these as equitably as possible. When I teach with someone who prefers lecturing, I can balance that inclination (which many students will appreciate) with my preference for group work (which others will appreciate just as much). My lecturing colleague can also alert me to times when I need to make a presentation to clarify or introduce difficult subject matter to students. When I teach with someone who exhibits a confrontational demeanor, my more laid-back approach helps keep the confrontation from spiraling out of control. On the other hand, the colleague with a confrontational impulse helps ensure that I don't dwell longer than necessary on a wholly congenial activity and that I move in a timely way to a more challenging learning task. Without such a colleague, my concern to affirm students might lead me into an educational dead end. The students in my classes might be enjoying themselves in a safe environment, but they would probably not be learning very much.

As a person who relies on words to communicate, it is useful for me to co-teach with someone who is more visually attuned than I. As a technophobe my teaching needs to be counterbalanced by working with someone proficient in computer-assisted instruction. On the other hand, my commitment to continually researching how students are experiencing their learning counterbalances the tendency of some of my colleagues to assume that things are going well if students are not actively complaining. In multiracial classrooms I need to teach with colleagues who are from the racial groups represented, or to involve cultural brokers to help me understand students' behaviors and to vouch for my trustworthiness and competence.

Unfortunately, what often passes for team teaching is sometimes only an agreement amongst a group of colleagues to divide a course into several discrete and different segments, each of which is the sole responsibility of one of the team. This is sequenced solo teaching, not team teaching. In true team teaching *all* activities are planned, conducted, and evaluated by all members of the team who are also all present for all class time. It is most emphatically *not* an agreement to teach only those classes in which one has expertise and then not to show up for the rest of the classes taught by ones' colleagues. True team teaching takes more time and energy than solo teaching because now all decisions have to be talked through with colleagues rather than remaining one's own judgment call. It is also more costly. Not surprisingly, autocratically inclined teachers don't like it, nor do cost-conscious administrators. But students often appreciate the energy generated by team teaching and the chance to work with different faculty who exhibit a range of identities and skills. If the norm in college was for diverse teaching teams to front diverse classrooms, we would be going a long way to addressing this issue effectively.

Mixing Student Groups

Teachers faced with students who exhibit wide variations in their backgrounds, identities, motivations, abilities, learning preferences, and temperaments sooner or later face the choice of how to group such individuals to accomplish specific learning tasks. Do you cluster together individuals who are roughly the same and who you think will therefore work well together? Or, do you create a pedagogic bouillabaisse—a mix of different experiential, racial, and personality ingredients, as well as students of different ability levels, who are stirred together to produce a satisfying blend? I would argue that both approaches are necessary and called for at different times.

Grouping students together who share a common curricular interest, or who are at the same ability level, allows them to learn without having to accommodate interests that are not their own or to be asked to work in ways that are too slow or too fast for them. This is something that is usually appreciated by students, particularly early on in a course. One exception to this is the reaction of White students to those students of color who choose to work together. White students may quickly conclude that Black or Brown students clustering together is a form of inverse racism, and feel excluded and rebuffed when making what they feel are good faith efforts to be inclusive. Although allowing students of color to work together in a group may discomfort the White majority, it often creates a safe haven for those students who share similar experiences of racism in the college, who understand the nuances of each other's communicative style, and who do not have to worry about always speaking circumspectly so as not to be misunderstood by or offend the White majority. Students working in groups comprised of similar racial identities or temperaments often find the experience much less jarring than when they are asked to work with students from different racial backgrounds or students with radically different personality types.

On the other hand, deliberately mixing students of different ability levels, interests, racial backgrounds, learning styles, and personalities also brings benefits. Firstly, it matches the reality of life outside the classroom where always choosing whom we will work or associate with is not an option. Most of us are required to work closely with people who are very different from ourselves. For that reason alone a major learning project of college should be that of learning how to work in groups of difference. Secondly, there are many learning tasks where a diversity of group members is an enhancement. For example, deepening our understanding of diverse perspectives in discussion can only happen when we are confronted with confident and credible expressions of those different perspectives.

Learning tasks that require creative problem solving also benefit from a mix of people who process information in very different ways, have varying approaches to understanding and responding to problems, and bring a range of priorities and experiences to the activity. It is interesting that whenever I preassign small-group membership in class, the balance of comments about this on the weekly CIQs is invariably favorable. Students say they appreciate being invited to work with peers they have not worked with before and that this brings an interesting experiential dimension to the course. It also often allows students to reappraise in a positive way the abilities and contributions of peers who had previously been dismissed.

There is often a developmental trajectory to mixing group membership. At the outset of a learning activity, students are understandably nervous about what waits ahead for them. In particular the anxieties of impostorship are very strong. When students encounter difference early on in a course, when they find themselves working with peers who clearly have more experience in the subject and are at a more advanced level, then their impostorship is raised to excruciating levels. In such a situation it is natural for people to seek out those they perceive as similar to themselves. However, as students get to know each other, become more familiar with the subject matter, and start trusting the teacher's credibility and authenticity, they are usually more open to working in mixed groups. So a prudent approach is to start by allowing students to cluster in groups characterized by similarity and then gradually to increase the amount of diversity of group membership they have to accommodate. The CIQ responses will give you a good sense of how fast to proceed in this matter.

Mixing Modalities

The most obvious response to encountering educational diversity is to employ the widest possible mix of pedagogic approaches and learning modalities within the classroom and to include the broadest possible racial and cultural diversity on the teaching team. As we know, this is much easier said than done. First, all the teachers on a teaching team may belong to one racial group. Second, external pressures may force us to move students through the curriculum at a prescribed pace that eliminates any experimentation with pacing. Third, as more and more students are placed into fewer and fewer classrooms, the possibilities for individualizing instruction or for temporarily grouping students by learning style, race, ability level, or focus of interest simply disappear. Nonetheless, we cannot do nothing. With some creativity it is possible to work towards including two or three different learning modalities into many of our lessons.

A helpful approach is to think of the different instructional choices open to most of us in our teaching. Teaching can be predominantly visual or oral, silent or speech filled, emphasize instructor demonstration or student experimentation, focus on abstract conceptualization or practical implementation, favor teacher talk or student talk, rely on teacher direction or student self-direction, be kinetic or static, and prefer independent study or group projects. Mixing activities along each of these axes is complicated and can sometimes appear confusing to learners. But if the rationale for our instructional choices is explained to students as part of our attempt to try to address as many different identities and styles as possible, and if our experimentations are monitored by the CIQ, then this confusion can be kept to a minimum.

Visual or Oral Communication

My own teaching style is heavily oral, and it is a real struggle for me to teach visually. This is why team teaching with a visually inclined person is so helpful to me and to my students. When this is not possible and I am on my own, I try to use visual handouts, PowerPoint presentations, video clips from films, video streaming from the Internet, and cartoons. An oral teacher like me will tend to use lots of stories and place great energy in selecting exactly the words she wishes to use to explain complicated ideas. A visual colleague can help by expressing these ideas graphically and by encouraging students to provide their own visual depictions of central concepts. For example, my writing partner and friend Stephen Preskill has experimented with an exercise called "Drawing Discussion" (Brookfield and Preskill, 2005, pp. 121–122) in which students depict their flow of talk visually, either two dimensionally or through collages of photos, cloth scraps, and other textured materials.

As an oral teacher I will also assume that when I've said something that I consider to be important that students will hear it in exactly the way I mean it and remember it clearly. I have been burned on numerous occasions when this turned out not to be true. I have given careful instructions for assignments in class, clearly (at least to my mind) set test dates, and painstakingly explained the criteria for judging A, B, or C papers, only for students to tell me later that I had never given them any of those messages. After having had several conversations with advisees in which I thought clear agreements had been reached, only to discover at a later date that these were unremembered by those same students, I started to insist that all my conversations with advisees be taped and that within a week of the meeting the students concerned provide a typed summary of the agreements we made that were recorded on the tape. I also make sure that important pieces of information are put in boldface in the course syllabus and then give students a graded test on that syllabus early in the semester.

Silent or Speech-Filled Classrooms

In the chapters on discussion I described the invisible norm that automatically privileges speech and teachers' implicit perception that student silence is a problem indicating either misunderstanding or lack of commitment. One of the easiest yet most dramatic ways to broaden learning modalities in the classroom is simply to plan silent periods when students are told that speech is not permitted. I do this in lectures by stopping talking and asking students to consider a question for two or three minutes, to write down some responses, and then to follow this up by talking over their responses in buzz groups. In discussions I often call a halt every fifteen to twenty minutes for a silent reflective pause when students write down the most important point made in the last fifteen-minute period of talk or the discussion theme that most needs pursuing in the next segment. The discussion resumes by my asking students at random to read out what they have written down.

One quiet exercise—newsprint dialogue—is a particular favorite of mine. I use this exercise as a silent way of debriefing small-group conversations when I want to return to whole-class discussion. Small groups summarize their conversations on large sheets of newsprint in the usual way and then post these around the classroom. I then post a blank sheet of newsprint next to each group's posting. I provide each student with a marker and tell him or her to wander about the room reading all the responses and adding comments. They do this as individuals, not in groups. Any time a student notices something she wishes to affirm or support, she records that directly onto the original posting or on the blank sheet posted next to it. Any time she disagrees with something, or needs clarification about something that's written, she writes that down too. She can also record any thoughts or ideas that the postings prompt in her. This exercise usually takes about ten minutes and happens in almost complete silence. Talk is not prohibited, it's just that people are very intent on reading and understanding what's written on the newsprint. When the whole class reconvenes, I tell them that we've just conducted the whole-class debriefing but that it's been done in writing rather than speech.

Teacher Demonstration or Student Experimentation

When helping students to acquire, and then apply, specific skills, teachers often spend considerable time demonstrating the required skills to students with the intent that students will then learn by imitating this performance. In this approach complicated intellectual and instrumental procedures are broken down into an incremental sequence of discrete steps, and teachers demonstrate how to perform these expertly at each stage of skill development. This is an approach I have used when teaching in such different contexts as little league soccer, recreational guitar, or when explaining how to undertake a critical analysis of literature in a Harvard graduate seminar. In the early stages of learning, providing this kind of scaffolding is important to students who appreciate having a clear image of what they are being expected to do. Demonstration as a teaching approach has the additional advantage of teachers modeling their own participation in, and commitment to, the learning activities they are asking of students. Given that students need to feel they are in the presence of a teacher who knows what she is doing, demonstration also helps build the kind of teacher credibility discussed in Chapter Four.

Problems arise, however, when the demonstration approach is emphasized so much that it allows the student little chance to try out the skills she is observing. An exemplary demonstration of skill early on in a course can be a double-edged sword. On the one hand it can provide a model of excellence that students may well find inspirational and to which they can aspire. On the other hand it can also be an off-putting display, a dazzling performance so apparently flawless that it ends up intimidating, rather than encouraging, students' desire to learn. Things are complicated further by the fact that different students in the same classroom may have these two different reactions to the same act of demonstration. If demonstrations are going to be used in teaching, then they are best conducted early on in a new learning sequence, before students have the chance to integrate bad habits into their skills repertoire. As with all other teaching approaches, they should also be monitored continuously through such mechanisms as the CIQ.

Abstract Conceptualization or Practical Illustration

To a large extent the degree to which teachers emphasize abstract conceptualization over practical implementation is determined by the content or skills they are trying to teach. But even in highly abstract subjects a measure of practical illustration will be appreciated. One of the most frequently mentioned themes in students' evaluations of teaching (and this applies across the disciplines) is the helpfulness of practical examples. As a general rule every new concept that is introduced into the curriculum should be accompanied by at least three practical illustrations from the teacher followed by the students' attempt to provide a fourth.

In order to give helpful examples of new concepts, it helps if the teacher knows something of the student's world. There is little point giving brilliant illustrations of difficult ideas if only the teacher understands their full resonance. As students in my classrooms become increasingly diverse (and younger!), the examples, metaphors, and analogies that make sense to me are rendered increasingly irrelevant.

Music, films, sitcoms, novels, and lines of poetry that are part and parcel of my cultural milieu are in no sense universal. Quoting thirty-five-year-old Monty Python sketches to students not even born until fifteen years after these sketches were first aired is not really an option for me these days. And even the contemporary pop culture examples I use will reflect my own racial and class membership. Some of my most embarrassing moments these days come from my attempts to quote dialogue from films or hip-hop lyrics and getting them hopelessly wrong. As a result I tend to stick to everyday tasks for the source material for my practical examples, such as riding the subway, going online, or shopping in supermarkets.

Teacher Talk or Student Talk

Teacher talk predominates in American higher education, and for many students this is just fine. If the teacher does all the talking, then the need for students to think or to take responsibility for their own meaning-making, understanding, and learning recedes. Teacher talk should not just be thought of as a sign of a teacher's arrogance or self-obsession, however. As Chapter Four emphasizes, many students need to feel they can trust the teacher, and to know that she is credible, before they will take learning seriously or participate in class. One of the chief ways that both credibility and authenticity are established is through teacher talk. This talk can show students that you know what you are doing and that your words are matched by your actions.

However, student talk is also crucial. First and foremost it is correlated with learning. The more that students speak out loud their emerging understandings, or raise questions that represent where they are in their struggles as learners, the more they are engaged. Even if their understandings and questions are confused, the fact that they are articulated bolsters the affective connection to learning. It also provides teachers with valuable information on which learning needs should be addressed next. Second, student talk is necessary for democratic classrooms. If you have any interest in your classroom being some kind of democratic analog, then there is no escaping the fact that there must be a great deal of student talk. Third, when student talk features prominently in class, and is listened to and responded to seriously by a teacher, it shows a true respect from the teacher for the student's opinions and concerns. Note, though, that we don't show respect by agreeing to and affirming every student comment. Rather, we show it by letting students know that we have listened carefully to them, have tried to understand what they are saying, and are ready to give our response to their comments in the clearest way we can. This good faith effort to understand another's perspective is at the heart of the communicative action so valued by Habermas (1992) as the foundation of democracy. Student talk is also necessary if teachers are to gain any sense of how students are experiencing their learning. Relying on nonverbal cues and gestures from students as indicators that allow us to "read" the emotional tenor and levels of understanding in a classroom is, as pointed out in Chapter One, very risky.

Teacher Versus Student Direction

In Chapter Four I indicated that an important element of credibility was teachers' being explicit about the rationale behind their classroom, curricular, and evaluative decisions. I also argued that making full disclosure of expectations, agendas, and criteria regarding teaching purposes and the assessment of learning was integral to authenticity. Giving clear teaching directions speaks to both of these factors by indicating to learners that the teachers concerned have a clear idea of what they are trying to accomplish and possess enough knowledge to make sure any directions given are clearly relevant to learning purposes. However, the giving of directions is not, in and of itself, always a good thing—it is all in how the directions are communicated. Directions can be confusing, baldly stated, issued as diktats, or seem to be arbitrary. The important point is that the directions provided must be perceived as clear, justified, and linked to educational purposes deemed important.

Students perceive teachers who give clear directions in very different ways. Some students see such teachers as authoritarian and arrogant, as focused only on their own agendas at the expense of students' needs and concerns. These same teachers are seen by other students as authoritative or clearly organized, as respecting the fact that students' time is not an unlimited resource, and as being concerned to work as productively as possible with them given the time available. Many Asian students will expect strong teacher direction and be confused if this is not forthcoming, at least initially. Field-dependent learners and syllabus-bound learners will also be drawn to such teachers. Even students who come in with suspicions of the teacher (perhaps they have been burned in high school or in other college classrooms by professors who look or sound like you) may also appreciate initial teacher direction since it gives them a chance to check out how consistently your words match your actions (a prime indicator of authenticity). Generally, student socialization is such that students will expect teachers to be directive, particularly about how best to secure that always desired A grade.

I grew up (professionally at least) fighting against this idea of directive teaching. The humanist-progressive paradigm of teaching, strongly influenced by Carl Rogers ([1961], 1995) and his notions of nondirective facilitation, was predominant while I was in graduate school in the 1970s. I felt the task of the teacher was to be a resource person in the service of student learning. My concern was to get out of the way of learners, to let their interests and motivations determine the course of their studies, and to be ready to step in with suggestions when consulted. Not surprisingly, my doctoral research was into independent learning conducted by learners outside the school system (Brookfield, 1981).

Over the years, however, my position has changed quite dramatically. I now agree with Freire's (Shor and Freire, 1987) view that "education always has a directive nature we can't deny. The teacher has a plan, a program, a goal for the study. But there is the directive *liberating* educator on the one hand, and the directive *domesticating* educator on the other" (p. 172). Myles Horton puts it (characteristically) more colloquially: "There's no such thing as just being a coordinator or facilitator, as if you don't know anything. What the hell are you around for, if you don't know anything. Just get out of the way and let somebody have the space that knows something, believes something" (Horton and Freire, 1990, p. 154). In other words, if you're a teacher you should stand for something. You should be honest about admitting that you have something to teach and some idea as to how learners can best learn it. The key points are whether or not your directions are (a) transparent to learners who can understand what your direction is and why you deem it important for their learning, and (b) open to being critiqued and challenged by learners.

A classroom assessment technique such as the CIQ can be used to judge how students perceive teachers' directions. If directions are seen as confused, arbitrary, pointless, or unfair, then these perceptions will pervade students' anonymous CIQ responses. At that point the teacher clearly needs to rejustify why the directions are being given and what they are intended to achieve, as well as trying to explain them more clearly. If the intent is to encourage students to take more responsibility for conducting their own learning, then this should be viewed as an incremental process of initiation—something that happens over time as students become more tolerant of ambiguity and increasingly knowledgeable about the learning options and resources open to them. True responsibility for learning can only be exercised when students have a full command of what Peters (1967) called the grammar of the learning activity; that is, an awareness of the criteria we use to judge whether something has been learned well or badly and a grasp of the essential concepts and skills that comprise the building blocks of knowledge in the learning area.

Diversity can never be fully addressed to the satisfaction of all involved. There are just too many variables to be accounted for, too many choices, too many contradictions. But neither can we just throw up our hands in bewilderment and refuse to acknowledge that we are working in increasingly diverse classrooms. If our purpose is to help people learn, then we must be open to constantly varying our activities in response to what we find out about the range of students in our classrooms. Of course, variations and experimentations are always bounded by our personalities, abilities, knowledge, and experience. We cannot constantly transform ourselves into something we are not. I cannot become an extraverted, large-gestured teacher fired by evangelical fervor. If I am working with large numbers of students from racial backgrounds other than my own, I cannot morph into someone of another race, using styles of communication and illustrative examples drawn from a different racial experience. For example, an African speech pattern such as call and response drawn from experiences of chain gangs, slave ships, and Black preaching traditions does not come easily to a White Anglo-American such as myself. It would be condescending and dishonest in the extreme for me to try to act like Cornel West or Jesse Jackson in a misguided attempt to identify with African American students. If I tried to play at being something I clearly am not, then the disjunction students perceived between who I am and who I am pathetically trying to be would be so glaring as to compromise my authenticity beyond repair.

Of all the approaches mentioned in this chapter, I find that team teaching with colleagues who share different racial backgrounds, personalities, and learning styles is the most helpful. I also rely on the CIQ to give me an accurate sense of what I am dealing with and how students view my efforts to address the range of styles, backgrounds, and desires in my class. In designing classroom activities and course assignments, I try to vary things (a rough rule is that each class I teach should have at least three different learning modalities evident) so that one learning style is not privileged too much. I also talk out loud to students the rationale for mixing modalities the way I do and constantly report back to them the spread of different responses each of these modalities produces on the CIQ. Throughout my classes I frequently remind students that the activity we're engaged in at any particular moment will be of interest only to a portion of the class and that soon we need to vary things so others feel included. But doing all these things doesn't remove my fundamental awareness that addressing diversity will always be only partially successful. Like democracy, inclusiveness is an ideal worth pursuing but one that will never be fully realized. But, like trying to work democratically, the effort to teach for diversity contains its own justification.

10

Giving Helpful Evaluations

Evaluating students' learning is when the power relationship inherent in teaching becomes public and undeniable. This is when the rubber of teacher authority hits the road of the student's learning journey. To evaluate is to judge, quite literally to assign value to something. Such acts of judgment invariably reveal the power and commitments of the judger. As teachers we may wish to have collegial relationships with our students and to be as supportive as possible of their learning efforts, but in students' eyes our power as evaluators of their learning means we can never be quite the same as them. We always have the power of the grade, of the evaluative commentary, of the ability to name publicly whether or not someone is working to the required standard. For teachers fired by a democratic impulse to deconstruct teacher-student power imbalances and a desire to view teachers and students as co-learners, co-creators of knowledge, this is a particularly troubling reality. As long as we work in hierarchically organized institutions with clear lines of command flowing from accreditation agencies to senior administrators, to department heads, to teachers, and then to students, the need to pass evaluative judgments that reflect someone's idea of what looks like effective learning cannot be avoided. Adopting a pass/fail grading system only blurs the sharp edges of this contradiction, since the passing or failing grade itself is based on notions of what constitutes acceptable levels of performance. In the words of one's student's remonstrance to me after I had declared my commitment to teaching democratically, "Your So-Called Democracy is Hypocritical Because You Can Always Fail Us" (Baptiste and Brookfield, 1997).

For those of us who wish to build collegial, supportive relationships with students, giving evaluations is one of the most difficult, demanding, and complex tasks we face; yet, done well, it is also one of the most significant spurs to learning. Through having their work evaluated, students learn to deepen their understandings, improve their skills, and become aware of new learning projects. They learn to internalize criteria for judging their work and practice that alter significantly how they approach these activities. So we should never forget that students invest enormous significance in teachers' evaluations of their work. Even students who have created confident social faces and built strong protective walls around their egos will find a negative comment from a teacher to be quite devastating. Alternatively, an appreciative comment from the same teacher can deepen commitment to learning. In terms of experiencing impostorship, receiving a poor evaluation may well be the moment when students conclude that their essential incompetence, their fraudulent entry into the community of learners, has finally been discovered and publicly revealed. Not surprisingly, then, giving evaluations is (quite appropriately) the feature of practice that gives rise to some of the most protracted and tortuous soul-searching among college teachers over the course of their careers. And this is how it should be! If we forget for a moment the impact our evaluative judgments have on students, or ignore the tremendous difference these judgments can make to the direction, intensity, and emotional tenor of students' learning, then we lose much of our sensitivity as teachers. For this reason, constantly asking yourself whether your evaluative judgments are fair and helpful, whether they are expressed understandably, and whether you're avoiding the traps of favoritism or prejudice is one sure sign of critically responsive teaching.

Giving evaluations is also important because it affords us the chance to exemplify aspects of the credibility and authenticity that, as Chapter Four pointed out, are so valued by learners. One important indicator of credibility—teacher conviction—is recognized when teachers make it plain to learners that they feel the subject matter, content, or skills being taught are so crucial that they want to explore every possible way they can to make sure students have learned these properly. The most common indicator of teacher conviction mentioned by students is the receipt of individual feedback or attention. The degree of detail, the clarity, the frequency, and the extensiveness of evaluations are correlated with learners' perceptions of the importance of the learning being judged. The more these features are present in evaluations, the more students see that teachers really believe this learning is important.

In terms of authenticity, the indicator of responsiveness—of the teacher clearly basing her practice on what she learns about how students are experiencing learning—is also addressed by evaluation. When teachers give students frequent evaluative information, and when they show how their evaluative judgments shape their learning, they are demonstrating responsiveness. Evaluation also speaks to the indicator of full disclosure, to the teacher's regularly making public the criteria, expectations, agendas, and assumptions that guide her practice. When students know what standards, criteria, and expectations they are being judged against, they are more likely to feel that they can trust the teacher to deal with them honestly and openly.

To evaluate something is to judge its worth. Concluding that one paper is better than another (because it is written more clearly, argued with more evidence cited, able to critique accurately the reliability of sources reviewed, and so on), or that one instrumental performance is more skilled than another (because it is closer to a professionally prescribed norm, adjusts well to unforeseen interferences, or produces the desired result in a shorter time) is to make a judgment on the basis of certain criteria. As argued earlier, these criteria are sometimes externally imposed on teachers by ministries of education, licensing boards, accreditation agencies, or department heads, and it may be that the teachers concerned believe these criteria are mistaken, ill-informed, even harmful. If you feel that you are teaching to indefensible criteria, then you have four options. First, you can grin and bear it and end up teaching to criteria you disagree with, a situation so contradictory as to produce anger, self-hatred, cynicism, and resignation. Second, you can quit your job. Third, you can work to alter these criteria by organizing with colleagues to change the requirements set by external licensing bodies. And, fourth, you can do what most settle for—move back and forth between your own agenda and that of the sponsoring authority, making sure your learners are equipped to move forward institutionally by doing enough of what is required of them while simultaneously undermining, subverting, or at least critiquing (and encouraging your students to critique) what to you are nonsensical evaluative criteria.

Some teachers try to escape the undeniably judgmental nature of evaluation by seeking refuge in the notion that evaluation is the value-free measurement of performance (a horrible word to describe learning with its connotations of going through one's paces in a circus ring, or of mounting a false show of competence to impress people) that can be judged according to objective criteria and indicators. But such criteria and indicators are never completely objective if that is taken to mean they are free of human judgment. In the last analysis evaluative criteria always rest on someone's belief that acting and thinking in certain ways is better than acting and thinking in other ways. To teach is to judge. As Freire (Shor and Freire, 1987, p. 2) argued:

> Education always has a directive nature we can't deny.
> The teacher has a plan, a program, a goal for the study.
> But there is the directive *liberating* educator on the one
> hand, and the directive *domesticating* educator on the

other. The liberating educator is different from the domesticating one because he or she moves more and more towards a moment in which an atmosphere of camaraderie is established in class. This does not mean that the teacher is equal to the students or becomes an equal to the students. No, the teacher begins different and ends different. The teacher gives grades and assigns papers to write. The students do not grade the teacher or give the teacher homework assignments! The teacher must also have a critical competence in his or her subject that is different from the students and which the students should insist on. But here is the central issue: In the liberating classroom, these differences are not antagonistic ones, as they are in the authoritarian classroom. The liberating difference is a tension which the teacher tries to overcome by a democratic attitude to his or her own directiveness.

Three important points concerning evaluation are made in Freire's comment. The first, and most obvious, is that teaching, and by implication evaluation, is always value-laden. The criteria we employ to decide that some educational approaches and curricular directions are more useful, just, important, relevant, humane, effective, or equitable than others are, at root, value judgments. Teachers always have an agenda, a direction in which they wish to take students that they believe is more worthwhile or important than the alternatives. In Freire's words, "Education is always directive, always. The question is to know towards what and with whom it is directive" (Shor and Freire, 1987, p. 109).

Second, Freire speaks of how liberating educators move towards collegial, collaborative modes of practice. In evaluative terms, this is seen when teachers and students evolve evaluative criteria and specify indicators together, when teachers encourage self-evaluation and peer-evaluation among their students, and when evaluative criteria and indicators established by teachers are placed before learners for their critique, scrutiny, and negotiation. Third, there is the difference Freire implies between authoritarian and authoritative teaching. The former imposes its will by the sheer force of tradition or institutional power. The latter imposes its will through the credibility, trust, and authenticity teachers establish in students' eyes (what Freire describes as the critical competence that the students should insist on). When teachers exhibit critical competence, they display expertise of a sufficient depth and breadth to convince students that they are sure to find their learning enhanced by being in the teacher's presence. Teachers with critical competence are aware of how their teaching contributes to making the world a better place, either as part of a broader social and political vision, or through the development of their individual students' capacities. Finally, they are able to engage in a constant critique of their vision and their methodology, and are eager to engage students in this critique. Teachers who possess these attributes of critical competence are authoritative but not authoritarian.

Helpful and Unhelpful Evaluations

Evaluation is not, in and of itself, a helpful thing. Evaluations can be done hurriedly and inaccurately, and they can be communicated poorly, confusingly, or condescendingly. This is as true for evaluations that praise as it is for those that criticize. Poorly conducted positive evaluations leave the learner feeling affirmed without knowing precisely why she should feel this way. Poorly conducted negative evaluations leave the learner feeling ashamed without knowing precisely what to do to improve matters. An evaluation is helpful to the extent that it clarifies for the learner what is meritorious about her work and what needs further effort. A helpful evaluation provides clear directions for the future and instills in the learner the desire to engage in further inquiry. It is written understandably and invites the learner to discuss with the teacher anything that strikes her as unfair, unclear, or unjustified. As a way of illustrating what I mean, let me give two examples of favorable evaluations—one unhelpful, one helpful.

Unhelpful Favorable Evaluation

This paper is terrific, well done. You've made a lot of progress this semester, and you can feel well pleased with your efforts. Keep up the good work.

Helpful Favorable Evaluation

This paper is terrific, well done. You've made a lot of progress this semester, particularly in three important areas:

1. You're much more careful about citing evidence in support of your arguments. For example, at the bottom of page 12 you quote three sources to support your contention that critical thinking is a contested concept. Then, on pages 17–19, your discussion of how textbooks ignore ethical dilemmas in critical thinking is illustrated by reference to most of the chief texts in the area.

2. You've taken much greater trouble to acknowledge viewpoints opposed to, and critical of, your own. A good example of this is your discussion on Skinner's work on page 7.

3. You're cutting down on your use of unnecessary jargon. Pages 4–6 and 11–13 were models of clear writing. The only time I felt I couldn't understand your argument was when you described the principle of falsifiability on pages 14–15.

Next time you try an assignment like this try to build on these improvements and see if you can cut down on the jargon even further. When you edit your next paper, try to pretend that you're reading it to a friend who knows nothing about the topic. If you come across a phrase you think this friend wouldn't understand, think about deleting this or rewriting it to make it more accessible. If it's a crucial concept, try to give two or three clear examples of it your friend would appreciate. For example, would she know what the term *praxis* (used on page 10) means? Overall, however, you can feel well pleased with your efforts. Keep up the good work.

––––––––––

Since both these evaluations are favorable, I'm assuming that students would be happy to receive either of them. However, only one of them—the second—is helpful. What are the differences (apart from length) between the two of them that make the second one so much more useful than the first? The individualized nature of the second evaluation is one clear difference. The student reading this evaluation knows the instructor has paid careful attention to her work. The first one, by way of contrast, comprises a number of generic comments that could conceivably be made about several papers from the same group. The second evaluation also clearly specifies which aspects of the student's work were so favorable. The first evaluation leaves a student with a warm glow but contains nothing from which she can learn. She knows she has done well and that the teacher likes her work. But exactly what it is about the work that is so improved and impressive is never made clear. By way of contrast, the second evaluation leaves her in no doubt about these things. The second evaluation also has a strong future orientation. The student knows she has done well, but she is also directed, in clear and specific terms, to work on particular items the next time she writes a paper like this one.

Let's turn now to two examples of negative evaluations. Both of these focus on a graduate student's behavior in a course on critical thinking.

––––––––––

Unhelpful Unfavorable Evaluation

I need to write to you about your behavior in class a couple of weeks ago. I don't like to say this, but I'm afraid your interruptions and comments in class discussions are having a really unfortunate effect on the group's dynamics. If you carry on with this disruptive pattern of behavior, I'm going to have to ask you to leave the group. The legitimate learning needs of the majority must always take precedence over any individual quirks. So please try not to be so disruptive in the future.

Helpful Unfavorable Evaluation

I need to write to you about your behavior in class yesterday. Please view my comments as being offered in the spirit of assistance. I don't think you're aware of how your behavior is being perceived by others in the group, and I'm concerned that you're losing the goodwill of your peers without your knowing this is happening.

I think you could be a terrific member of this class. Your enthusiasm, drive, and experience are valuable assets to any group, and I'm glad we have them as resources. But some things are happening to obscure the value of these assets. As examples, let me mention three things that happened in class yesterday that are worth your attention:

1. In the small-group exercise when your group was discussing the different intellectual traditions informing concepts of critical thinking, you spoke so much that in the fifteen minutes allocated for this exercise I noticed the other three group members speaking only once each. You are entitled to have your voice listened to seriously, but you spoke so quickly and confidently yesterday that the other group members could find no space in which to make their own, less forceful, contributions.

2. During the whole-class discussion of the small-group conversations, you nominated yourself as your group's reporter and then spoke as if all the points made in the report came only from you. I think your colleagues in the group would have liked some recognition.

3. When Stephanie was reporting her group's comments, I and the rest of the class heard you make a joke about "a woman's place" and men "being on top" that distracted the group's attention, threw Stephanie off her stride, and was clearly sexist.

If these kinds of behavior continue I'm concerned that your credibility in the class will be completely destroyed. It would be a real shame if class members closed their ears to your insights just because of some unfortunate behaviors on your part of which you're probably unaware. So I'd like you to begin a self-conscious pattern of behavior change when the class meets again next week. As a start, please try to do the following things:

1. In any small-group exercise in which you participate, don't be the reporter who gives an account of the group's discussions to the larger class.

2. When you've made a contribution in both the small- and large-group discussions, please wait until at least three other people have spoken before you talk again. You can forget this rule if someone asks you a question directly.

3. For the next three weeks don't crack jokes while other people are making their group's presentations to the whole class.

Let's try this for three weeks and then meet to talk about what each of us thinks has been happening.

If anything I've said in this memo is unclear please feel free to call, e-mail, or visit me personally to talk it over. My number is 651-962-4982 and my e-mail address is sdbrookfield@stthomas.edu.

Both these evaluations would be hard for a student to take, leaving him or her feeling threatened, not to say devastated. There is no way to entirely anesthetize against the pain of receiving negative instructor evaluations. But there are some important differences between the two examples given. The first evaluation probably leaves the learner overwhelmed with feelings of shame and anger, but with no sense of exactly what it is that she is doing wrong. The only message conveyed is that the student is bad and needs to stop being bad as soon as possible. But why she or he is bad, what it is that must be stopped, and how the student can change for the better, are never revealed. Note also that the first evaluation is given two weeks after the events described, by which time the learner's memory of the class will probably be dim.

By way of contrast, the second evaluation is given very soon after the events, which heightens its significance for the learner. The evaluation specifies which particular actions the teacher finds objectionable. It then suggests in clear and concrete terms what the student might do to improve the situation. Instead of only being condemned for bad behavior, the learner is told why it is in his own best interests to consider changing. The teacher also acknowledges the student's experience and enthusiasm, a fact that should help him feel respected while being criticized. The student also has the possibility of reacting to the evaluation after the next three weeks of classes and can contact the teacher for further clarification and discussion. The student does not have to bottle up feelings of shame, anger, or embarrassment but can talk through these with their instigator.

Characteristics of Helpful Evaluations

From these four examples of favorable and unfavorable evaluations we can discern key characteristics of evaluations that can be described as helpful.

Clarity

Be as clear and transparent as possible in your evaluative judgments. Let students know from the outset what criteria you are using to judge their efforts. Describe specific actions you find favorable or unfavorable and those on which you want students to concentrate. As an example of my attempt to do this, here is the grading rubric I used in a graduate education class I taught while writing this chapter:

EDLD 913: POWER, FREEDOM, AND CHANGE

Criteria Used to Grade Essays

Your essays will be graded according to the following criteria:

1. *The clarity of the writing.* —Are your ideas clearly stated, organized into paragraphs with linking statements, and grammatically correct? Do we as readers struggle to understand what you're saying because we can't follow your sentences or comprehend your meaning?

2. *The accuracy of your ideas.* —When you describe concepts central to the course, are these clearly and accurately elucidated? Do you illustrate your understanding of these central ideas by providing frequent illustrations and examples?

3. *The degree to which your assertions are supported.* You will be making claims regarding the ideas of the authors you are summarizing in your essays. Are these claims and assertions fully supported by references to specific elements in their work? Do you give at least three quotes and citations, as well as specific page references, to support each of your summaries of authors' key ideas? Is the bibliography accurate?

4. *The degree to which you place the ideas you review in the contexts of your own life and experiences.* Do you show how the authors' ideas are confirmed or contradicted by your experiences? Do you place ideology, hegemony, disciplinary power, automaton conformity, repressive tolerance, democratic process, and so on in the context of your life and support your analysis by providing appropriate illustrations and examples?

5. *The critique you supply.* Do you identify the assumptions undergirding authors' positions and your own conclusions? Do you critique the accuracy and validity of authors' assumptions and also of your own arguments?

A+ Your essay is almost ready for professional publication in a major journal in the field with only a few minor editorial changes. It excels in meeting all 5 criteria.

A   Your essay satisfactorily meets all five of the criteria described above.

A- Your essay satisfactorily meets criteria 1, 2, 3, and 4.

B+ Your essay satisfactorily meets criteria 1, 2, and 3.

B   Your essay satisfactorily meets criteria 1 and 2.

B- Your essay satisfactorily meets only criterion 1 described above.

C   Your essay meets none of the criteria described above and requires major revision.

Immediacy

Give any evaluative judgments you make as soon as possible for the learning events on which you are commenting, before the pressures of life outside the classroom (or other teachers' evaluations of the student's work in other courses) flood in to distract the learner's attention.

Regularity

Try to comment regularly on students' work. Even if all you do is acknowledge that learners are doing their best to follow your suggestions, this is still important for them to hear. When you are asking the learner to make major changes in her work, you need to monitor her efforts closely, especially in view of the learning rhythm of incremental fluctuation (two steps forward, one step back) described in Chapter Five's discussion of roadrunning.

Accessibility

Give your comments in language and with examples people understand. Also, provide opportunities for students to discuss with you the meaning of your evaluations. Students may misinterpret your comments or be so demoralized with impostorship that they focus only on the negative aspects. For students reeling from the shock of negative evaluations, it is important to know they have the chance to respond to your comments, to seek clarification, and to discuss with you any aspects of the evaluation that disturb them.

Individualized

As Chapter Four established, the more individualized the feedback the student receives the more she feels it is important to learn the abilities or skills the teacher is trying to develop. Giving detailed, clearly individualized attention to learners' efforts makes it clear that you consider it important that they learn the desired content and also shows that you respect the effort they have made. Of course, when individualizing evaluations it is important to focus on the student's actions, not her personality. People should not feel their whole being is under assault.

Affirming

Always try to acknowledge students' efforts and achievements, however slight these might seem to you, before making critical comments about their work. At times it might seem like a stretch to find something positive to acknowledge, and, if someone clearly has not taken an assignment seriously, there is no point dishonestly praising something that is not really there. But effort should always be acknowledged, even if you feel it has been badly misdirected.

Future-Oriented

Give clear suggestions about specific actions students should take to make progress in the short and long term.

Justifiable

Do your utmost to show how attending to the evaluative comments you make will be in the student's best long-term interests. People have the right to know why you're praising or criticizing them. More particularly, they need to be sure that your criticisms spring from a concern for their learning, not from your own obsessions or from personal dislike.

Educative

Keep asking yourself "What can this person learn from my comments?" A good evaluation is one from which students can learn. Evaluations should not leave students just feeling good or bad about what they've done; they should inform learners about the valuable parts of their work and provide guidance for future actions. If students only feel warmed or ashamed by your evaluation, then it isn't educative.

Improving Your Evaluations

In contrast to the reams of advice available in textbooks concerning how to improve instruction, there is relatively little attention given to how you might improve the way you give your evaluations. Yet, from the student's point of view, your evaluations represent a major learning moment, one that can be confusing or demoralizing, clarifying or inspirational. Consequently, trying to improve how she gives evaluations should represent a major professional development task for any committed teacher. Two possible ways this task might be undertaken suggest themselves. First, teachers can reflect on their own experience of being on the receiving end of evaluations and try to identify what it was about the experience that was either helpful or demoralizing. They can then try to build some of these features into their own practice. Second, they can ask their students to comment on which evaluative behaviors and approaches were most helpful to them and then do their best to make sure these are contained in the evaluations they give to students.

For a teacher to experience being evaluated provides an invaluable window into the visceral, emotionally charged reactions this process induces in learners. To receive another's evaluations of your work is a powerful, often humbling, and always enlightening experience. If those who regularly give evaluations of others' efforts receive regular evaluations of their own endeavors, they can hardly escape the visceral significance of such scrutiny. Being on the receiving end of an evaluation is an excellent way to sensitize yourself to those aspects of evaluation that affirm and illuminate, and those that demean and confuse. For example, as a writer who regularly submits his work to academic journals and conference panels as part of a blind review process, I am subject to frequent critiques. My manuscripts are criticized for their unnecessarily obscure language, their lack of practicality, their tendency to repetition, and their political tone (or sometimes for their lack of political analysis). When I first receive these criticisms, I usually act emotionally to them. Often, my first impulse is to fire off an angry e-mail broadside haranguing the editors for their lack of judgment in choosing such obviously uninformed reviewers to comment on my work. Even though, rationally, I know I am being unfair and reacting instinctively and defensively, the strength of my reaction has not diminished much with time.

Gradually, however, I settle down and give the reviews a second, third, and fourth reading, and it is then that I start to make some judgments about the helpfulness of these evaluations. If a review of my manuscript is wholly negative and overlaid with a tone of personal insult, then it loses credibility for me. For example, if a reviewer called one of my books vacuous nonsense, said it had no content, contained nothing specific to teachers, and was replete with hollow chapter and section titles, it would obviously be hard for me to read this. But if the reviewer supported these criticisms by making a strong case that critical reflection and critical thinking were irrevocably disciplinary based processes that could not be spoken of as generic mental processes in the way that I had, then I would be open to learning from them. However, if the insightful challenge of this critique was sabotaged by comments such as that students in teacher training courses were "not the brightest people around" and that the "drivel" my book represented would leave them more confused than ever, then the credibility of the critique would be damaged in my eyes. A review that pointed out my conceptual confusion but omitted the personal tone would be one I would take far more seriously.

Being aware of my own reactions to negative evaluations reminds me to scrutinize the evaluations I give to students for any derogatory personal comments I might unwittingly be making, and to make sure

I acknowledge that even though their efforts might be misguided, at least they tried to do their best. If I pay more attention to reviews of my own work that show some evenhanded recognition of my efforts, then I reason that students will have the same reaction. Again, if I receive an evaluation that makes blanket criticisms (for example that my work is drivel or vacuous nonsense), but that gives no specific examples of where my efforts are in error and could be improved, then I am left with no fruitful directions to pursue. Knowing that generalized criticisms do little other than frustrate or demoralize me helps me to remember to focus on specific errors when I am evaluating my own students' work, to suggest items that they can work on in the future, and to give students the chance to react to my criticisms by seeking further clarification of any ambiguities.

A second option to improve your evaluative skills is to ask students to evaluate the evaluations you give them. This sometimes happens as part of end-of-course student surveys of teaching. Such surveys assess a variety of instructional activities including the evaluative behaviors of the teacher. The problem with many of these end-of-semester student opinion forms is that students fill them in at the last class meeting as summative course evaluations, giving the teacher no opportunity to work at improving her evaluative skills as they apply to those students who completed the forms. Sometimes information about your evaluative behaviors will be offered throughout the semester on the CIQ form without any need for prompting by you, particularly if you have returned marked assignments in class that day. At other times it may be necessary to add an item to the CIQ focusing only on how you give evaluations. You can also ask students individually to tell you what they found most helpful in your evaluations, or you can conduct a conversation about this in groups. My own preference is always for students' comments to be made anonymously, since this increases the likelihood that such comments will be honest expressions of opinion. The characteristics of helpful evaluations specified earlier in this chapter have come, in large measure, from anonymous students' comments to me about the aspects of my evaluations that they particularly appreciated.

11

Teaching Online

Since the first edition of this book appeared, several profound changes have occurred in higher education. Its clientele has broadened to include students from a wide range of ethnic and racial diversity, there has been an enormous growth in proprietary higher education (the University of Phoenix being the most prominent example), and the need to do more with less (as budgets are continually shorn while student numbers are expected to grow) means faculty are under increasing and unending stress. For most college teachers, however, I would imagine that the biggest change in their lives has been the requirement for them to integrate some measure of online teaching into their practice. Many colleges now offer whole degrees online, and even those faculty who still teach primarily face to face have to take account of students' desire to have course resources posted on the web, syllabuses and course announcements distributed to them electronically, and some opportunity provided for them to communicate with each other online about course activities. So many colleges have purchased WebCT or Blackboard programs that course registration and grade posting is conducted electronically for a majority of students. These days no college teacher can avoid teaching in a hybrid manner, combining electronic and face-to-face communication. The only question remaining is the degree to which electronic communication is integrated into course activities.

My initial reaction to this development was political, intellectual, and pedagogical skepticism. Politically, online education seemed to commodify learning, to turn it into an external object marketed for a hefty price to save cash-strapped programs trying to stay afloat. To me it appeared to embody some of the typical excesses of capitalism by turning a dynamic, fluid, and unpredictable phenomenon—the process of learning and teaching—into an objectified product, something to be bought and sold on the open market. I also felt that the exclusionary patterns built into face-to-face education would be magnified even more online. Instruction was overwhelmingly in English, students without experience on, or access to, computers would be penalized, and there would be little opportunity for any kind of remedial counseling. Intellectually, I feared that standardizing courses for online delivery to a wide audience would mean dumbing them down—removing all ambiguity that could not be resolved via e-mail and focusing only on accessible, simple materials that could be used by students with a wide variety of ability levels. Pedagogically, I felt that online teaching took the personal dimension out of teaching, removing the relational element that I always believed to be so important to learning. How could students learn to trust someone they never saw in person or spoke to directly?

These fears ebbed as some interesting things started to happen. First, students began to tell me that some of my classroom exercises (such as newsprint dialogue) paralleled online teaching processes (such as threaded conversation). That made me realize that online teaching was not necessarily qualitatively different from its face-to-face counterpart. Indeed, various introductory guides to e-teaching explore many of the exact same problems (how to engage students, respond to racial differences, take account of different learning styles, and so on) that engage the attention of teachers in face-to-face classrooms (Palloff and Pratt, 2003; Conrad and Donaldson, 2004). Second, I realized that one of my chief preoccupations as a classroom teacher—to avoid one or two powerful voices dominating the discussion—might be differently (and maybe more easily) addressed in an online environment.

In asynchronous discussion learners would have the time to think through their responses without the pressure to come up with an impromptu contribution or response to a teacher's question that would make them look good in class. Students who struggled with language, who were introverts, or who needed time to process information and create meaning, as well as those who were intimidated by the theater of the classroom (particularly having to play the role of the smart, capable, committed student), would all benefit from online learning's privacy. The online environment also placed a greater degree of control into the student's hands over when and how fast learning happened, something Piskurich (2003) argues increases both retention and self-directed learning. Finally, whenever I did engage in some measure of online teaching, the students involved stressed the importance of feeling a member of some kind of learning community in exactly the way that students in my face-to-face classrooms did—a dynamic explored by Palloff and Pratt (2004) and Lewis and Allan (2005).

However, although a case can be made that the dynamics of online teaching are not intrinsically different from those of the face-to-face classroom, there are contextual features that need to be borne in mind since they give online teaching a particular resonance. First, the learner's physical isolation means that the importance of individualized evaluation is more crucial than ever. Given that online course materials are usually prepared well in advance, the main teaching actions that happen online occur in the giving of evaluative comments. Not only does evaluation help the student learn, it also convinces her of the social presence of the teacher in cyberspace (a notion I will say more about later in the chapter). Second, the time spent in giving extensive feedback is, itself, considerable. One of the greatest misconceptions about online teaching is that it is somehow a "quick and dirty" version of the much more complex reality of classroom teaching. Nothing could be further from the truth. Teachers who have taught online will usually say that their face-to-face classrooms are far less time consuming.

Third, the possibility of reading and giving visual and tonal cues in classroom communication is obviously rendered almost impossible. Despite attempts to develop a visual and tonal shorthand for online communication (smiley faces, exclamation points, dots for pauses, boldface and capitals to express importance, and so on), the scope for massive misinterpretation of comments exists. Words written are very different creatures from words spoken with a warmth or frigidity of tone, accompanying gestures of emphasis or dismissal, and lively facial expressions that communicate interest, empathy, or contempt. It is also the case that real-time or live conversations held online exhibit distinct dynamics (Hoffman, 2003, 2004). At a very basic level, fast typists enjoy a distinct advantage over those with little keyboard experience. Also, unlike a live face-to-face conversation, there is a delay (sometimes rather prolonged) between the individual typing the words she wants to convey and all other chat participants seeing the words projected on the computer screen. Such delays often result in responses that overlap with each other, leading to multiple lines of communication that can be confusing and disorienting. Since live chats cannot work at all unless the group of participants is small, the instructor who decides to rely heavily on them may find herself, particularly in a large class, committing to as many as five or six one-hour chats a week. In Palloff and Pratt's (1999) opinion, live chat "rarely allows for productive discussion or participation and frequently disintegrates into simple one-line contributions of minimal depth" (p. 47).

Almost by default, then, the primary mode of student-to-student and student-to-instructor interaction in an online course occurs through asynchronous discussion. The advantages of this kind of interaction include its flexibility and convenience, the time it affords learners to think things through, and the fact that participants in hard-to-reach locations can be accommodated. However, an online course can seem a very "cold" emotional climate for some learners, particularly extroverts who crave the synergy of people in a room arguing, clarifying, disagreeing, and encouraging each other in learning. Similarly, students from cultures in which collective decision making is the norm, and in which individual identity is considered as something that can never be separated from racial or tribal group membership, will find it a deeply unnerving experience to sit by themselves, stare at their screen, and respond to words typed by others at a different time and in a different place.

Familiarizing Ourselves with the Online Experience

Before teaching in cyberspace for the first time, it is a definite advantage if you can take an online class as a learner. Noticing what affirms or demeans you, and what helps or hinders your learning in an online environment, helps you understand what will make for a supportive learning environment in your own online course. A minimum recommendation for all teachers working online is to secure a special ID that will allow them to view their class through their students' eyes. To enter your own course as if you were a student, without the capacity you possess as the instructor to manipulate and alter the online environment, provides a valuable new perspective on the course. It also brings to the surface the learning approaches you most favor and the knowledge and skills you most value which may, or may not, match those favored and valued by your students.

It is also helpful while planning your own online courses to have access to similar courses taught by online veterans. Being able to access a colleague's class while it is in progress, see how she organizes the course and handles student-to-student and student-to-instructor interaction is enormously helpful in putting your own course together. Once your own class is up and running, it is equally valuable to have an experienced colleague sign on as a student or teaching assistant, something that can be easily done through WebCT or Blackboard. Your colleague can take a quick peek at the class as if she were a student much more easily and conveniently than is the case in a conventional class. Unlike face-to-face peer observation, there is no need to coordinate complicated schedules or require colleagues to fight traffic in the effort to observe your class. Your colleague can sign on as a guest and offer observations about the course's content and organization. It is especially helpful for a colleague to negotiate the menu of resources you have posted and to review the discussion postings or chat records to assess how well class conversations are deepening students' understanding and promoting student participation.

One of the major complications surrounding the introduction of online teaching is that many teachers (including me) who teach online have spent most of their years as elementary, high school, and college learners in conventional face-to-face classrooms. This learning history inevitably frames the approach they take to teaching in an environment fundamentally different from the one they know as learners. This is why I advocate taking a class online before teaching one. In an ideal world any enthusiastic dean, vice president, or president who urges an expansion of online education in their institution should provide teachers with at least two course releases; one in the semester or quarter prior to beginning online teaching so that the prospective teacher may take an online course as a learner, and one in the semester or quarter that the course is being taught to take account of the large investment of time needed to prepare for and conduct online teaching well. But since we don't live in an ideal world, we have to work with what we have—and this chapter examines how teachers new to online teaching can help create the conditions for student learning.

Skillful Teaching Online

As argued earlier, online teaching does not represent a qualitatively different form of practice that renders irrelevant any insights drawn from classroom practice. The three core assumptions of skillful teaching (good teaching is whatever helps students learn, good teaching is critically reflective, and the most important knowledge teachers need to do good work is how students experience their learning) apply equally online and face-to-face. Credibility and authenticity in teachers are just as important to online learners as they are to those in classrooms. And students in online classes feel like impostors, run the risk of cultural suicide, lose innocence, and experience incremental fluctuation, while also needing the sense of community felt by their face-to-face counterparts. In particular, the need to research how students are experiencing learning and the importance of demonstrating teacher responsiveness are as crucial in the online classroom as they are in the conventional one.

The Importance of Research

As described in Chapter Three, the Critical Incident Questionnaire (CIQ) solicits information from students about how they are experiencing the course. In online environments this works in exactly the same way as in face-to-face teaching. After collecting students' anonymous opinions at least once a week, instructors regularly report a summary of these to students and consider what they mean for the online environment. Because of information gained from the CIQ, teachers sometimes change features of the online class to make it more satisfactory for students. At other times they have to rejustify and reexplain why they can't change the course organization and why activities that are disliked by learners are integral to students' intellectual development. As with its classroom variant, it is essential that CIQ feedback from students be captured in the form of anonymous, written responses, and securing this anonymity initially posed problems for me in my early efforts teaching online. However, two ways to address this problem are available. First, students can go to the Discussion Postings on a WebCT page and check a box that automatically records all responses for that particular posting as anonymous. An alternative is to have a students-only course listserv or chat room where students post their CIQ responses to each other and then have one of their number compile these and post the summary to faculty.

Since most online class activities are asynchronous, it is important to specify on each CIQ the inclusive dates that constitute the "week" in question. Otherwise the questions are the same as for the face-to-face version:

_____

1. At what moment during this week of online class were you most engaged as a learner?

2. At what moment during this week of online class were you most distanced as a learner?

3. What action that anyone took during this week of online class did you find most affirming or helpful?

4. What action that anyone took during this week of online class did you find most puzzling or confusing?

5. What surprised you most about online class during this week?

_____

After analyzing the CIQ responses using the same procedure outlined in Chapter Three, the results are reported in a prominent place on the course welcome page (or in an e-mail posting to all learners) to ensure that students read them. Students are then invited to post written reactions, questions, and elaborations regarding the CIQ summary that all students in the class can view and consider. Then, based on what is received, the instructor proposes, if necessary, a course of action to address the concerns raised.

Being Responsive

Instructional responsiveness is central to the creation of an effective online learning environment. Such responsiveness is evident when instructors seek out student concerns, share those concerns publicly with students, and take action to address them. Examples of such action are building on students' comments to reorganize the course for ease of navigation or addressing what students say in online discussions. These actions underscore that student issues are heard, taken seriously, and acted upon. Responsiveness is probably the most important factor contributing to the success of a discussion-based, online class.

It is important to acknowledge, however, that it is neither possible nor desirable to give students feedback every time they contribute to an online class. First, there are not enough hours in the day to make this work. Second, such an obsessive level of responsiveness only causes students to become more dependent upon the instructor's comments and approval. However, my experience supports Fein and Logan's (2003) observation that "from the very beginning of the course, the instructor should foster a high-quality feedback environment by establishing an expectation around the importance of instructor-student and student-student feedback" (p. 53). The reason for this is simple. Learning online can be a lonely, unrewarding experience. It can also breed uncertainty and loss of confidence. When instructors are relatively absent from discussion, students begin to wonder: Why aren't I hearing more from the teacher? What is she doing as I slog my way through these learning modules? What does she think about the quality of my work? Why should I be taking so much time to express my ideas when she takes so little time to acknowledge them?

The number one complaint from online learners is the low level of instructor responsiveness. Students clearly need to hear from us on a regular basis. For those students who tend to be less engaged, or at least less participatory, it is particularly important to receive frequent responses from the instructor, often in the form of simple acknowledgments or requests for further information. One advocate of online discussion (Bender, 2003) urges teachers to be up-front about their likely level of participation. She writes, "Making explicit the frequency of your participation in class helps students to anticipate when they will be hearing from you, and also will not give false impressions that just because the class is available 24/7, that you are, too" (p. 57).

One theme stressed in the literature concerning the importance of responsiveness to online teaching is the "social presence" of the instructor, defined by Gunawardena (1995) as the extent to which someone "is perceived as a 'real person' in mediated conversation" (p. 151). Gunawardena and Zittle (1997) argue that social presence has two major components, intimacy and immediacy. Intimacy is the sense the learner enjoys that the instructor is responding in an individualized way to her efforts and has an awareness of her as a person. Immediacy refers to the speed of instructor feedback. Both elements help bridge the physical and psychological distance that exists between instructor and students in online environments. The evidence is fairly strong, according to Gunawardena and Zittle (1997), that "social presence is a strong predictor of satisfaction" in computer-mediated conferencing environments (p. 23). Drawing on the research of others, Aragon (2003) claims "that social presence facilitates the building of trust and self-disclosure within an online learning context" (p. 61) and urges instructors to enhance their social presence by remaining actively involved in the discussions taking place on discussion boards, providing frequent opportunities for students to respond to instructor comments, giving timely feedback (responding to all student e-mails within a day), striking up conversations with students who arrive early for live chats, and including their own personal experiences in responses they post to students' stories.

Creating Participatory Discussion Online

One way to warm the climate for online learning, and to give students the sense they are part of an active learning community, is to stimulate as much participatory discussion as possible. A participatory discussion is one in which most learners participate, in some form, at least part of the time. Without broad participation in online discussion, students suffer a sense of isolation, a sense of lacking membership in a virtual learning community. Yet a feeling of belonging is reported as crucial to keeping students in online programs (Lewis and Allan, 2005). Students also need practice in expressing their ideas cogently, and participating in online discussion allows them to have access to the diversity of viewpoints that helps them make connections between different aspects of content. One strategy to increase participation online is to hold occasional real-time conversations in which each person in the group, in turn, has a chance to make a comment about the topic under discussion without interruption from anyone else. In this online variant of the Circle of Voices exercise, more free-flowing conversation ensues once all the participants have had an opportunity to post their initial responses. Each person's contribution, however, must somehow refer to what someone else has said during the first round. This helps ensure wider online participation, but it does create two additional problems. First, the discussion sometimes becomes rather stilted and can sap energy as the group waits for each person to post. Second, once the more open dialogue resumes, the same problem can arise of a few people dominating the exchange.

The technique known as Circular Response also prevents a few people from dominating the exchange and helps bring focus to participants' contributions. Circular Response requires all speakers to begin their remarks by commenting on the previous participant's observations and to use those observations as a springboard for their own contributions. Once again, online environments are particularly conducive to this process. Contributors to the conversation can actually see and read what the previous speaker has said and thus more easily frame their comments to explore the themes that were raised. Indeed, Circular Response is so well suited for online discussion that it would be quite appropriate to require that all online exchanges begin with a reference to a previous contribution.

According to learners, online instructors need to be present and participate even more than do instructors in face-to-face discussions. However, this emphasis on teacher participation raises the danger of too much teacher voice. The crucial variable is the manner of the instructor's participation. Declarative statements, mini-lectures, overly extensive and lengthy corrections of students' misguided understandings are all to be discouraged and kept to a minimum.

A wide variety of brief, concise observations, questions, clarifications, affirmations, and acknowledgments are the best ways for teachers to maintain "social presence," while keeping students coming back for more conversation and participation.

Keeping Online Discussion Focused

As is the case with face-to-face classroom discussion, its online variant can easily get sidetracked by one or two particularly strong individuals whose agendas, passions, or fixations determine what the rest of the class focuses on. In an online context (as in a face-to-face classroom), discussion is focused when participants' exploration of the topic entails them offering evidence to support their point of view, explaining the basis for that view, recalling and summarizing some of the multiple viewpoints that have been shared, attempting to identify connections between contributions already made, and showing how the discussion has changed their thinking or added to their knowledge. The initial responsibility for creating such a focus lies with the instructor who can work to keep students connected to the topic by inserting questions and comments such as:

> How does your observation relate to the topic of discussion?
>
> What is the connection between your comment and what was just said?
>
> Can you explain how your idea is helping us to make sense of this subject matter?
>
> We seem to have wandered away from the main topic. What do we need to do to get back on track?
>
> Who has a comment or question that can help us regain our focus?

A teacher's attempts to model keeping discussion focused, and letting students know this is what she's doing, is crucial. In different ways it is both easier and harder to encourage these behaviors online. It is easier because students can read comments the instructor has made and see clearly how the instructor has responded to their ideas. What makes it harder is the fact that the instructor often cannot intervene in the middle of an exchange and may even find that once she has responded, the rest of the group has moved on to another topic or issue. There are two ways to deal with this problem. One is to orient students from the outset toward the idea of focused discussion by including references to it in the syllabus and deliberately attempting to practice it during a required face-to-face orientation. The other is to be persistent and consistent in asking the kinds of questions that are listed above while letting students know your purpose is to keep the discussion as focused as possible.

An important element in keeping online discussion focused is fostering dialogue that is evidence-based or clearly grounded in some explicit reasoning. Again, it is important that teachers initially model questions and comments such as those below to get students in the habit of thinking through and supporting their responses:

How do you know what you say is true?

What evidence do you have to support that claim?

What is the source of that point of view?

Whose work that we have studied confirms what you are saying?

By what process of reasoning did you reach that conclusion?

Students should be supported when they pose such questions to their classmates and hold one another accountable for backing up comments with evidence, logic, experience, justifications, rationales, and so on. An important indicator of success is when students apply these same standards to assessing the teacher's contributions. Online instructors can help this process along by publicly subjecting their own comments to these focusing questions.

Keeping focused in online discussion is also helped when participants can summarize what they have learned from the conversation. One way to encourage summaries is to pose a final synthesis question to the group in real-time online chats. The synthesis question offers the added bonus of creating a thinking pause in the conversation. Once the final synthesis question is posed, everyone must withhold comment until a minute or two has elapsed. Participants are invited to write their final thoughts as a way of slowing down the pace of the discussion thus giving participants more time for reflection.

Examples of synthesis questions are:

How has this discussion changed the way you are thinking about this topic?

What is the most memorable thing you have heard here today?

What question or questions does this discussion prompt you to ask?

What is something that you learned or relearned here today?

What do you know now that you did not know before this dialogue began?

What assumptions that you had about this topic have been confirmed or questioned for you by this discussion?

Note that these synthesis questions are not summarizing questions in the sense of giving a précis of the discussion. Instead they provide a final reflective moment to think about what has been learned and what new learning projects have been suggested. Once the habit of responding to final synthesis questions becomes ingrained, learners often develop greater proficiency in commenting on the discussion as a whole. Synthesis questions also heighten the feeling that the effort participants have put into the dialogue has been worthwhile.

Online environments are especially well suited to practicing this kind of disciplined dialogue. Unlike live, face-to-face conversation, asynchronous exchange permits learners a relatively leisurely review of everything that has been said. This makes it easier for them to look for recurring themes, essential questions, and emerging understandings. The challenge is to build in ways to redirect students to previous discussions, so they can review everything that has been said and record their reflections. Sometimes the online assignments are so numerous that there isn't time to revisit previous postings. Johnson and Aragon (2003) note that one of the biggest problems with online courses is a tendency toward "information overload" (p. 37). The solution is, of course, to slow the pace and require fewer assignments.

The learning pause that occurs in the wake of the synthesis question has special value in addressing the problems of live online chat. Instructors who are interacting in real time online with a small group of students can leave ten to twelve minutes at the end of the chat for responses to a final synthesis question. When the question is posed, all activity in the chat is suspended and participants are asked to spend the next two or three minutes quietly scrolling back through the whole dialogue. Each student in turn then offers a response, taking about a minute to address the synthesis question. Some sort of rotation should be worked out ahead of time—assigning numbers to learners may work best. Each respondent attempts, in some manner, to take account of the content of the dialogue just reviewed. This has three advantages. First, participants have the opportunity to review the entire dialogue that has occurred, thus producing more focused, disciplined, and thoughtful comments. Second, this procedure avoids the problem of overlapping dialogue. Third, it brings a more relaxed sense of closure to what can sometimes be a disorienting and frenetic experience.

Organizing the Online Course for Discussion

In order for an online class to work it must be well organized. Good course organization is evident when (a) students understand clearly from the beginning the expectations for the class, the criteria they are being judged by, and how and when assignments are due;

(b) students are assigned to small, deliberative groups to promote interaction in discussion boards and live chat; (c) students see clearly how the opportunities for interaction are linked to the content modules of the class; and (d) ground rules for participation on discussion boards and chat rooms are public, openly discussed, and subject to change based on CIQs and other ongoing course evaluations. Let's talk a little more about each of these in turn.

Clear Expectations and Requirements

Online learning can be a bewildering experience, particularly for first-time learners (not to mention first-time teachers!). Consequently, instructors need to create and maintain a sense of stability and order from the very beginning. In any teaching situation, it is disconcerting when the instructor is constantly shifting the requirements and expectations. In an online environment, this is doubly distressing. The construction of the chief outline of an online course should be completed by the time of the initial course orientation. In this way, students are not "ambushed" by additional assignments and can map out their time for the run of the course. They can read the syllabus, access the online calendar, and review all the content modules to find out when everything is due and what criteria are applied to evaluating learning. If online discussion participation is graded, the criteria for this should be stated up front.

Assigning Students to Small Groups

It is not uncommon for teachers to have to teach thirty or forty students in an online course. In a face-to-face environment this may not seem like such a large class, but online it is overwhelming, requiring multiple postings to thirty or forty individuals. Given such a large class size, it is essential to assign students to smaller, more manageable groups for many of the interactive opportunities online. For example, the instructor can divide a class of forty into five groups to make chat work. Alternatively, students can assign themselves to a group discussing a topic (from a list suggested by the teacher) that interests them. If all the students opt for only one or two topics, the instructor obviously has to intervene to distribute students more equitably.

Posting messages on an asynchronous board works best if there are no more than ten or twelve students per group. Though it might seem best to maintain the same groups for all forms of discussion, it is actually rather stimulating and broadening (and only a little confusing) for students to be assigned to one group for the asynchronous discussion board and a different group for live chat. However it is done, students should know when they are to participate in their groups and what their individual roles are. The responsibility for facilitating small-group discussion can be rotated so that each member of the group has this opportunity at some time during the course. The instructor usually suggests how to do this and checks in occasionally to ensure this is happening.

Linking Interaction to Content Modules

Whenever questions are posed as prompts for discussion postings, or chats, teachers should show how these questions emerge from the course content. The ability to answer such questions should be understood to be determined by how carefully students have reviewed and understood the course content. Discussion questions should also be sequenced, so that issues explored in one posting are the basis or prompt for subsequent conversations. Consequently, students gain a sense that although many of the topics assigned are challenging, none is arbitrary or viewed as "coming out of left field." The course content may be perplexing but the organization of postings and required assignments are seen to have a logical structure.

Evolving Public Ground Rules for Discussion

The value of evolving ground rules applies online as much as in face-to-face classroom discussion. Adapting the ground rules exercises described in Chapter Eight, online learners can talk about their best and worst discussion experiences and then use these to suggest ground rules that are clearly transferable to online situations. These ground rules can then be supplemented by instructors who have accumulated a rich store of "letters from online successors." In the "letter to successors" exercise, current students are asked to compose a letter that will be sent to new students who are entering the same course the next time it is offered. The letter puts into print the departing students' insights about how to survive the experience.

Such letters often suggest that contributions to online discussion should be concise, leave room for others to contribute, include plenty of responses that affirm and build on what others have offered, combine personal stories and anecdotes with broadly applicable conclusions and generalization, focus on questions as much as answers, emphasize responding as much as initiating, and build in time to circle back and revisit discussion postings which participants have contributed days before. Instructors can propose specific ground rules that ensure such behaviors are present, as well as building on students' suggestions that emerge.

Concerns About Online Teaching and Learning

Online teaching has tremendous potential for accessing hard-to-reach students whose geographical, social, and occupational locations make it impossible for them to attend regular college classes. It provides opportunities for introverted learners to participate in discussions that deepen their engagement with complex questions and challenging topics. It is also well suited to those students who prefer self-paced learning formats and who dislike the theatrical aspects of face-to-face learning. However, online formats, like face-to-face ones, are far from perfect. I dislike entire degree programs done online since the spontaneity of live instruction can contribute so richly to student learning. Also, given the importance to learners of trusting in a teacher's authenticity, a learning format in which the other person is rarely, if ever, glimpsed face-to-face does raise problems. As people have discovered to their cost, cyberspace is a place where identities can be easily falsified. Online courses can also be abused by institutions wanting to capitalize on their cost effectiveness and convenience for students. Also, students invariably suffer when instructors who are not interested in, or comfortable doing, online teaching are increasingly pressured—some would say frog-marched—to create web-based courses, as such courses appear to be so advantageous to their home institutions.

There are also problems posed for instructors engaged in online teaching. Instructors who teach online often have less time to chat informally with their students and may therefore overlook the personal and professional challenges they are experiencing. Also, since instructors cannot physically see how students are reacting to what they say online, they may ignore the impact of the tone or choice of their words on students. Furthermore, because there is so much preparation that goes into an online course, there is a tendency to believe that, once the course design is in place, that the bulk of the work has been done. This may cause the teacher to think that her frequent participation is unnecessary.

Other problems with online courses are largely logistical. It is, for instance, very difficulty to ascertain exactly who is actually assuming responsibility for doing students' work in cyberspace. There is virtually no way to know when students designate someone else to do a particular assignment for them or even to take the entire course in their place. Additionally, online courses are not a good environment to develop the ability to think spontaneously on one's feet or to practice and hone oral communication skills. For someone who likes to use films in teaching, the online environment remains technologically ill-equipped for such media, and securing copyright permission for videostreaming films continues to be prohibitively expensive.

None of these problems are, however, insurmountable. Teaching online is not qualitatively different from teaching in more traditional face-to-face classrooms. Online teaching certainly exhibits its own particular features that need to be recognized. Because students and teachers can't see and hear each other speak their words, the ability to write clearly and appropriately becomes doubly important. Stripped of tone and gesture, some comments can seem abrupt, confrontational, rude, or disrespectful. But such comments are hardly a rarity in face-to-face classrooms. What is crucial is that teachers take the lead in modeling online contributions that are thoughtful, disciplined, and self-critical.

A final comment. Online education is sometimes caricatured as an alienating, disembodied process in contrast to the warmth and fluidity of bodies gathered together in face-to-face classrooms. But the assumption that traditional classrooms are relaxed and congenial arenas brimming over with interpersonal empathy and respect, while online classrooms are lonely and isolated, needs hard scrutiny. Many face-to-face classrooms I have participated in as both student and teacher have been (from my perspective) lonely, isolating, uncongenial, and disrespectful. As a learner I have suffered in such classrooms from disrespectful, unresponsive, and uninterested teachers and from being expected to study disembodied content in a lonely and stress-inducing competition with peers. In her critique of this false dichotomy between supposedly warm face-to-face classrooms and chilly online environments, Hess (2005) argues that "we actually have more to fear and critique in our current classroom practices of *disembodied* learning than we do from our experimentation with online learning" (p. 68). Castigating learning online as the poor cousin of face-to-face learning in "traditional" classrooms allows teachers a convenient opting out from the need to ask hard questions about their practices in both environments.

12

Responding to Resistance

Trying to understand why and how students resist learning is probably something I've spent more time pondering than any other facet of my life as a teacher. Early in my career I believed that by sheer force of will I could galvanize the natural learning energies of students whose spirit had been cowed by the system. Needless to say, this conviction suffered a series of severe experiential shocks. My constant efforts to dismantle the formal curriculum and encourage students to take responsibility for their education (by asking them to design and evaluate their own learning) were met with a mix of bemusement and resentment. The bemusement was caused by my not bothering to explain what I was doing and by my not bothering to check that students did indeed feel the sense of frustration I assumed was inhibiting their learning. The resentment was produced by my apparent unwillingness to do the work I was being paid for—to teach them. This was compounded further by some students' belief that by showing up for class they deserved an automatic A. For someone like me who tends to assume that everything that happens in the classroom is my responsibility, encountering this kind of resistance is particularly troubling. If I've caused resistance (so my thought process goes), then it's my responsibility to dismantle it. It has taken me many years to realize that resistance to learning is not something that can be removed from the classroom in the same way that a stain can be washed out of a garment. Resistance is stubborn and persistent and frequently confounds our attempts to defeat it.

Why people resist learning is a puzzlingly complex question, particularly when such resistance appears to come out of nowhere. Sometimes students appear to be truculent from the start of a course, seeming determined to sabotage our best attempts to engage them. At other times, however, they appear to be going along quite well and then suddenly resist doing something that to us seems like a fairly simple operation. However, if we can get a sense of where resistance springs from, then we are in a better position to make an appropriate response. Even if no easy resolution suggests itself, knowing what's causing resistance is sometimes helpful, decreasing the demoralizing frustration we can easily slip into when it's encountered. Specifically, it helps us fight the myth (well chronicled by Britzman, [1991]) that everything depends on and is caused by the teacher. We come to realize that in some situations cultural factors (such as the fear of committing cultural suicide, the culture of entitlement, or an ethnic or racial difference between teacher and students) that we have absolutely no control over can create deep and sustained resistance rendering all our careful planning completely useless.

It is important to remember that in many situations where students are resisting learning the best we can hope for is to contain the resistance displayed by some so that it does not completely take over the classroom. We should also be ready to admit that the resistance displayed might be completely justified. Resistance should not automatically be equated with mindless truculence or vindictive sabotage. In the face of unreasonable teacher demands, pedagogic misjudgments, broken teacher promises, or clear incompetence, it is often principled and justified. I have been a resistant learner myself in situations where learning was prescribed for me without any attempt to justify how this would be in my own best interests and where the person teaching me seemed to me to be unqualified.

Being forced to learn something that I regard as a waste of time, and that is taught by an incompetent to boot, is hardly likely to produce a motivated state of learning readiness. So it would be naïve to imagine that we can wave a magic wand and remove the resistance-inducing frustrations, anxieties, and cruelties students have suffered before they arrive in our class. If people are determined not to learn something, there is often little you can do to convince them that such learning is worth their effort. Indeed, one of the biggest mistakes we can commit when encountering resistance is to fall into the trap of conversional obsession. Conversional obsession is what happens when you become obsessed with converting a small and easily identifiable minority of hard-core resistant students into becoming enthusiastic advocates for learning.

Imagine the scene. You walk into the classroom on the first day of a course and, as soon as you start to teach, you see all the familiar signs of resistance displayed by a knot of students sitting at the back of the room. They put on Walkmans and open up magazines as soon as you start talking. They fall asleep, arrive late, leave early, take cell phone calls in the middle of class, and spend the time passing notes or holding a series of private conversations. Eyes roll, glazed or angry expressions dominate, and there is a complete absence of questions, comments, or any other signs of interest. When you notice these signs, a switch is turned on in your head. It's as if the students have walked up to you, slapped your face with a glove, and challenged you to a pedagogic duel. The duel is one in which they are saying "Do your best to motivate me—I'll bet you won't succeed." You enthusiastically accept their challenge and start to do everything you can to engage them in learning.

As the weeks go by and this cabal of learners refuses to crack a smile, display any interest, or participate in any way, you feel your reputation is on the line. You say to yourself "If it's the last thing I do, I'm going to break this resistance." You become obsessed with their faces—will they ever laugh at your jokes? Can you plan an activity so irresistibly engaging that they cannot help but show a flicker of interest? You pour all your energy into provoking a response from this group, visualizing them leaving your course at the end of the year wreathed in beatific smiles of self-actualized gratitude for the wonderful transformations you have wrought in them. In your fevered imaginings these same students will be writing you notes of thanks, telling you that they were initially skeptical about the course but that in the future they will urge all their friends to take your class because of your personal charisma as a teacher.

There are two problems with this situation. First, the transformation you envisage will almost never happen, leaving you feeling that you've failed in your quest to motivate students. In acknowledging that the students have won the duel, you start to call your competence as a teacher into question. Second, and even more troublingly, in enthusiastically accepting the challenge the resistant students have offered you, all your efforts are poured into converting a relatively small number of individuals to being enthusiastic advocates of learning. Along the way the legitimate learning needs of the majority of students take second place to your efforts to prove to yourself that you're a *real* teacher because you can win over hardcore resisters. You are so concerned to show that you can be a motivator of resistant learners that what happens to the majority of motivated, or potentially teachable, students becomes of little interest to you. So watch out for the trap of conversional obsession. Left unchecked, it can come to dominate your life.

The basis of resistance to learning is the fear of change. Learning, by definition, involves change. It requires us to explore new ideas, acquire new skills, develop new ways of understanding old experiences, and so on. No one is the same after learning something. The change might not be very dramatic or even evident. But even incremental and imperceptible change carries its own discomforts. Given that change is threatening, some people much prefer to remain in situations that to outsiders seem wholly unsatisfactory. Abusive marriages, oppressive workplaces, and autocratic regimes are all systems of domination that maintain their power through a mixture of repression from above, self-monitoring not to challenge the status quo, and the fear of learning new ideas, skills, and behaviors. As teachers we need to remember that learning entails change and that the prospect of such change is often highly threatening. To this extent it would be highly unusual for teachers not to face student resistance to learning on a continual basis.

In my own life the prospect of learning something new—particularly if that learning has been forced on me by changed external circumstances—is rarely something I embrace or seek. When I review my own experiences as a learner, it is helpful for me to recall what it was that was helpful to my efforts to overcome my own resistance. For example, a learning task of my forties—learning to drive—was resisted by me for years. I only embraced this task when its necessity became abundantly clear. When I moved from New York to Minnesota, the abysmal lack of public transport meant that not driving was not an option. Cars have always seemed to me like sophisticated instruments of death as much as transportation devices, so for many years I avoided learning to drive them through a combination of sneakiness (pretending I'd lost my temporary permit) and luck (living mostly in cities).

The fact that everyone I knew seemed to be able to drive effortlessly did not, as one might imagine, ease my anxiety; rather, it increased it, since I was convinced that if I tried to learn I would be revealed in all my shame, ineptitude, and embarrassment as the one person in the world who showed a total inability to acquire this skill. Eventually, my wife agreed to use part of a sabbatical to teach me and, as I learned under her direction, I was alerted to some of the reasons for my own resistance. For example, because this was a sabbatical we were far away from friends and family. This was a boon to me because it allowed me the privacy to make mistakes without these being noticed by people whose approval I wanted. I had never thought of the ways my insistence on group work might strengthen or even inculcate students' resistance to learning until I was given this welcome opportunity of conducting a major learning effort in relative solitude. I realized that my freedom to make mistakes in private meant I would be willing to take more risks, and endure more shame, than if my learning had been situated wholly in groups. My own welcoming of the chance to make errors in private alerted me to the need to pay more attention in my own teaching to create private opportunities for learning (and the mistakes that this would inevitably entail) along with my usual classroom discussion and group project activities.

Two other things were helpful. First, my wife set realistic limits regarding learning rather than creating high expectations. This ran counter to what I had believed about learning. My assumption had always been that learners would rise to the highest challenge I set them. Now I started to doubt this insight. Because I had been told that my three-month project was to learn the essentials of driving on quiet country roads and then to be able to drive the car into a local town and back again, I had no fears of being expected to engage in freeway driving or undertake overly complicated maneuvers. As it happened, I achieved this three-month goal in more like three weeks, a fact that increased my confidence considerably since I assumed I was galloping ahead of schedule. Had I been told at the outset that this was the three-week goal, I would have felt intimidated and fearful. As a result of this experience, I now realize that my setting high expectations can sometimes inhibit and demoralize as well as inspire. The other important feature in this learning effort was my wife's clear, calm, and supportive style of teaching. She didn't push me too fast, she broke a complex skill set down into a series of small, incremental chunks, she gave clear instructions, she praised frequently those things that were done well, and readily admitted that when she was learning to drive she had all the fears and anxieties I was experiencing. That alerted me to the importance of teacher disclosure and to the need to provide sufficient scaffolding for learners early on in a learning effort.

Understanding Resistance to Learning

One of the most frequent complaints I hear on campuses around the country is that students aren't what they were, that they want an easy grade for no work, that they have no attention span, and that they lack any intrinsic interest in learning. In this analysis resistance is framed as personal truculence, a choice made by individuals who just can't be bothered to work and who have no natural aptitude for learning. Now this may be the case with some students, but as a universal explanation for why students resist learning it's a simplistic and somewhat lazy cop-out. The truth is that resistance is a multilayered and complex phenomenon in which several factors intersect. In the following section I explore a number of possible explanations for students' resistance to learning. The section begins with factors having to do with the student's self-image and rhythm of learning and then moves into an analysis of social factors and teacher behaviors.

Poor Self-Image as Learners

Many college-aged learners who have managed to negotiate a path to higher education have been stigmatized in their previous school careers as being too dumb for college. They may well have suffered persistent sarcasm, systematic humiliation, and peer ridicule for their apparent lack of intelligence or commitment. Others might have a command of academic skills but be full of self-doubt regarding their abilities. For all these learners the smallest disappointment, the least bump in the road, will quickly be taken as incontrovertible evidence of their unsuitability for college and lead to them either dropping out (at worst) or struggling unconvincingly through a course (at best). They will resist efforts to move them forward, believing themselves incapable of the level of work conducted by their peers.

Developing a strong self-image as a learner—regarding oneself as someone able to acquire new skills, knowledge, behaviors, and insights—is a crucial psychological underpinning to learning. It tends to function as a self-fulfilling prophecy. If people see themselves as learners, if this is a part of their identity, then the prospect of new learning is within their horizon of possibility.

Fear of the Unknown

Change entails unknowability. Since any learning episode entails broadening horizons, knowledge, and skill sets, there is the presumption that we will be in an altered state at its end. The fear of the unknown (which is what this altered state represents) is often a massive inhibitor to learning. For many people routine, habit, and familiarity are leitmotifs for the conduct of their lives. Learning is framed as a quest for certainty, for a system of beliefs or structure that they can commit to for life. Consequently, any teacher who invites people into learning by emphasizing its transformative power is unwittingly only strengthening their resistance. Erich Fromm's books (1941, 1956a, 1956b) chronicle the human desire for security, for *not* learning, that is manifest in people's striving for automaton conformity and their willingness to submit to authoritarian rulers.

The human capacity for denial—particularly for denying the need to change—knows no limits. People committed to eternal verities can withstand years of dissonant experiences and mountains of contradictory evidence that call these into question. Perversely, a law of inverse commitment sometimes seems to apply whereby the more contradictory the evidence discovered, the more people assert the self-evident truth of their beliefs. Given this dynamic it should not be surprising when we encounter students who display a revulsion for change. Even students who appear to be committed to learning and who are enthusiastic in its pursuit sometimes reach a point where they are overwhelmed by a grieving for lost certainties and a trepidation about what awaits in the future.

The Normal Rhythm of Learning

Some instances of resistance to learning are simply examples of the incremental fluctuation rhythm of learning identified in Chapter Five in which the two steps forward, one step back pattern entails regular moments of temporary collapse (when Wile E. Coyote crashes to the floor of the canyon). As students learn something new, they find that their initial enthusiastic embrace of new skills, ideas, or practices is followed by a disturbing period of confusion as they realize just how complex and unfamiliar is the new territory they are entering. This realization is followed by a yearning to return to the comfortable certainties of old skill sets and attitudes. Not surprisingly, when students are in this state of yearning, they resist any attempt by the teacher to move them forward. Although this stage is temporary, it is experienced as permanent until some external prompt or support reignites their movement forward.

Disjunction of Learning and Teaching Styles

Sometimes it is not learning new content or skills that students resist but the style in which these are taught. If a highly oral or text-based teacher like me is teaching a visual learner, it is hardly surprising if that learner resists the tasks she is being set. Alternately, an anal-compulsive, extremely organized learner who is taught by an improvisational, intuitive teacher will resist that teacher's tendency to make changes in the middle of a planned activity because of some change of classroom mood or teachable opportunity she detects. Students who have been used to learning by conducting web-based analyses, listening to lectures, and reading independently may well be confused and irritated at the sudden prospect of having to participate in a role play. Field-independent learners with little patience for group process will strenuously resist case studies, simulations, and debates and will view class discussion as a waste of valuable time. So if we rely on only one method of teaching, we are bound to engender resistance in those students who don't learn in a manner matching that method.

Apparent Irrelevance of the Learning Activity

People will generally resist activities for which they see no justification. If the learning that students are asked to undertake seems to have no purpose or connection to their own interests and concerns, they may well resist it. This holds true for all kinds of students, but it is particularly apt for adults who have entered college after a period in the workforce. For such students college demands a heavy price. If someone has dipped deep into their financial reserves, taken out massive student loans, resigned from a secure job, undergone all kinds of convolutions to arrange child care or work coverage while they are learning, and also faced resistance from unsympathetic spouses, friends, or colleagues, then they are going to be frustrated and annoyed if they think that they are being asked to perform exercises or undertake assignments that have no meaning for them.

Level of Required Learning Is Inappropriate

It is easy for teachers to misinterpret students' levels of learning readiness, particularly if there has been no attempt to use some kind of classroom assessment tool to find out what and how students are learning. Even in the most benign of classrooms, people are understandably unwilling to admit they are confused about content or don't understand instructions. If the teacher interprets a lack of student questions as a sign that learners are in full command of the material, she may well set assignments that are pitched at too advanced a level. Resistance will also likely arise if the language used to describe new learning activities is too abstract or conceptually sophisticated. Teachers in love with their subjects and caught up in the passion of communicating the elegant beauty of scientific reasoning, literary insight, or historical theorizing can easily overestimate how far students have progressed. Enthusiastic teachers who travel too far, too fast for their students, and who don't check in regularly to see if students are keeping up with the pace, can easily leave learners behind.

One of the most common mistakes teachers make in this regard is to ask students to take responsibility for organizing and conducting their own learning before they are really ready to do this. To the teacher this seems like a laudable attempt to work democratically that students should welcome. To the student, however, this is an unreasonable attempt to force them to make learning decisions in a confusing vacuum of misinformation and lack of knowledge. Not surprisingly, it can be perceived as a deliberate trick setting them up for failure. Many times in my own teaching I have made this miscalculation of asking students to design their learning activities before they had a full grasp of the learning terrain they were traversing and have then been surprised when students didn't thank me for my efforts to respect their intelligence. In their place, however, I would have had the same reaction. My feeling would be that without a thorough grounding in the grammar of the subject—an awareness of the criteria used to determine legitimate knowledge, an understanding of the chief concepts studied, and a grasp of the building blocks of content—it would be ludicrous to expect me to plan my own learning. How on earth could I make an informed choice? I would anticipate that being expected to design my own learning plan before I was familiar with the content was only priming me for the public humiliation I would inevitably endure as I floundered around in an unfamiliar subject area making a fool of myself.

Fear of Looking Foolish in Public

Many people (including me) have a perverse wish only to learn things they know they already can do well. They will only play games they stand a good chance of winning, and they will only try to learn something new and difficult if they know this can be done in private. Students' egos are fragile creations and, as the discussion of the impostor syndrome in Chapter Five showed, this fragility is as characteristic of those who appear confident and successful as it is of those who have struggled with previous learning. So students' resistance to a particular learning activity may simply reflect their feeling that it is taking place in an overly public forum, rather than their dislike of the focus of the learning itself.

Cultural Suicide

Participating in higher education is valued highly in some subcultures, viewed suspiciously in others. A student's decision to attend college entails many social and psychological changes. One of these is the risk of being regarded with mistrust in their home cultures and of facing eventual exclusion. This is the risk of cultural suicide discussed in Chapter Five. These cultures may tolerate educational participation better if it is felt that the student's learning helps support the culture's interests and values. Additionally, students who can communicate about their learning using language that is easily understandable within the culture decrease the risk of cultural suicide. But if students are pushed too quickly into learning skills or considering ideas that the culture views as radical and unfamiliar, they run the risk of being viewed as betrayers who have rejected their allegiance to their own culture.

There is also the problem of teachers from one culture asking students from another one to learn in ways that represent only the teacher's cultural mores and traditions. Asian students who are asked to challenge the teacher's authority as evidence of their ability to think critically, aboriginal students who are asked to speak only of their own independent opinions and judgments as if these had no cultural formation, African American students who are told to speak one at a time in contradiction to the layered and simultaneous speech patterns of the West Niger delta—all these are being asked to learn in ways that go against their own cultural traditions. This is an impossible Catch-22. To succeed they need to do something that denies practices constitutive of their identity.

Faced with the psychologically devastating prospect of losing their cultural supports, many students (not surprisingly) choose not to pay the price required of learning. I have seen this dynamic with working-class students for whom taking education seriously (that is, demonstrating interest in ideas for their own sake rather than as a source of future income) is taken by some of their peers as a betrayal of solid, unpretentious working-class values. I have seen it in fundamentalist groups for whom a member's consenting exposure to new spiritual ideas is regarded as tantamount to blasphemy. I have also seen it in racial groups in which a commitment to learning past a certain point is seen as indicating that the learners have joined the dominant White supremacist culture. In all these situations students' resistance to learning will spring from their perception that if they go past a certain point they will commit cultural suicide.

The culture of entitlement, described graphically by Sacks (1996), is another factor. This culture operates when students feel that by showing up in class they deserve to receive an A grade for the course irrespective of the amount or quality of their work. It is seen in students' belief that it is the teacher's responsibility to get them through a learning task and, consequently, that if the learner fails it is the teacher's fault. The mentality is that the student is a customer paying for a service and that the customer is always right. If the service or product (usually an A grade) is not delivered, then in the student's mind the teacher should be held responsible. One aspect of the culture of entitlement is the students' belief that the teacher should be endlessly accommodating to their circumstances, such as being willing to accept work being completed late for assignment after assignment. Another is students' feeling that it is their right to choose to arrive late, leave early, and ignore teachers' instructions. This culture is underscored by marketing materials that emphasize that if a student chooses a particular college, its teachers will do all they can to ensure her success. This is a laudable and appropriate commitment but the other half of the equation—the student's responsibility to make a reasonable effort to persist at learning in the face of difficulties and problems—often goes unmentioned.

Lack of Clarity in Teachers' Instructions

As we saw in Chapter Four, learners appreciate teachers making the fullest possible disclosure of their teaching intentions and the criteria they use to evaluate learning. Wherever students experience ambiguity or confusion regarding teachers' expectations, resistance is the predictable consequence. If students perceive themselves as failing after faithfully following teachers' instructions, only to discover that these were so poorly communicated that students completed what was essentially the wrong task, mistrust explodes. So receiving the clearest possible instructions is something that is crucial in students' eyes. In Critical Incident Questionnaire reports, the perception of teacher ambiguity or duplicity—of students being unsure what teachers want or of suspecting that a secret agenda exists that students are denied access to—is reported time and again as being particularly demoralizing for learners. To receive unclear instructions is to feel that you're being set up for failure. Consequently, any learning task that appears unclear will likely be resisted.

Students' Dislike of Teachers

This is a hard one to contemplate. The brutal fact though is that sometimes students just take a personal dislike to us no matter how credible or authentic we might strive to be. This may be due to any number of factors, some of which (such as our race, gender, or personality quirks) may be totally beyond our control. At other times the dislike is entirely justified. Teachers may use humor inappropriately, belittle students, show up unprepared, make racist or sexist remarks, dismay some by their informality and offend others by their inapproachability, exhibit favoritism and discrimination, or appear arrogant and cynical. Sometimes these behaviors and predispositions are unclear to the teacher. Given that learning is a highly emotional phenomenon, a student's dislike of a teacher can become so overwhelming that it permeates all their interactions with that teacher. After all, teachers' personalities are inevitably reflected in their pedagogic actions. If they like to use humor they will crack jokes, if they feel like impostors they may be overly self-deprecating, if they are dour or low key they will soothe some and bore others.

Responding to Resistance

In the first edition of this book, this section was titled "Overcoming Resistance to Learning." This was unfortunate in that it set readers up to expect that resistance could be overcome. What I should have emphasized, of course, is that resistance can sometimes be contained, and its worst effects mitigated, but it can never be completely overcome. And, as I have argued already, we should not make the mistake of judging our competence as a teacher by the extent to which we remove resistance to learning from our students. However, the intensity and longevity of resistance stands a better chance of being reduced if you follow some of the general practices explored throughout this book—making a deliberate attempt to create diversity in your teaching, regularly trying to get inside students' heads, making sure you try to balance credibility and authenticity, creating learning communities, and so on.

Try to Sort Out the Causes of Resistance

Since resistance to learning is such a complex phenomenon, an important first step is to gain some sense of what combination of factors is causing this in a student or group of students. Before any thought of making an appropriate response to resistance, you need a clear sense of the origins of resistance; otherwise you risk spending time and energy pursuing irrelevant solutions. The various classroom research instruments discussed in Chapter Three are very helpful in this regard, although if the resistance runs wide and deep there may not be many who take these seriously. CIQs, one-minute papers, and learning audits are not much use if they are returned as blank sheets of paper. If that's the case, then you have other options: you can speak to resisters individually and privately (when the culture of cool is less likely to stop them speaking), you can consult colleagues about their "read" of the resistance you're facing, you can regularly invite students to voice their concerns and problems, and you can find out what the history of the course has been at the college. Was there a previous instructor who created much of the resistance and skepticism that new students bring to the course? Was the course changed from an elective to a requirement after the students were already committed to their program? What kind of instructor turnover rate has the course exhibited in the past? All these factors are likely to cause resistance.

Ask Yourself If the Resistance Is Justified

As mentioned previously, we should not jump to the automatic conclusion that resistance is a symptom of truculence, boorishness, or laziness. Think about your own autobiography—haven't there been times when your resistance to new learning has been justified? You should at least consider the possibility that if you felt that your resistance was principled, then that displayed by your students might be just as reasonable in their eyes. If the only justification for learning that students hear is that institutional routine, history, or protocol require it, and if students are being asked to work at too advanced a level with no introductory preparation, it would be surprising if extensive resistance did not exist. When we ask ourselves "Why do my students need to know this?" we should not have to wait long for a strong and convincing response to suggest itself. If you can't come up with one, then the chances are good that any resistance displayed is, indeed, justified.

Research Your Students' Backgrounds

The more we know about those we teach, the better placed we are to respond to any resistance they display. If we know something about the different values, expectations, experiences, and preferred learning styles of our students, we can adjust our teaching approaches, assignments, and forms of assessment accordingly. The more information we have about these things the more likely we are to choose materials and use approaches that our students find congenial. Knowing these things also helps us make a better case for the learning we are asking them to undertake. This is the whole point of the third core assumption of skillful teaching discussed in Chapter Two and of the adoption of the various classroom research techniques described in Chapter Three.

Involve Former Resisters

In trying to convince new students of the importance of learning, we are always working against the fact that our own expressions of its importance will be met with some skepticism. Students will say, "Of course you're going to tell us it's important that we learn this—after all, teaching it is how you earn your living!" The voices that will have far greater credibility than ours are those of former students who were themselves resistant to learning but who came to appreciate its value for them. As described in Chapter Two, organizing a first class alumni panel made up of three or four resistant students who were in the course in previous years can be very effective in puncturing early resistance. A few words from these former resisters will have a much greater effect than any appeals you can make.

Model

The missing link in much college teaching is the regular attempt by teachers to model the learning behaviors and dispositions they have requested of students. Far too often students are told that a certain task or learning activity is good for them but have never seen the teacher engaged in the very activity that is being urged on them. One of the mistakes I have made many times is to walk into a classroom on the first day of a new course, announce to students that I believe in discussion, and tell them why the experience will be good for them. Then I assign topics to students and put them into small discussion groups. The trouble with this scenario is that it omits a crucial element. I have neglected to model in front of the students an engagement in the very activity—participating in group discussion with peers—I am prescribing for them. As teachers we have to earn the right to ask students to engage seriously in discussion by first modeling our own serious commitment to it. If we want students to believe us when we say discussion is good for them, we have to show them how it's good for us too. So, in any course in which we're intending to use discussion methods, it's a good idea to invite a group of colleagues into the classroom at an early stage in the course. We can then hold a discussion in front of the students about some aspect of the course's content in which we try to show the kinds of behaviors we'd like students to exhibit in their own subsequent discussions.

When Appropriate, Involve Students in Educational Planning

If students feel they have a say in determining the curricular focus, specific content, pedagogy, and evaluative approaches of a course, they may well feel a greater connection to learning. How far this is feasible will depend on the state of students' previous knowledge, accreditation requirements, and the complexity of the knowledge, skills, or content to be taught. Sometimes these factors mean everything has been prescribed beforehand. But if students can be involved, several benefits are likely. At the very least they will be unable to say the teacher is unresponsive or has arbitrarily imposed meaningless requirements on them. Of course, some will still maintain this is the case! But it will be that much harder for them to convince their peers that resistance is justified if there has been a concerted effort to consult them. It may also reduce students' fear of the unknown and increase the chances that your teaching will have some meaning for them.

Use a Variety of Teaching Methods and Approaches

When resistance is caused by teachers working in ways that support only a limited range of learning styles, the obvious solution is to use a greater variety of teaching approaches. This has already been discussed extensively in Chapter Nine, so I will not go into detail on this point here. However, it is important to reiterate that we should not expect ourselves to be fully competent in a range of very diverse methodologies. Most of us can probably broaden our repertoires somewhat beyond where we are, but we cannot become something we are not. I could no more turn myself into a highly visual, extraverted, charismatic, kinetically inclined teacher than colleagues I work with could become as organized, or committed to group process, as I am. But we should all work to create at least three different learning modalities within each teaching segment we have control over, whether this lasts fifty minutes or three hours.

The importance of pedagogic variety raises once more the crucial issue of team teaching. When a course is taught by a team comprised of different personalities, learning styles, and pedagogic orientations, the chances are raised that most students in the course will find that their own learning preferences are addressed for a reasonable amount of time. Of course, this teaming must be done properly; that is, all planning, teaching, and debriefing must involve all team members all the time. If we keep dividing the curriculum into discrete segments, each taught by individual members of the team (as in "You do this week, I'll do the next, and Stephen can do the third week"), the effect can be confusing to students. Properly conducted team teaching involves teachers constantly explaining to students how their different activities fit together and are designed to be complementary.

Assess Learning Incrementally

If their resisting learning means that students will incur a low grade, they need to know this as early as possible. Students have a right to resist, but they also have a right to know what the consequences of this resistance are for them. If you assess students' progress only by administering a mid-term and then final exam, resistant learners have no way of knowing (until it's too late to do anything about it) that their lack of commitment means they will not achieve the grade they may feel entitled to. I like to break up the assessed work that students have to do into as many incremental tasks as the course structure allows. If I had a ten-week course I would ideally have ten homework or class assignments, each of which carried ten points, with the first of these being the test on the syllabus I mentioned earlier. By the third or fourth week it would then be clear to resistant students that—with 30 or 40 percent of the assigned points now gone—their chance to receive the kind of grade they wished was rapidly disappearing. Of course, many subjects do not break down neatly into ten or so assignments, but the principle of continuous assessment holds true; if students learn as early as possible the negative consequences of not taking learning seriously, it may help decrease their resistance. At the very least it gives them full knowledge of the consequences of their actions—a crucial component of an ethical pedagogy.

Check That Your Intentions Are Clearly Understood

Repeatedly throughout this book I have emphasized the importance of teachers making their expectations, agendas, and rationales as clear as possible. I don't think it is possible to overemphasize why you are asking students to develop certain skills, explore areas of knowledge, and participate in activities you have devised. Regularly collecting Critical Incident Questionnaire responses, administering an early test on the syllabus, and finding any way you can to check that students have understood your intentions will help avoid confusion and the needless creation of resistance. Any time you give out an assignment, distribute as much information as you can about the criteria, indicators, and grading policies used to judge students' work. It is often difficult for students to challenge teachers directly about their actions, and we should never assume they have understood why we are asking them to do something. Check, check, and check again that students have fully understood what you are asking them to do.

Build a Case for Learning

Because as teachers we see clearly the value of learning, we all too easily assume students can see this too. The reason why certain understandings or skills are important is so obvious to us that we may feel they need minimal justification. Nothing could be further from the truth. You should never be too proud to say why in your view it's important for students to learn something. Although the first class alumni panel will do a much more convincing job (at least in the eyes of new students) of justifying why learning is necessary, that doesn't mean you don't need to address this too. As much as you can, try to describe the benefits you believe learning brings in terms that make sense to students—using language, examples, and reasons that are familiar to them. When it's appropriate, a simulation held early on in a course can make an effective case for new learning. If the simulation is one the students recognize as credible, and if it's clear that the only satisfactory way out of it is for the student to learn something she does not know already, then the simulation builds the case for learning. It might also be possible to take students to a location outside the classroom where the desired skills or understandings are clearly being put to good use.

Create Situations in Which Students Succeed

Success is addictive, failure demoralizing. The more students succeed, the more their resistance may weaken. One good idea is to find a failure-proof task for students to complete at the first class meeting. An early experience of unexpected success can reduce the level of resistance enough to create a connection with the learning process. Such failure-proof activities are, admittedly, sometimes hard to discover. Indeed, you may regard these as particularly trivial. But, from a student's perspective, to be able to experience a small success—particularly if she has convinced herself that a subject is beyond her and that therefore there is no point in her trying—can make all the difference. Nothing is more heartening or effective in decreasing resistance than to feel one is moving forward successfully.

Connected to this, it is also important to acknowledge students' efforts, to congratulate them on their progress, and to stress whatever is meritorious in their performance. Remember that what may to you seem like a very small incremental step forward may, to the learner concerned, represent a progression of enormous significance. Any sense that we are moving forward and building momentum helps lessen our fear of the unknown.

Don't Push Too Fast

As shown in Chapter Five's discussion of incremental fluctuation, periods of movement forward in learning are often followed by periods of stasis. Such plateaus or apparent regressions are normal rhythms of learning that do not signal some sort of irretrievable breakdown. Sometimes, however, teachers rush prematurely to conclude that any kind of temporary halt in a student's progress is always a danger sign that calls for immediate intervention. The problem is that students may well experience such interventions as an annoying increase in pressure that only serves to create anxiety and inhibit learning even more.

So we need to be realistic about what we can expect from students, particularly when they seem to resist activities that to us flow naturally from what just went before. To students, reaching a certain point in learning may have taken such energy and determination that there is a real need for them to catch their breath before moving on. Such a necessary interlude builds up energy for the next stage in learning. Also, if students are experiencing the lost innocence described in Chapter Five, they may be grieving for the disappearance of old certitudes—ways of thinking and acting that were familiar and comfortable. They may need to return temporarily to familiar intellectual territory to develop courage for the next learning effort. This will probably require more time than you have allowed. To push too fast in this situation just leaves students exhausted.

Admit Resistance Is Normal

Sometimes confronting the likelihood of resistance publicly works to defuse it. When a teacher acknowledges that resistance probably exists, and when she describes how she has addressed it in the past, it helps normalize the phenomenon. It is sometimes helpful for teachers to describe their own resistance to learning—to talk about its causes (such as the fear of looking foolish in public) and how it was kept under control. We can also talk about former learners and what typically caused their resistance. Doing these things may strike a chord within some students to the point where they will talk openly about why they are unwilling to learn something new.

Acknowledging that resistance exists and admitting to its normality might seem like an embarrassing thing for teachers to do. In the long run, however, it will probably make everyone feel much more relaxed if the reality of the situation is made public. Far better to do this than to practice a massive suspension of belief where you pretend that everything is fine when in fact you feel you're facing serious and sustained resistance.

Acknowledge the Right to Resist

In most college classrooms there are limits to how much we can force people to learn something they wish to avoid. Baptiste (2000) has argued that coercion is a natural part of learning and that it can be exercised in a principled and ethical manner. But if people are resolutely opposed to your efforts, your options are limited. My experience is that past a certain point it's a waste of effort to try to force learning. Ultimately, the learner has to make the internal commitment to become involved.

This does not mean that you should not explain, with all the force and conviction you can muster, why you think it's in students' own best interests to learn something new. But if all your reasoning means nothing to learners, then you have to grant people the right not to learn something that you are convinced is important. Maybe you can strike a bargain with hard-core resisters that allows them to work in ways that do not interfere with the learning of others. I have sometimes devised group projects with the intention of removing the most destructive resistance from the room. This happens when I group all the hard-core resisters into one team and set them a project to work on outside of the classroom. They can then go off, vent together, and eventually implode into a black hole of negativity while the rest of us can get on with some work.

Ultimately, students have the right to resist learning something we're urging on them. Just as in the past we may well have refused to learn things for reasons that are quite legitimate to us, so we must acknowledge that our own students will do the same. If students resist learning activities that we feel are important, this doesn't mean we're incompetent or unconvincing. It may be that at a later date the relevance, necessity, or delight of the learning will become as clear to them as it is to us. It may be, too, that we are mistaken in the emphasis we place on a particular act of learning and that subsequently we will come to see the legitimacy of students' complaints. Remember that resistance to learning is normal, natural, and inevitable. The trick is to make sure it interferes as little as possible with classroom activities that others see as important and helpful.

13

Dealing with the Politics of Teaching

Many teachers probably don't consider teaching to be a political activity. Their main concern is to make sure that their students acquire a predetermined body of useful knowledge and/or required skills. Colleagues with this conviction frequently tell me their job is to teach their subject, assess their students' progress, and pick up their paycheck. They are extremely bemused when I suggest they are political actors since it has never occurred to them to think of their work as having any political dimensions. This perception of college teaching as having nothing to do with politics is shared by most of the general population. To many people outside the academy, professorial life is thought of as one step short of monastic seclusion. College teaching is deemed to be the practice of high-minded intellectual ascetics ensconced in an ivory tower of pure thought and interested only in the pursuit of truth and beauty. Sometimes higher education is thought of as a refuge for those frail individuals too sensitive to participate in the maelstrom of daily existence. Novels such as David Lodge's *Nice Work* (1988) caricature the view of business that teaching is a shielded occupation suitable for those unable to survive the harsh vicissitudes of commercial life. Both these beliefs—that teaching is apolitical and that teachers have retreated from the conflicts and anxieties of daily existence—are fundamentally misconceived.

Let's talk first about the belief that teachers are somehow above politics. It's true that many teachers never mention political ideologies, or discuss contemporary political issues, in their classes. There is a good chance that such teachers have never used the word political when describing what they do to friends and colleagues. However, just because teachers don't see their work as political does not mean that this element is absent in their practice. I contend that any teacher of any subject is engaged in politics since he or she is exerting influence and coercion in the organization of classroom activities. In our pursuit of educational curricula or the inculcation of skill sets we deem to be intrinsically worthwhile, all of us treat students in certain ways that can be considered political. Sometimes we view students as passive recipients waiting for knowledge to be poured into them, sometimes as active co-creators of knowledge. In the organized pursuit of educational objectives we inevitably exercise persuasion, manipulation, even coercion, and politics, at its root, is all about the exercise of such power.

A political process is one in which someone attempts to persuade, direct, or coerce someone else into devoting scarce resources to a particular activity. Teachers are people who constantly try to influence learners into devoting their resources—their money (in the form of tuition), their energy, their time—into studying a particular subject or developing a particular skill. As they pursue these objectives, they exercise power to organize the classroom a certain way. Sometimes the classroom resembles an autocracy where the teacher speaks most of the time and makes all substantive decisions. At other times the classroom looks more like an oligarchy where the teacher, plus a few committed, articulate, or favored students, take up 90 percent of the time available for discussion. In the best of all possible worlds (from my point of view), the classroom is closer to a democracy as participation is equalized and teachers and learners take joint responsibility for deciding what and how to study, and how to evaluate learning. And, of course, all teachers evaluate their students' learning, a process (as Chapter Ten makes clear) in which the exercise of teacher power is seen at its most naked. If teachers who don't think there are any political dimensions to their work could hear how their students talk about being evaluated, they would know just how powerless those students sometimes feel.

The essence of teaching and learning is change, and change always has political dimensions. For teachers and learners, nothing is exactly the same after a learning event as it was before. Making a dent in the world is the inevitable consequence of teaching, irrespective of the subject area concerned. You cannot teach without in some way changing yourself, your students, and the world around you. Trying to avoid changing people while you teach is like trying to walk on a bright sunny day without casting a shadow. As a teacher, the question is not whether or not you cast a shadow (for you can't avoid doing this) but what form this shadow takes and on whom it falls. Sometimes teachers seek to escape their shadows by espousing as their aim the promotion of students' growth or development, as if these processes were somehow neutral, lacking moral, social, or political dimensions. But endemic to growth and development is the sense that these must always be in some direction, towards some end. Growth cannot occur in a vacuum. Nothing develops in a directionless way.

Most teachers who subscribe to ideas of growth and development have strong implicit ideas of what these processes look like and what they should lead to. For example, they would probably resist the idea that students should grow into a greater lack of criticality or that they should develop a perspective that is more closed and narrow-minded than was previously the case. Indeed, many of them would say that growth and development implies students being increasingly open to new ideas, ready to acquire new skills, and interested in considering broader viewpoints than they had previously been exposed to. They would probably disagree with the aim of developing bigotry or that strengthening their students' belief that they are innately superior to all other races, classes, and cultures was a valid educational objective. In rejecting some directions for growth and development while supporting others, teachers are acknowledging that teaching intended to encourage students' growth and development is inevitably infused with moral, social, and political dimensions.

All teaching activities spring from an idea of what a properly run classroom, or a properly educated person, looks like. Having a prescriptive vision of what comprises a fulfilled, mature, or healthy person, or what a properly run, academically rigorous, participatory classroom looks like, is normal and inevitable. Many teachers, if pressed, would say they believe in values such as honesty, compassion, respect, fairness, and inclusion in the classroom. Show those same teachers a classroom in which some students are consistently excluded from participation, publicly humiliated, or punished for disagreeing with conventional, received wisdom, and those teachers will generally condemn these practices. So, whether they acknowledge it or not, those teachers are operating under the influence of political values—openness, respect, compassion, inclusion, fairness, equity—that are central to the democratic tradition.

Now let's examine the second widely held belief, that teachers live in some sort of placid, tranquil, apolitical ivory tower. This is so far from the truth as to be a dangerous caricature. The reality is that teachers do not practice their craft in a cocoon insulated from political pressures. Instead, they constantly have to deal with a number of political factors affecting whether and how they teach. Getting, and then keeping, a job is partly a political matter often involving whom one knows. If you have the resources to attend conferences and cultivate a network of influential contacts, then you are much better placed to find job openings and to know how to present yourself in interviews. Once you get to the college, you realize just how ubiquitous are the politics of the classroom and staffroom. From C. P. Snow's novel *The Masters* (1951) to David Mamet's play *Oleanna* (1993), novelists and dramatists have long recognized that higher education is fertile ground for the analysis of political battles exacerbated by racism, sexism, and personality conflicts.

Of all the issues illustrating the political nature of teaching, academic freedom is probably the one that grabs most attention outside the academy (closely followed by matters having to do with promotion and tenure). Anytime a new course is proposed, particularly if it challenges conventional notions of what constitutes appropriate curricula or teaching methodology, a political fight is likely to ensue. Women's Studies, African American Studies, Peace Studies, Alternative Healing, Popular Culture—all have had to fight to establish themselves as legitimate areas of academic inquiry within higher education. When it comes to matters of employment, things really start to heat up. Securing tenure is as much a political as an academic process, involving teachers in researching the culture of their institutions. They must know which of the holy trinity of tenure criteria (scholarship, teaching, and service) really matter, whose opinion on the tenure committee really counts, whether co-authorship is frowned on as less credible than solo authorship, and which journals need to be targeted for publication since they are most highly regarded in the department. Journals are like baseball cards—you can trade three articles in a less prestigious journal for one article in a leader in the field. Battles over tenure, hiring, and firing are sometimes long and bloody, marked by a deep sense of grievance, and with divisive effects felt for many years.

The daily decisions of a teacher's life—such as whether or not a new program should be approved, an assessment procedure be changed, or a new teaching approach be introduced—can easily and quickly turn into political conflicts fought against the backdrop of participants' memories of past hurts and humiliations. When a foundation or corporation awards a large grant to a department, program, or college, the scramble to obtain juicy pieces of this makes Machiavelli seem fainthearted and overly scrupulous. If several departments are competing for their positions to be funded, the lobbying and infighting is as vicious and sustained as anything seen on Capitol Hill. When a budget cut means that a percentage of employees must be fired, then the gloves are off as past friendships are sacrificed and strange new alliances emerge.

In a broader context, political changes in the wider world have their effects in the classroom. Changes in government often

have immediate policy effects, forcing teachers to become bureau-
crats, raising the importance of test-taking, focusing attention on
one or another underrepresented group, or switching institutional
priorities as a pot of money becomes available for a pet initiative.
The ascendancy of a new national leader or a change in the balance
of power in the state house may seem like events pretty far removed
from a college class in biochemistry, English literature, or theology.
In reality, the impact of such events trickle down to individual
teachers as contracts are not renewed, pressure is applied to become
expert in an area where state or federal grant monies are suddenly
available, or the need to create new programs and deliver programs
in new ways becomes urgent. In C. Wright Mills' (1959) terms, the
private troubles of a teacher trying to deal with ever larger and more
diverse classes whilst being forced to take on a heavier committee
and advisement load is directly connected to the public issue of an
administration's desire to divert resources from education to military spending or to fund a new program of tax cuts.

Of course, what one is allowed to teach, and how one is allowed
to teach it, are matters over which college teachers are often the
last to exert control. When governments decide that certain subjects or skills are important to economic growth or ideological
socialization, then these areas inevitably receive preferential fund-
ing. What comprises a core, national curriculum, which skills are
overemphasized or need development, how cultural literacy is
defined—all these issues are subject to guidelines and legislation
developed by people far removed from the college classroom. So
educational institutions are prime battlegrounds for the culture wars
fought in the wider society, with teachers caught in the midst of
numerous battles.

The Political Purposes of Teaching

In a very broad sense college teaching can be considered as a political activity. By this I don't mean an activity concerned to teach a
particular ideology, but one in which students are encouraged to ask

awkward questions about why things (including college curricula, definitions of what constitutes learning, or criteria for judging academic excellence) are organized the way they are. In political activities people are asked to consider whose interests are served by the way these things are organized and how they might be organized differently. Challenging official definitions of what issues and problems are central to a curriculum or subject and substituting teachers' and learners' own notions of these is a political process. Anytime teachers encourage students to think in new and different ways, to explore alternatives to commonsense interpretations of their experiences, or to challenge the accuracy and validity of society's givens, their teaching is, in this sense, political.

Political teaching not only encourages people to develop a critically alert cast of mind, it also helps them develop a sense of agency. Students with a sense of agency see themselves as creators of events as much as reactors to them. Agency helps people to construct their own meanings and then try to live by these, rather than having these constructed by someone else. Creating these meanings occurs through the arduous process of testing our emerging insights and understandings against our experiences. College classrooms are one of the settings where people can do this without needing to fear where this process of meaning making may take them. When students learn that their opinions and interpretations matter because the teacher and other students take these seriously, important changes in self-concept can occur. An enhanced feeling of self-worth can be the affective underpinning to students' attempts to change aspects of their personal, occupational, and political lives.

Teachers who encourage students to ask awkward questions regarding dominant ideas run real risks. Such students will likely end up mistrusting simplistic solutions, be alert to political deception and able to resist propaganda, and earn from their teachers a reputation as troublemakers. In some societies scholars are routinely tortured and murdered because they foster critical questioning. The consequences of encouraging students to critique prevailing assumptions in this country are not likely to be imprisonment, exile, or death at the hands of paramilitary vigilantes. But an inability to get one's work published, progressive isolation within one's own institution, or the denial of promotion and tenure are all common penalties for teaching politically. So, rather than teaching being the last refuge of the politically disinterested, it is actually one of the most immensely politicized occupations people can choose.

Surviving Politically

Surviving politically within your institution means being able to keep teaching in creative and purposeful ways with a minimum of external interference. Doing this means negotiating and retaining enough physical resources, fiscal support, and institutional credibility to do good work. Learning the arts and skills of political survival is something that is not usually a part of the curriculum of teacher education, but rather learned on the job. This chapter focuses on general principles that seem to me to hold true across different contexts, although every department, college, and political situation exhibits its own idiosyncratic features.

All of us work in settings in which power plays and shifting organizational priorities affect how we practice our craft. So many times I have visited campuses as a speaker or consultant and been told that particular campus is unique in its history of political disputes and personality conflicts. Each campus feels it stands alone in its history of dysfunctional conduct. In truth, my experience is that every campus is dysfunctional in that squabbles based on personality differences and exacerbated by ideology and history exert great influence over day-to-day life. The rarity is to find a team, department, or whole faculty that works collegially and respectfully. A significant number of college teachers I speak to also feel they practice on the margins of their institutions. As new teachers they are increasingly hired on temporary contracts with no guarantee of renewal. Then, when they scramble on to the tenure track, they are given mixed messages concerning the kinds of behaviors that are *really* rewarded within the institution. Facing tenure decisions in a few years, they have to make numerous daily calculations as to when to hold their tongue, when to speak truth to power, how to express a threatening idea in a nonthreatening way, who to trust and who to steer clear of, and when requests made of them are diktats masquerading as innocent suggestions.

Working on the margins can sometimes be exhilaratingly edgy and creative. In times of economic austerity, or in situations of professional isolation, it can also soon become debilitating and demoralizing. So a degree of tactical shrewdness, including the ability to read the political culture of one's institution, is a political necessity for college teachers.

Become a Political Anthropologist

The first rule of political survival is to know what you are up against. As a newcomer to an institution who finds herself in an unfamiliar and possibly hostile situation, it is important to spend some time getting the lay of the land. I would suggest spending the first three to six months in a new job drawing a political map of the department, school, or college. In departmental meetings, in the cafeteria, in e-mail conversations, and in senate gatherings try and work out what reward system is in place, whose voice is taken seriously, where the power really resides, what organizational symbols are revered, and the language, arguments, and justifications that feel most congenial to staff, administrators, and faculty. You also need to learn something of the cultural and political history of the institution. As Shor (Shor and Freire, 1987) points out, there is nothing worse than blundering in with a well meant supposedly "new" suggestion for college policy only to find out later that the faculty has just spent six months considering and then rejecting something very similar.

If you do your anthropological work well, you will be better placed to follow some of the suggestions contained later in this chapter. It will help you choose which battles to fight and when and how to take a stand on controversial issues without being fired. It will also mean you are able to frame an intervention to have the greatest organizational effect. You will know who to seek out as allies, how to build up deviance credits (institutional brownie points you accrue by taking on tasks others are reluctant to perform), and when to cash these in. Finally, you will know which strategies and tactics are likely to have the greatest effect as you pursue your ends.

One of the most important dimensions of this anthropological work is researching the culturally approved language of the institution. A junior member of an organization who wishes to persuade those in power of the merits of a new and potentially threatening initiative she wishes to sponsor would be well advised to couch her proposal in accessible terms. In doing this it is immensely helpful if you know the language that is spoken and approved by those in power. It is surprising how much you can accomplish with no one objecting to, or even noticing, activities that are strongly alternative as long as these are described in terms that are familiar and approved. If the rhetoric of "learner-centeredness," "academic rigor," "critical thinking," or "responding to emerging needs" is adapted to describe teaching practices that challenge institutional norms, chances are nobody will visit the close attention on your classroom that would otherwise stifle your creativity.

Building alliances is also an outcome of the sort of anthropological research I am advocating. Change rarely happens as a result of wholly individual effort (though one person armed with sheer dogged determination can outlast and outwit people with strategic sophistication who don't want to put in the hours of sitting through committee meetings) but rather tends to be linked to some sort of collective initiative. So, for activist effect, as well as for the emotional sustenance it provides, we need to build alliances with like-minded peers. How do we find such peers? One way is to make sure we attend faculty meetings and watch who speaks out on issues about which we feel strongly.

Note, however, that a faculty member's speaking out doesn't necessarily mean that anyone is listening. We all know of colleagues who talk a lot at faculty meetings but who are rarely heard. This is in contrast to those who talk only occasionally but whose opinions often have greater credibility as a result. Such faculty have what the

English political observer Simon Hoggart (1981) calls TATBTS (TABS for short)—The Ability To Be Taken Seriously. TABS is defined as "an ability to impress your colleagues, a knack of convincing them that you are someone to whom it is worth paying attention, the kind of man (*sic*) of whose remarks people might be heard muttering 'y-e-e-s, that could well be the case,' rather than sniggering behind their hands" (p. 46). If you can find colleagues in your institution who have TABS and who share your convictions, these are potentially very valuable allies. They can vouch to colleagues regarding your sincerity and competence, they can provide crucial information on how to move an initiative through the organization, and they can help you frame a contentious view in ways that will be heard and considered (rather than being dismissed out of hand).

Watching and learning—a kind of radical patience—are the precursors to effective action. Shor describes this process as follows: "If you do a careful institutional profile, a map of who is on your side politically, then you can find allies, scout your enemies in advance, get a feel for what terrain offers some political opening. This preparation not only reduces the chances of miscalculating the room for opposition, but it also starts knitting you into your location" (Shor and Freire, 1987, p. 66). One particularly helpful piece of advice he offers is the merit of earning deviance credits.

Deviance credits are institutional kudos, organizational brownie points, earned by publicly performing tasks crucial to organizational functioning, such as serving on the alumni, library, or diversity committee or helping to organize fund-raising events. Undertaking these tasks earns you a reputation as an organizational loyalist. They help you bank a large number of deviance credits in the account of your organizational credibility. Then, when it comes time for you to take an oppositional stand, you cannot be dismissed out of hand as a troublemaker clearly disloyal to the institution. This is because your voice carries with it the institutional credibility of having performed these approved tasks. Cashing in your deviance credits at a strategic moment means you pry open a gap in which your concerns receive serious attention.

Choose Your Battles

Martyrdom is often appealing, a seduction to those who see themselves as change agents single-handedly fighting an oppressive system. However, as teachers with limited resources and precarious contracts we need to choose our battles carefully. We need to learn when to bend and when to stand firm and in particular when to bank our deviance credits to greatest effect. We need to realize it is easiest to get through an apparently impenetrable brick wall by finding the stones with the least mortar around them and chipping away at those weak areas rather than by trying to push the whole wall over. Sometimes it is best to skirt the whole wall altogether rather than try to force a way through the center. All of us only have a limited amount of energy after surviving the inchoate diversity of classroom life. So you need to choose the struggles that are significant and that contain within them the prospect of success or progress.

A good general rule is to focus on battles that are fought over some structural change. It's a fact of institutional life that individuals come and go, but structures and policies stay the same, unless a deliberate attempt is made to change them. And it is structures and policies that in large measure determine how we act. Battles that focus on the reward system are usually worth fighting. After all, the reward system of any organization determines 90 percent of the behavior of its members. Change the reward system and you change the behavior. We know this truth applies to students (which is why we spend so much time generating evaluative criteria for our courses), but we sometimes forget it applies also to teachers. A simple change in organizational policy can have deeper and more long-lasting effect than hours spent trying to persuade someone to agree with your point of view. This is why it is always worth volunteering to serve on any committee that has as its charge the redesign of the reward system governing faculty behavior. In this I build on two of Myles Horton's insights: that the point of social action is to change structures and that systems determine behavior (Horton, 1990; Jacobs, 2003).

We need to remember, too, that there are times and situations when it's best to say "There is very little I can do about this right now, so I may as well recognize this fact and use my energies for something I *can* do something about." Or, to say, "These circumstances mean that I can either live with an unsatisfactory situation or get out of teaching. So I may as well live with these circumstances as best I can, doing what little I can to change them, but mostly conserving my energies for a later date when more purposeful and fundamental change is possible." Such stoicism is, admittedly, not always possible and can be a comfortable rationalization for cowardice. Sometimes there are clear-cut situations where moral imperatives mean you have to fight a battle even with little hope of success. But in many other situations, teachers fail to choose their battles wisely and waste their energies by individually battling immovable forces to achieve little other than a fruitless martyrdom noticed by no one but themselves.

Generate External Recognition of Your Efforts

When we fight organizational battles, it is easy to focus all our attention on internal foes and obstacles and forget the world outside. Yet one of the most important hedges against our efforts being squashed is having those same efforts be noticed approvingly by eyes outside the college. If people external to the institution are talking favorably about a program inside it, then it's much harder for the institution to shut that program down. So one of the greatest assets teachers can call on in support of their internal activities is that of external recognition. When an organization knows that people outside it are watching the activities of a particular program, the teachers working within that program are less easily dispensed with. Nothing disturbs an institution so much as knowing that if a program is cut or closed, or its staff are sacked, that there will be an outcry from institutions and individuals outside the organization.

My own career as a writer stemmed from this realization. At one community adult education institution where I worked I faced great pressure to cut the educationally valuable but financially negligible community services I was overseeing. As a way of staving off the inevitable day of closure, I began to write articles describing these services for national educational journals. Many of these services focused on nontraditional forms of education (a supporting autonomous learning groups scheme, a walk-in educational advisory clinic, a home study service, a precollege study skills program for so-called "disadvantaged" adults) and consequently caught the imagination of editors. I also cultivated relationships with local journalists, and as a result features on these services were written up in local papers and broadcast on local radio. Although the program was eventually closed, I did buy a couple of extra years for the program's operation and some breathing time to consider my next move.

In pedagogic terms this means that whenever a student tells us just how much a particular course meant to them, or how much they've learned from us, or how they admire some aspect of our teaching (such as our ability to explain difficult ideas, the amount of attention we give to each student's work, or the degree of responsiveness we demonstrate regarding students' concerns), we should respond in a certain way. First, we should thank the person concerned for their feedback, letting them know how it fuels our motivation to keep working in the face of student resistance or whatever other obstacles we face in our teaching. Second, if the person concerned has already left the institution, and therefore has nothing to gain from pleasing us, we should suggest that they send a letter documenting their satisfaction with us to the head of our department, copying this to us as well as relevant senior administrators (such as the dean, division head, or vice president for academic affairs). One letter documenting an alumnus' satisfaction with and appreciation for our efforts is worth fifty such conversations we might have with a superior trying to convince him or her of our value to the institution. When questions are raised within the institution regarding our efforts, these letters of appreciation are worth their weight in gold.

Create a Paper and E-Mail Trail

Many of the agreements we make in the course of our daily life are verbal. We agree whose turn it is to get milk today, who will be responsible for getting the kids off to school, which of the many pressing bills we should try to pay first, and so on. Because we know and trust those we are making agreements with, there is no need to write these down. You don't usually write down agreements made around the dinner table, TV set, or in bed. This reliance on good faith verbal negotiations usually extends to the professional agreements we make as teachers.

There are two big problems with this extension. The first is that words are notoriously slippery and opaque. Postmodernism teaches us that the words we use to communicate our thoughts never capture exactly what we are thinking and that we have no control over the meanings others take from our words. So an agreement we make with students, colleagues, or superiors may be understood in one way or deemed to extend to one set of circumstances that is clear to us, but be understood in very different ways or seen as applying to a much broader range of circumstances by those we are coming to agreement with. When this difference exists we are often completely unaware of it. We continue along quite happy and secure in our knowledge of what we think we have agreed to until something happens that causes us to realize that those we depend on, or those who have power over us, are expecting us to act in ways we feel contravene the understanding we had. Then a situation arises in which we feel abandoned by those we previously had trusted. This is because we perceive them now as having betrayed a clear agreement we had made. They, in turn, start to view us as uncooperative, recalcitrant troublemakers who say one thing on one day and then refuse to abide by this on another day.

This difference of interpretation is particularly frustrating when it arises in the context of decisions in which the continuance of employment is at stake. Most grievance hearings sought by those who feel they have been unjustly denied an extension of their contract, or the award of tenure, boil down to the teacher feeling she has had no clear, unequivocal prior warning of a problem while her superiors feel that numerous verbal warnings were issued to her. The grievance hearing then becomes a "he said-she said" matter, in which the benefit of the doubt usually goes to the superior who has been at the institution for a much longer period of time. Because the conversations at issue are usually one on one, with no witnesses present to testify at a later date as to which person is remembering the conversation correctly, no clear resolution suggests itself. This is why documentation of prior warnings is so crucial in decisions to fire someone.

The second problem with relying on verbal agreements made at work is that those we have made agreements with often move out of their positions to be replaced by people who were not party to the original conversation. A colleague on your teaching team leaves or an administrator is promoted to another position or reaches the end of their term of office, with the result that the original verbal agreements you reached with those people are now rendered null and void. However, we often act as if they are still in place, naïvely assuming this to be the case. The new colleague or superior, on the other hand, has a quite different understanding of your role and obligation, and this understanding sooner or later (usually sooner) comes slap up against your own. The relationship then sours as you feel this person is unfairly trying to take advantage of you, while your colleague or superior feels you are dragging your feet and trying to get out of work.

Although perfect transparency of communication, in which each person clearly and fully understands exactly what the other person is saying, is probably impossible, we can certainly get closer to or further away from it. One thing that helps us move closer to this unattainable transparent ideal is the existence of a written record. This is why one of the most important pieces of advice I give to colleagues newly arrived to the profession is to create a paper trail of agreements made. Every time you have a conversation that involves you coming to an agreement on some aspect of your responsibilities, or that entails a team dividing up their labor in as efficient a way as possible, this should be written down and distributed to all involved in the conversation. Every time you agree on a set of responsibilities with an administrative superior, this should be written down and communicated with that person.

Because most administrators have a thousand and one things to take up their time, they may well feel that the verbal conversation is sufficient. However, I urge teachers to write up any conversation involving a discussion of their roles and responsibilities and to send a dated copy of this message to the administrator concerned. This message or memo should also ask for a quick reply indicating whether or not the administrator feels this is an accurate record of the conversation. If no response is forthcoming, then the dated memo or message should be sent a second time, along with a note saying that if no reply is received within a week that this will be taken as an indication that the administrator agrees that the memo or message accurately summarizes the understanding reached. This does not have to be done in any kind of confrontational way. You should say you are writing this merely for the historical record and to make sure both parties understand what they have agreed to.

It's also a good idea to keep a paper trail of your efforts to adhere to agreements that are made. If you have agreed to a new set of responsibilities but there is dispute as to how these might be met, you should write a quick memo each time you feel you have worked to meet these responsibilities and send a copy of this to the relevant administrator or colleague. This can be marked FYI (for your information) rather than as needing a response. If this message is sent in e-mail form, then the absence of an "undeliverable message" automatic e-mail response indicates the message has been received by the person you intend to read it (though it does not guarantee the person has actually opened and studied its contents!). If at any later date you are then accused of not having performed whatever tasks you agreed to, you have a paper trail or electronic record of how you have assiduously undertaken and reported these.

Finally, a paper trail should be created that documents any of your noteworthy accomplishments that can then be produced in times when people accuse you of not pulling your weight. Keeping a file documenting our accomplishments is hard for those of us who feel that teaching should be about helping students learn not about trumpeting our own achievements. But if you want to keep helping students learn, you need to be in an arena—a college classroom—where you can accomplish this while still being paid. Having a paper trail that comprises a public record of your achievements along with any external recognition you have received for these is invaluable in helping you stay in a situation where you can continue your work. Anytime a superior jots you a quick "well done" note acknowledging your successful completion of a task, copy it and file it for later possible use. Anytime you receive an unsolicited letter of thanks or recognition from a student or colleague (both inside and outside your institution), copy and file it. Anytime you achieve a particular goal—getting a paper published, giving a presentation at a conference, being asked by other faculty groups inside or outside your institution to come and address them regarding the particulars of your practice—this should be recorded in a message or memo that is sent to your superiors on an FYI basis.

All of this advice stems from Brookfield's Law of Employment. This law holds that for any job you take you should act as if one day you will face some kind of situation that involves pressure to remove you from this same job. Taking the kinds of steps described above in anticipation of that day may well mean that day will never come.

14

Surviving Emotionally

I f, as this book has argued, the purpose of teaching is to help students learn, then the focus of your efforts clearly needs to be on understanding how students are experiencing their learning and on responding appropriately to this information. From this perspective it may seem that attending to your own survival is selfish, narcissistic, and self-indulgent. Nothing could be further from the truth. Unless you find a way to navigate the roiling sea of emotions that the experience of college teaching generates, you run a real risk of drowning in swells of frustration, disappointment, or self-loathing. And if you do go under, of course, you are of no use to your students. So, in your students' best interest, you need to pay attention to your own emotional health. In this final chapter I explore three ways to help ensure your emotional survival as a teacher: (1) developing a working philosophy for teaching, (2) forming a support network of peers, and (3) remembering the maxims of skillful teaching.

Developing a Working Philosophy of Teaching

To some teachers developing a working philosophy of practice may seem a complete irrelevance, an intellectual game played by a few teachers in the humanities and social sciences who consider themselves intellectuals and who have the time to indulge in this academic fancy. My position is that, like it or not, we all operate according to a working philosophy of teaching. To me a philosophy of practice is a daily reality that shapes much of what we think and do. We may not acknowledge the reality of this philosophy, and we may call the intuitions, assertions, and convictions influencing us something other than a philosophy. But the reality is that, to echo Gramsci (1971), we are all philosophers, at least where our educational practice is concerned. For example, all teachers possess a set of beliefs concerning what their role should be in the classroom. They may not express this very clearly to themselves or to others, but they will probably employ various metaphors to speak about how they are coaches, cheerleaders, enforcers, or sparkplugs for learning. The beliefs that lie behind these metaphors may not be at the forefront of teachers' minds; indeed, these beliefs may only become apparent when circumstances seem to be pushing teachers into behaving in ways that feel unfamiliar and uncomfortable. In trying to understand why they feel so uncomfortable with a certain course of action, teachers sometimes realize it is because they are contravening a belief that they were unaware they held.

In the same vein, every teacher has an intuitive sense of what a good class looks like, of when they have taught well, and of who is a good student. Again, any time teachers feel that they, or their students, are wasting time, this necessarily implies a notion of what they think represents a proper and effective use of time. This notion of how to use time and energy to good effect reflects, at heart, a philosophical commitment to an ideal of what constitutes good education.

The collection of implicit beliefs outlined above (that, as I say, all teachers possess whether they admit it to themselves or not) constitutes a working philosophy of practice. Such a philosophy addresses the role teachers should play in the classroom, what a good class or good student looks like, what it means to have taught well, and what it means to have wasted time. Beliefs about these practices seem to be objective and purely descriptive. In reality they are normative; that is, they are based on preferences and values comprising what we think should happen in the world. Even teachers who say their practice is based on objective, empirically grounded notions of education—for example that a good class is one in which students display predetermined behaviors and competencies—are acting normatively. They are implicitly supporting one vision of learning and teaching contained in a particular set of standards to the exclusion of other possible visions.

Of course, any working philosophy can be full of contradictions, unrelated to real life, or just plain immoral. The fact that we have a philosophy does not make that philosophy good, useful, or right. Perhaps we act in the way we do because a superior has told us to. Or, perhaps our actions are purely mimetic—we are trying to look like our peers on the assumption that our peers' behaviors constitute an ideal we should realize. It could also be that some implicit beliefs we hold about what we, or our students, should do contradict each other. For example, we may sincerely desire our students to be self-directed learners capable of planning and conducting peer learning without teacher assistance, while equally sincerely believing it to be our duty to intervene as soon as we see a student in difficulties. Also, actions flowing from beliefs that seem right to us—perhaps concerning the best ways to use our power or to discipline students—may to others seem immoral or naïve. My point is that all teachers act according to a philosophy of teaching, whether or not they choose to acknowledge that fact. The ideal is to be aware of that philosophy so that its morality, accuracy, and utility can be judged by the person subscribing to it.

Why a Working Philosophy Is Important

A working philosophy is a set of values, beliefs, insights, and convictions about the essential forms and fundamental purposes of teaching. Embedded in it are criteria for judging how far your practice exhibits features you feel are essential to good teaching and a set of purposes towards which your efforts are geared. When you consciously hold to such a philosophy, you have an organizing vision of what you are trying to do, how you are trying to do it, and why doing it is important that you can present to your students, your colleagues, and yourself with conviction and clarity. This is important for several reasons: it helps you maintain a sense of stability and coherence in the face of constant chaos, it acts as a hedge against being forced into uncongenial, immoral, or harmful practices, and it imparts a confidence-inducing sense of direction to colleagues and students.

One way to think of a working philosophy is to compare it to the kind of computerized navigation instrument that allows air or sea pilots to maintain direction in the midst of a storm. Classrooms are like storms or squalls—full of surprises, of unexpected events that throw our neatly conceived plans into confusion. To teach while constantly feeling that things are out of control, or that life is constantly sabotaging your carefully conceived plans, can be extremely debilitating. It's the pedagogic feeling of flying into a hurricane with no cockpit navigation devices and no air traffic controller to guide your progress. Without the steering device of a working philosophy, it's much easier for others to define your path, your aims, and your roles and functions for you. You will be like a rudderless vessel tossed around by the winds, waves, and currents of whatever political whims and curricular fashions are prevalent at the time.

We will never lose the sense that classrooms are full of surprises, but holding a working philosophy will help us endure the episodes of apparently directionless confusion that are the inevitable accompaniment of such surprises. Even if no clear resolutions suggest themselves during such episodes, you can resolve to conserve your energies for the time when practicing your philosophy will become more possible. At times when we feel we are swimming against a massive tide of pointless, immoral, or harmful institutional imperatives, a working philosophy is likely to suggest small, contained steps we can take that will allow us to feel we are staying true to ourselves. So a distinctive organizing vision—a working philosophy of why we're doing what we're doing that we can call up in times of crisis—is crucial to our personal sanity and professional morale.

Politically, a working philosophy is a useful hedge against institutional pressures that are trying to force us into working in compromised ways. Just as conscientious objectors need a strong spiritual or secular rationale that can be articulated as a defense against conscription into an immoral war, so principled teachers need to express a strong rationale that explains why certain things asked of them are impossible. Sooner or later (hopefully later) you will find yourself pressured by powerful figures in your institution to do things (such as introduce poorly developed, inaccurate, and exclusionary curricula, apply evaluative standards that are irrelevant or harmful, or adopt teaching methods you find ineffective or immoral) that you feel strike against what you think it means to be a teacher. Sometimes there is little you can do short of quitting. At other times, however, your working philosophy, which you have repeatedly and clearly expressed over the months and years you have worked at the institution, can be strongly cited in your defense. At the very least this can buy you time while you build alliances, make necessary reforms, or look for another job. And occasionally it may help you win your case.

When combating pressures imposed from above, it is enormously helpful to express your opposition in terms of a confidently articulated rationale. Even if you don't win your case, you will be communicating a credible and clear-headed sense that you know why you are a teacher. Opposition to wishes of superiors that is clearly grounded in a well-developed and carefully conceived philosophy is less likely to be interpreted as sheer stubbornness or a lazy desire to get out of doing more work. You may not win over your enemies, but they will be more likely to respect you for taking a consistent and principled stand and less likely to conclude that you're not a team player or just looking for the easy life. Being respected for the strength of a thought-out commitment is important both for your own self-esteem and your long-term political survival.

Pedagogically, having a clear rationale for practice helps you judge whether you are having the kind of effect you wish on the world around you. The criteria for judging good teaching embedded in your philosophy may sometimes diverge from those that are institutionally applied to determine whether you deserve reappointment, promotion, tenure, or merit pay. When this happens you may find yourself on the receiving end of poor evaluations. Let's assume for the sake of argument that these evaluations are not a sign that you're lazy or incompetent but are due instead to the fact that the institution's aims have started to diverge from your own. Developing a clear working philosophy—being able to say to yourself, "Well, even though no one else seems to understand what I'm doing, at least I know it's right for me and my students, and I can explain to anyone who asks precisely why it's so right"—is one important layer of the thick skin you need to protect yourself against the temporary debilitation of a poor evaluation.

Knowing clearly why you feel it's so important to teach in a certain way also helps when you are forced to choose between the conflicting claims and priorities advanced by superiors, colleagues, and students. When your department head warns you to teach in one way and your students ask you to take another approach, it is important that you have some criteria you can use to help you make your choice. A large part of teaching is finding partial resolutions—the best we can come up with at the time—to essentially irresolvable dilemmas. In the struggle to balance the risks and consequences of different courses of action, it is very helpful if we can assess the consequences in terms of how they connect to what we view as the essential purposes of teaching.

Finally, a well-thought-out, clearly articulated working philosophy has a powerful effect on learners. When students are suffering confusion and uncertainty about what they're doing and why they're in college, they can draw strength from the clarity of your conviction. Students have the right to ask you to explain why you feel it's important that they should learn something and why you're asking for that learning to be conducted in a certain way. They may be worried that the content you're proposing to cover is irrelevant to their learning needs. They may feel that the learning activities you're asking them to engage in are inappropriate or that the criteria their efforts are being judged against are unfair or unrealistic. In response to students' expression of such legitimate concerns, it is very reassuring to them if you can demonstrate that you have a clear and well-worked-out reason for each of the things you're asking them to do. Even though they may not agree with your explanations and justifications of your actions, they are likely to feel reassured if you can express these clearly, confidently, and understandably.

Demonstrating that you have a well-developed and deeply felt conviction about the importance of your teaching is an important element in imbuing students with a perception of your credibility. Showing that you know where you're taking students, and why you believe it's important for students to get there, plays a big part in developing confidence on their part. They realize they are under the direction of an experienced, insightful, and committed professional. This is essential if they are venturing into perilous intellectual and affective terrain (which is how many students view new learning). When embarking on what is likely to be a difficult journey, no one wants to feel that the guide is inexperienced, unsure, or unconvinced as to whether the journey is worth the effort. Having a clear working philosophy that explains where the journey is leading and why it's important to take is crucial when students feel lost, afraid, and confused along the way.

Forming a Supportive Network

The importance of college teachers having a group of peers to whom they can turn for support and nourishment has been stressed at various points earlier in this book. In the preceding chapter I outlined the importance for political survival of building alliances, and I mentioned in passing the emotional sustenance these provided. In Chapter Five I mentioned the role that membership in a peer learning community played in helping teachers (as well as students) survive the risks of impostorship, cultural suicide, lost innocence, and roadrunning. Additionally, my discussions of the benefits of team teaching throughout this book have referred to the way that team members can encourage each other and keep each other on an emotionally even keel. So in this final chapter I will only briefly reprise this theme.

College teachers spend so much time teaching solo behind the closed doors of their classrooms that this isolation can induce in them a distorted perception of their own failings. When teachers talk together in staff meetings, their conversations usually concern administrative necessities and procedures. Rarely do they talk about the rhythms and dilemmas of their day-to-day teaching practices. Yet, private and informal talks with your peers about situations that confound you usually reveal that these situations are equally confounding to others! Realizing that other colleagues regard themselves as inept and inadequate—the same way you regard yourself—is enormously reassuring.

Let me emphasize this point regarding the benefits of teachers belonging to a peer learning community. Such a community may not suggest new resolutions to long-standing problems. You may outline whatever problems keep bedeviling your practice (such as a dominant student who shuts everyone else down in class, students who show up late and leave early, discussions that fall flat because no one has done the prereading, learners who hand in substandard work but expect an A, students who go behind your back to complain about the apparently unpatriotic views you express) and find that everyone else has these same problems and wanted to talk to you because they were hoping *you* would have the answer! It is the fact of knowing that you're not alone in your struggles that is the point. When you talk about dilemmas and frustrations that you thought were unique to you and caused by your own particular shortcomings, and then you find that your peers share these exact same difficulties, you often feel a rush of relief as a weight is lifted off your shoulders. You realize you are not uniquely ill suited to teaching but that you're experiencing feelings and emotions that are almost banal in their normality.

This feeling of being part of a shared experience, of suffering the same pangs and anxieties your peers admit to, is enormously reassuring. You lose the sense that the whole world is set against you. You stop thinking that you're stuck in a race to become professionally competent in which everyone else is forging ahead successfully while you seem glued to the experiential starting blocks. Team teaching will usually cure you of such feelings, which is one reason why I am such an advocate of this practice. It helps you recognize that you are participating in a common reality when you felt you were the only one suffering. Stumbling across this realization of commonly shared reactions and experiences is such a pleasure to see emerge in a teacher reflection group. As soon as one person admits to feeling like an impostor, discusses how they obsess over the minority of poor evaluations they receive, talks about feeling powerless in the face of student apathy or contempt, or describes a problem they assumed occurred only in their classroom, the others in the group chime in with their own experiences of these same feelings. In an experiential domino effect, people realize that, far from being alone, they are going through emotional rhythms and experiencing anxieties or problems that are commonly shared, completely normal, and utterly predictable. This realization can make the difference between staying in the classroom and quitting out of a sense of personal failure.

Fifteen Maxims of Skillful Teaching

Finally, let me end this book by summarizing some of the major themes stressed throughout its pages. These comprise Brookfield's Fifteen Maxims of Skillful Teaching.

Maxim 1: Expect Ambiguity

Legislation that requires teachers to teach to the test, curricula that purport to be "teacher-proof," manuals of practice that take you through a sequenced application of prescribed tasks designed to induce certain predetermined competencies or outcomes—all these practices rest on the assumption that classrooms are essentially rational, ordered environments from which surprise and serendipity can be banished. As anyone who has been in a college classroom more than five minutes knows, this assumption is ridiculous. This is not to say that the elements of sequence, order, and reason do not have an important place in teaching. We couldn't teach without them, students can't learn without them, and institutions and licensing bodies operate based on them. But teachers quickly realize that teaching is a journey into uncertainty in which they gradually learn to recognize those times when they need to abandon their reliance on standardized practices and curricula.

As teachers we regularly cross borders of chaos into zones of ambiguity. For every event in which we feel things are working out as we anticipated, there are two that confound our expectations. It is difficult enough to predict one person's response to a classroom exercise, let alone to predict the multiple responses of a diverse group of students to a single lesson unit. Context and contingency will distort the most perfectly planned curriculum or project.

Maxim 2: Perfection Is an Illusion

Yes grasshopper, the image of the fully formed, omniscient teacher trained to respond immediately and appropriately to any and all eventualities is indeed part of the veil of illusion that comprises the physical world of pedagogic practices. Expecting perfection in one's performance as a teacher usually has one of three predictable consequences: you quickly develop an anxiety disorder, you quit the profession because you are so demoralized at what you perceive to be your constant failures, or you develop a disconnected cynicism that holds that your actions don't matter because nothing works out how you think it will anyway. So, David Carradine and Kung Fu aside, I do believe that perfection (at least as defined as never making a mistake) is a chimera. You will never achieve it, and in pursuing it slavishly you will become so obsessed with your own actions that you'll forget the real reason for teaching—to help students learn.

Seeking perfection in pedagogic performance is as dangerously narcissistic as seeking perfection in sexual performance. In both cases what is really important—what is happening to the other person—is forgotten as one becomes obsessed with living out an idealized version of perfection drawn from manuals, media portrayals, or one's own fevered imaginings. In trying to be responsive to students while covering important content, in trying to build credibility and authenticity in equal measure, and in trying to use multiple learning modalities to meet diverse learning styles—in all these situations you will never achieve a perfect balance. Indeed, the notion of balance in teaching is itself highly questionable. Perhaps the most we can hope for is to keep these seeming opposites in a state of congenial tension.

If you equate the achievement of teaching perfection with only receiving positive reactions from students, you are really on the road to nowhere. For every student who embraces change or welcomes learning, there will be one (or more likely many) who will doggedly resist your efforts. It is easy to become obsessed with these students who, stubbornly, seem unable to realize the validity of the learning you are urging on them. But be ever wary of the trap of conversional obsession mentioned in Chapter Twelve by which you mistakenly measure your success as a teacher by the extent to which you turn the most recalcitrant student into a passionate advocate for your subject. Remember, no teaching action ever produces universally felicitous consequences. Every teaching choice is a trade-off involving pluses and minuses. If the overall advantages of one course of action outweigh its disadvantages, it is probably worth pursuing.

Maxim 3: Ground Your Teaching in How Your Students Are Learning

If I had to choose one process that exemplifies skillful teaching above all others, it would be the extent to which teachers make a deliberate and consistent attempt to discover what and how their students are learning and then to use this information to inform their teaching choices. This is why I devote the whole of Chapter Three to exploring this process. We should certainly watch for nonverbal reactions that indicate interest or disinterest, and we should always listen to what students tell us in class. But the Rosetta Stone of skillful teaching is the anonymous data regularly given by students regarding how they are experiencing the course. The instrument I rely on in this regard is the Critical Incident Questionnaire (CIQ), but Chapter Three describes several alternatives.

Sometimes teachers become understandably impatient about this process of research, feeling that it takes valuable time away from what everyone is there for—to learn important skills or knowledge. I feel this impatience also. But I tell myself that this impatience springs from my conviction that what I'm teaching is important for students to know. If this is so, then it follows that I should work diligently to make sure students are actually learning what I think they should be learning. And one important way I can be sure this learning is happening—that students are acquiring an accurate understanding of concepts, assimilating correct knowledge, or developing skills in the way I want them to—is by getting weekly information from them that indicates precisely what is happening in their learning. So for me classroom research is a foundation of good, content-based teaching.

Let me reiterate a point made in Chapter Three. Sometimes you will receive anonymous responses from students that make it clear they don't wish to learn what you wish them to learn. I often find myself dealing with a majority of learner responses that say, in effect, "Enough with the critical thinking—just tell me what to think, what's the right viewpoint on this question. It's too difficult for me to think this through on my own so give me the right answer." In the face of comments like this my response is to reiterate why I can't give them the "right" answer and to reaffirm why I insist on critical thinking as a major learning process. In doing this I may be open to renegotiating how critical thinking is demonstrated, but I won't be open to renegotiating the process itself. To do so would mean I had no right to show up to work each day or to call myself a teacher.

It's also true that students often judge that certain prescribed content or skills are irrelevant to their needs, or too difficult to assimilate, at the time of their initial exposure to them. However, subsequent experience—perhaps the application of this content or skill in a work setting or its indispensability to success in a later course—often proves the relevance of the learning. A quickly arranged alumni panel of students who are working and using the skills or knowledge taught in a course to good effect can help rejustify to new learners why this learning is so important. Sometimes, however, this option is not possible, and you are left having to explain, in the clearest way possible, why you are asking students to engage in certain learning activities. This is when a well-articulated working philosophy of practice is so crucial.

Maxim 4: Be Wary of Standardized Models and Approaches

Teaching and learning are such complex processes, and teachers and learners are such complex beings, that no curricular model or instructional approach will ever apply to all people in all settings. Not surprisingly, peddlers of such things would have us believe otherwise. Their pitch is that if we just adopt their model or approach we will rid our teaching of ambiguities, problems, and contradictions. It ain't necessarily so. The truth is that a lot of fruitless time and energy can be spent trying to find the holy grail of pedagogy, the one way to instructional enlightenment. No philosophy, theory, or model can possibly capture or explain every single aspect of the idiosyncratic reality that is your own experience as a teacher.

You can, of course, draw much that is useful from models and approaches that are out there. Indeed, most practice is a stew of hunches and activities in which a pinch of Freire, a drop of Horton, a soupçon of Marcuse, a splash of Fromm (you can substitute your own influences in this sentence) are blended together, mixed with a generous tablespoon of your own, experientially-based insights, and then served up to your learners. When it comes to good teaching, there is no such thing as stealing. Or if there is, it is a morally justified theft in the cause of student learning. For once, ends justify means. In the cause of improving student learning, it is quite permissible for us to be nicking (as we'd say in England) ideas, techniques, and activities from books, workshops, and colleagues. Moreover, when we nick a good idea from someone we should feel no compunction about rejecting parts of it or changing other parts. Again, if this idea doesn't work out as we'd hoped it would, we shouldn't worry about dropping it. Practices nicked from other sources can be useful starting points for our own teaching, but they don't relieve us of the necessity to make endless choices and judgments about what works best and why. Making such judgments—sometimes rightly, sometimes wrongly—is at the heart of teaching. No model of practice will allow you to abdicate this responsibility.

Maxim 5: Regularly Reflect on Your Own Learning

One of the best ways to improve your ability to work with hesitant, intimidated, or just plain terrified learners is to remember what it feels like to learn something new and difficult. This is best accomplished by your regularly volunteering to learn something that scares you and then to observe what it is that helps you through this learning, and what it is that makes the learning even harder. There is a good chance that those things that help and hinder you are the same things that help and hinder your students. For example, as a result of receiving criticism of your own performance, you may well decide to temper how you give criticism so that it is not interpreted as a personal assault on students. You will probably be reminded of some typical rhythms of learning (for example, incremental fluctuation) that get in the way of smooth progressions in learning. Knowing this will, in turn, stop you making needless and even harmful interventions. Most likely you will gain some new insights into why and how people resist learning and what some useful responses to this resistance might be. I try to learn something new each year, to keep a journal of the highs and lows of this experience, and then to think about the lessons I've learned for my own teaching. In an earlier book (Brookfield, 1995) I include a detailed analysis of how my learning to swim in adulthood unearthed and challenged some of my securest assumptions about good teaching.

Maxim 6: Take Your Instincts Seriously

Many of us are socialized into believing that the knowledge and insights contained within textbooks and teacher training programs have a greater legitimacy than the knowledge and insights we ourselves generate in response to the particular crises and dilemmas we face in our daily practice. Although I don't want to decry books and teacher education unnecessarily (after all, I write books on teaching and work in a school of education), it is also true that in a very real sense teachers are the greatest experts on their own situations. No one is inside a crisis or problem in exactly the way you are.

Often you may feel instinctively that a particular action is called for in a particular situation, but you refrain from following this because it is either omitted from, or actually contradicts, good practice as documented in a teaching text or a teacher education class. Certainly, texts can be right when teachers are wrong. They can sometimes suggest interpretations of a situation, and possibilities for its resolution, that never would have occurred to you. But you should not immediately assume this is always the case. If your instinct screams at you that something is either right or wrong, even if this goes against the conventional wisdom you have learned, be open to taking this seriously and possibly acting on it.

This carries the risk, of course, that you'll find out that your instincts are completely misjudged and that you have seriously miscalculated the consequences of following them. But if this worst-case scenario does happen, at least you will have learned something about how to recognize when your instincts are misleading and when they are well-grounded in reality. So don't automatically shut off an instinct the first time it speaks to you in the mistaken belief that if it doesn't match the theories espoused in books and professional programs it must, by definition, be wrong.

Maxim 7: Create Diversity

Chapter Nine has dealt at length with this maxim, so I will only mention it briefly here. Every class, workshop, or learning event should contain at least three different learning modalities. This will raise the chances that at some point in the learning episode most students will find that their particular learning style or preference has been addressed, which will be reassuring and energizing for them. It will also broaden their repertoire of engagement with various learning styles thus allowing them to flourish in the future in a greater range of situations than would otherwise have been the case. If you are consistently working with multiracial groups, you should make every effort to find some way to do at least part of your teaching in multiracial teams. At the very least, try not to fall into habitual patterns of teaching that spring from your own preferred learning style.

Of course, the breadth of diversity you can employ will depend on a number of contextual variables—organizational resources, available planning time, students' levels of learning readiness, your own familiarity with each of the different learning modalities involved, the racial identity and availability of colleagues, and so on. There is also a limit to how far you can stretch yourself to work comfortably with methods that contradict defining elements of your personality. You can't be expected to change your style at the drop of a hat, particularly if it involves doing things with which you have no experience or training or that make you feel personally very uncomfortable. For example, my own self-consciousness and shyness makes it hard for me to participate in role plays. My suspicion of people who reveal their life story with no prompting means I am not the best person to run highly personal life-history exercises. But many of us could probably inject a greater degree of diversity into our teaching than is currently the case.

Maxim 8: Don't Be Afraid to Take Risks

Risk is endemic to skillful teaching. Good teachers take risks in the full knowledge that these will not always work. The more you take risks, the more you open yourself to making a mistake, to falling flat on your face in front of your students and colleagues. However, the more these things happen, the more adept you become at recognizing when risks are justified and likely to pay off. In particular, you become better at responding to truly teachable moments—those times when an unexpected event creates a high level of readiness amongst learners that can be seized on to help them grasp a concept at a deeper level, see the relevance of a piece of knowledge, or try out a new skill in a way that embeds it dramatically in their existing skill sets. When a teachable moment occurs, it is a real gift and, if possible, should be built on to greatest effect. This is particularly the case when you've planned what you thought would be supremely exciting activities only to find that they draw lukewarm responses or studied indifference. Often in my own Critical Incident Questionnaire responses, I have found that students remember most clearly events that were unplanned.

In this regard it is helpful to think of a good educational experience as resembling a good conversation. Good conversations cannot, by definition, be predicted in advance. They are characterized by surprise and spontaneity. If I knew what you were going to say before you said it, and if you could predict beforehand my responses to your comments, there would be no point in talking. A conversation—and a class—with this degree of predictability is forced and boring. It's true that students want to know what's coming in a course, particularly if they are juggling multiple commitments and have to carve time for learning out of a busy schedule, or if the course is one that will play a big role in determining their future. But within the reassuring structure or scaffolding provided by the syllabus or the teacher's directions, they also need elements of surprise. Knowing exactly what will happen at every single moment along the way robs learning of the kind of spontaneity that keeps learners engaged and alert.

Maxim 9: Remember That Learning Is Emotional

If you've ever read a collection of Critical Incident Questionnaires, or thought about the most beneficial or memorable learning episodes you've experienced, you can't help but be struck by the emotive nature of learning. Yet the language of educational policy, learning theory, or curriculum design is remarkably cognitive and rational. It's as if learning is conducted by bloodless ascetics rather than by flesh and blood human beings with frailties and enthusiasms, passions and dislikes. There is often little indication of the emotional peaks and lows, the visceral ebbs and flows, accompanying, and intermingling with, the process of learning. The truth is that learning is often highly emotional, involving great threats to students' self-esteem, particularly if they are required to explore new and difficult knowledge and skill domains. Even when progress is being made, there is likely to be a grieving for old ways of being and abandoned assumptions—the lost innocence of Chapter Five.

Being aware of the emotionality of learning helps prepare teachers for the inevitable outpouring of anger and resentment that some students express as they explore new intellectual arenas and new skill sets. This awareness stops you experiencing a more or less constant angst-ridden scrutiny of your shortcomings when some students inevitably greet your instructions with hostility rather than the enthusiasm you'd expected. You will come to see students' grieving for old ways of thinking and learning as a natural element of learning, and you will be less likely to interpret resistance to risk-laden learning activities (such as critical thinking) as caused by your own poor preparation or lack of charisma. Finally, remembering the emotionality of learning may help you keep your own impostorship under control when you receive negative evaluations of your teaching that are expressed in emotional terms. It is important that you know that your effort to move students beyond their comfort zones will often be met with strongly felt and negatively expressed emotions and that being on the receiving end of these can be one indicator that you're doing your job.

Maxim 10: Acknowledge Your Personality

Chapter Four has shown how students need to feel they are in the presence of an authentic teacher, one whom they can trust because "What you see is what you get." If you teach in a way that belies fundamental aspects of your personality, then you will probably come across as stilted and inauthentic. Despite the infinite malleability of human beings, there is a limit to how far most of us can go in pretending to be something or someone we're not. For someone as introverted as me, it would be a major mistake to try and pass myself off as the pedagogic equivalent of Groucho Marx, Robin Williams, or Graham Norton. I try to remember that some of my students are introverts too and that they will probably feel more comfortable with me than with a highly charged extrovert. After all, by appearing to operate at a superhuman and unattainable level of proficiency, charismatic teachers can inhibit as well as inspire.

If you feel uncomfortable about behaving in a certain way, it's probably best to acknowledge this to yourself, your colleagues (if you're team teaching), and your students. Be wary of spending valuable, nonrenewable emotional energy on trying to exemplify idealized behaviors of "the good teacher." For example, I find listening to students' questions and responding fully to these to be hard work requiring great concentration. To answer a complex question clearly, I need first to focus on listening intently to the question, often to the exclusion of everything else. This means that as I hear the question, or think through my response, I often close my eyes, stare at the floor or into middle distance, and generally ignore all eye contact other than maybe with the questioner herself. As an introvert, human faces distract me. In the midst of a class I am always struck by students' expressions and find myself wondering constantly about the meaning of a glazed look (deep reflection or wandering attention?), a smile (recognition of a truth or mockery of my incompetence?), or a frown (grappling productively with an intellectual challenge or indicating a deep dislike of an activity?). Shutting out external stimuli such as students' faces is necessary if I am to understand a question the way the asker has framed it and if I am to give a good response.

Now in terms of good classroom communication, looking at the floor or into middle distance, or closing my eyes while someone else is speaking, are all things to avoid. But for me they are necessary to giving a good response to a question. It may seem that by ignoring eye contact with the majority of students that I have forgotten that they are in the room. Quite the contrary. It is because I feel it is so important to answer questions well that I do these things. In effect I am treating the students with greater respect and attention than if I conscientiously rotated my head 180 degrees from left to right, making sure all corners of the room received equal eye contact from me. If I put my energy into doing this, rather than into understanding and answering the question, I would give a much more confused, and less helpful, response.

So I begin many of my classes by telling students that I value questions but that when answering them I will probably stare at my shoes or into space. I tell them that I do this because giving a good, thoughtful answer depends on me concentrating on words and temporarily forgetting faces. Far from forgetting their existence, looking at the floor means I am acutely aware of their presence because it means I am trying to give the clearest, fullest, most helpful answer I can to their question. Many times the Critical Incident Questionnaires (CIQs) my students complete indicate that my answering their questions is a particular engaging moment or helpful action for them, whilst they also acknowledge that if I had not warned them of my tendency to stop making eye contact when doing this that they would have felt confused and ignored.

Maxim 11: Don't Evaluate Yourself Only by Students' Satisfaction

Although I have consistently argued for the importance of situating teaching in an awareness of how students are experiencing learning, I believe it is a mistake to measure yourself by how much students like you. Many of us would be the first to acknowledge that we go into teaching inspired by an admirable desire to help others. What we would probably be much less ready to acknowledge, however, would be that we expect to be liked, even loved, by our students for this altruism. We might not always admit this to ourselves, but for many of us it constitutes a powerful underpinning of our practice. One consequence of this expectation is that when it is not met—when students greet our efforts with anger, resentment, or indifference—we immediately conclude that we have failed. It is as if we assume that being a successful teacher requires that our students love us and find our efforts to be deeply transformative in the manner portrayed in popular films about teaching such as *Mr. Holland's Opus* or *Dead Poets Society*.

We need to remember (as pointed out in Maxim 9) that when we are doing our job properly some hostile student evaluations of our teaching are to be expected. Of course, if we only receive universally hostile evaluations, this may indicate a real problem in our teaching. It is hard to imagine much learning happening if everyone involved is consistently full of anger and resentment. But as one predictable element in students' reactions, hostility should not come as a surprise. After all, students themselves report that significant learning episodes in their lives frequently involve pain, anxiety, and challenge. While these episodes are being experienced, they may inspire resentment against the apparent cause of these emotions, that is, against you, the teacher. Knowing that hostility can be read as a sign of your pedagogic competence as much as a sign of inadequacy is an important defense against the demoralizing depression that tends to accompany the receipt of poor evaluations.

Additionally, you need to remember that the relevance and utility of an act of learning is often not appreciated until long after it has happened and you are no longer on the scene. This is particularly true in professional and clinical education where there is a gap between the initial learning and the student finding herself in a work context where the content or skills of the learning clearly apply. The fact that in the immediate aftermath of a learning episode students view their participation as a waste of time does not mean that this is the case. Seeds planted sometimes flower long after the gardener has departed the scene.

Maxim 12: Remember the Importance of Both Support and Challenge

Of all the intractable dilemmas college teachers face, getting the balance right between being supportive of students and challenging them to go further than they think they are capable of is one of the most difficult. You will never get this balance right; indeed, as mentioned earlier, it is probably mistaken to focus too much on the notion of balance. Trying to keep things in a state of congenial, rather than disruptive, tension is probably a better way to think about this. Even when you are faced with the culture of entitlement, an attitude of supportive respect towards your students should underpin your practice. Students who feel they are in a hostile or indifferent environment will have their commitment to learning (fragile as it may be) seriously weakened. They may be physically present but mentally absent.

When we criticize students as a way of challenging them, this can be devastating to those students, even if their attitude of bravado, contempt, or nonchalance hides this realization from us. So an ever-present concern (discussed in Chapter Ten) should be to begin all evaluations with an acknowledgment of any effort students have made, even if this effort falls short of producing the standard of work you had been hoping for. This is not to say that students who have clearly blown off an assignment and handed in work that is an insult to you should be bathed in affirmation. In such instances it is clear that you need to let them know early and clearly what the consequences of this will be. My point is that a negative comment from us can be remembered by students for months, even years, as deeply wounding, so we need to make as sure as we can that when we make them they are truly justified.

On the other hand, if students receive only affirmation from you and are never challenged, then their encounter with you is not fully educational. Affirmation is an important precondition of challenge but is never the sum total of teaching. Without challenge students will never move beyond where they are—never develop new skills, grasp new concepts, encounter new knowledge, or explore alternative viewpoints and perspectives. Of course, keeping balance and support in a state of congenial tension is difficult enough with one person, let alone with a whole class comprised of students of varying backgrounds, abilities, racial identities, motivations, and states of learning readiness who are confronting a variety of learning tasks. What has helped me enormously in this regard is the Critical Incident Questionnaire (CIQ). Behind the impassive, stony masks of students' faces, emotions may be churning without our ever knowing it. The culture of cool will work to ensure that no indication of their panic, or enthusiasm, will slip out. But these feelings will be noted on the CIQ once students are convinced their comments are anonymous. CIQ data is one of the most helpful sources of information that allows students—week in, week out—to judge how well I am balancing support and challenge.

Maxim 13: Recognize and Accept Your Power

Teachers committed to a vision of themselves as nondirective facilitators of learning, or as resource people there only to serve needs defined by students, often adopt the "fly on the wall" approach to teaching. This approach assumes that through a variety of strategies (mostly staying silent and refusing to give direction) teachers can gradually wither away into insignificance to the point where students don't even notice they're still in the room. In the power-laden, hierarchical setting that is a college classroom, this is a naïve and unrealistic assumption. A teacher cannot be a fly on the wall if that means being an unobtrusive observer. If you say nothing your silence will be noticed by students and interpreted either as withholding approval from them or as tacit agreement with their actions. Students will always be wondering what your opinion is about what they're doing. Better to give some brief indication of what's on your mind than to have students obsessed with whether your silence means disappointment or satisfaction with their efforts.

Although many student-centered teachers are uncomfortable with the idea that they are the focus of attention in the classroom, the reality (at least initially) is that this will always be the case. As long as you hold the power of the grade, you control a part of students' destinies. I believe it is far better to understand and acknowledge that fact and then to work to make sure that your power is used to best effect and not abused for unethical or immoral purposes. You may not like it, but students will imbue the slightest of your actions with all kinds of significance. When it comes to building trust in a classroom, this most delicate of pedagogic projects can quickly and devastatingly be sabotaged if your words and actions are seriously discrepant.

So don't make promises to students you can't keep. Don't tell them that all viewpoints are welcome in a discussion and then shut some down because they seem too harmful or irresponsible in your view. Don't fool yourself into thinking that by saying to students you're treating them as equals that this will mean they will view you the same way. As Freire (Shor and Freire, 1987, p. 160) says, "Education is above all the giving of examples through actions." You have power, so you may as well accept it and use it to model publicly your own commitment to the kinds of learning you wish to encourage in students. To pretend you don't have power, that everyone in the class (including you) is friends with one another and all are on an equal footing, will only cause students to be suspicious of you and to wonder what your real agenda is.

Maxim 14: View Yourself as a Helper of Learning

This is perhaps the most fundamental truth of all. At the heart of skillful teaching is the attempt to find out how students are experiencing the learning we are overseeing so that we can make this as relevant and accessible as possible. The only reason we teach is to help someone else learn, and whatever we do to help them in that regard must be considered as good teaching, no matter how unprofessional or strange it may seem to an outsider. If a practice contributes to students' learning, we should do it, no matter how much it may offend against professional or community expectations regarding good teaching. Contrarily, if a practice hinders students' learning then we should stop it, no matter how much it may be expected of us by students, peers, and superiors.

Of course, we all have to make compromises in this regard. Much as I would like never to have to give a grade, there are times my institution requires this of me. Much as I am suspicious of the use of closed-book examinations as true measures of students' abilities or learning accomplishments, I cannot avoid having my students take these if a licensing board requires them. But when it comes down to it, when you're deciding whether or not something is an example of good teaching, the only question you have to ask yourself is "Does this help my students learn?"

Adopting this approach to teaching means we must consider as examples of good, skillful teaching all kinds of activities that fall well outside the "teacher as charismatic performer" paradigm. If teaching is helping learning, then textbook authors or software developers who never see inside a classroom or meet any of your students must be considered some of their most effective teachers. You can be a highly skillful teacher if you design well-conceived and richly illuminating role plays or simulations that students explore without you being present. In this electronic era the designers of online courses are some of the powerful teachers that students are exposed to, yet they are for the most part faceless. Again, being able to help students understand their learning difficulties in an area of learning is a highly effective teaching act, even though it may be carried out by someone who carries the professional label of diagnostician rather than teacher. Someone who puts students in touch with each other so that they can form learning communities is, as Chapter Five has shown us, one of the most effective teachers students can benefit from. Often it is the support staff in a program that students turn to because they know that these staff don't hold the power of the grade over them. And it is support staff that can be so effective in putting students in touch with each other and thereby building community.

So forget Robert Donat or Peter O' Toole in *Goodbye Mr. Chips*, Sidney Poitier in *To Sir With Love*, Edward James Olmos in *Stand and Deliver*, Robin Williams in *Dead Poets Society*, Jon Voight in *Conrack*, Richard Dreyfuss in *Mr. Holland's Opus*, Michelle Pfeiffer in *Dangerous Minds*, or Kevin Kline in *The Emperor's Club*. These are excellent fictional portrayals of powerful individuals whose personal authenticity and pedagogic brilliance illuminate the mediocrity surrounding them. But they are bad role models (at least for me). Teaching is not about charismatically charged individuals using the sheer force of their characters and personalities to wreak lifelong transformations in students' lives. It's about finding ways to promote the day-to-day, incremental gains that students make as they try to understand ideas, grasp concepts, assimilate knowledge, and develop new skills. All the small things you do to make this happen for students represent the real story of teaching. Helping learning is what makes you truly heroic.

Maxim 15: Don't Trust What You've Just Read

Everything in this book should be regarded with great skepticism. Just because words appear on a printed page doesn't make them right, helpful or, even more important, trustworthy. So don't trust what you've read in this book. What to me appear as truths and tenets of skillful teaching may, for you, be partially or entirely inappropriate. Keep in mind that in the time between writing these words on a computer and having them bound and printed in the book you are now holding, I may have significantly amended some of these maxims, deleted others, and added replacements. My continuing journey as a teacher through diverse contexts and irresolvable dilemmas is bound to generate new insights. The one thing I can expect with real certainty is that I will be surprised by what's coming. It would be a contradiction of what I have written in this book if I ended it by proposing a standardized set of maxims supposed to hold true across all the varied contexts in which readers work.

Obviously I feel these insights have some grounding in reality; otherwise I would not have allowed them to be published under my name! From responses I have received to the first edition of this book, I suspect that many readers will recognize parts of themselves and their practices as they read these chapters. But don't think that if some element of your practice contradicts what I'm saying that you're wrong and I'm right. The world is far too messy to conform to the analyses and suggestions of any single author or teacher. Listen to that inner, nagging voice that says you might be right and your superiors, your colleagues, your union, the professional code of conduct that you work under, and the writers of books like this one might be wrong. In a very real sense, you are the ultimate expert on your own experience so be ready (particularly if your CIQ data supports your hunch) to act on what this voice is telling you. And if you do act and find out that your hunch was wrong, you can remind yourself that continually making mistakes, and learning from these, is endemic to all good teaching.

Bibliography

Althusser, L. *Lenin and Philosophy*. New York: Monthly Review Press, 1971.

Anderson, L. W. *Classroom Assessment: Enhancing the Quality of Teacher Decision Making*. Mahwah, NJ: Erlbaum, 2002.

Angelo, T. A. (ed.). *Classroom Assessment and Research: An Update on Uses, Approaches, and Research Findings*. New Directions for Teaching and Learning, no. 75. San Francisco: Jossey-Bass, 1998.

Angelo, T. A., and Cross, K. P. *Classroom Assessment Techniques: A Handbook for College Teachers*. San Francisco: Jossey-Bass, 1993.

Aragon, S. R. "Creating Social Presence in Online Environments." In S. R. Aragon (Ed.), *Facilitating Learning in Online Environments* (pp. 57–68). New Directions for Adult and Continuing Education, no. 100. San Francisco: Jossey-Bass, 2003.

Astin, A. W. *What Matters in College: Four Critical Years Revisited*. San Francisco: Jossey-Bass, 1997.

Baptiste, I. "Beyond Reason and Personal Integrity: Toward a Pedagogy of Coercive Restraint." *Canadian Journal for the Study of Adult Education*, 2000, *14(1)*, 27–50.

Baptiste, I. E., and Brookfield, S. D. "Your So-Called Democracy Is Hypocritical Because You Can Always Fail Us: Learning and Living Democratic Contradictions in Graduate Adult Education." In P. Armstrong (ed.), *Crossing Borders, Breaking Boundaries: Research in the Education of Adults*. Department of Adult Education, Birkbeck College, London: University of London, 1997.

Baxter Magolda, M. *Knowing and Reasoning in College: Gender Related Patterns in Student Development*. San Francisco: Jossey-Bass, 1992.

Belenky, M. F., Clinchy, B. M., Goldberger, N. R., and Tarule, J. M. *Women's Ways of Knowing: The Development of Self, Voice and Mind*. New York: Basic Books, 1986.

281

Bender, T. *Discussion-based Online Teaching to Enhance Student Learning.* Sterling, VA: Stylus, 2003.

Bergin, D. A., and Cooks, H. C. "High School Students of Color Talk About Accusations of 'Acting White.'" *Urban Review,* 2002, 34(2), 13–34.

Bess, J. L., and Associates. *Teaching Alone, Teaching Together: Transforming the Structure of Teams for Teaching.* San Francisco: Jossey-Bass, 2000.

Biggs, J., Kember, D., and Leung, D.Y.P. "The Revised Two Factor Study Process Questionnaire: R-SPQ-2F." *British Journal of Educational Psychology,* 2001, 7 (Pt. 1), 133–149.

Bligh, D. A. *What's the Use of Lectures?* San Francisco: Jossey-Bass, 2000.

Brems, C., Baldwin, M. R., Davis, L., and Namyniuk, L. "The Imposter Syndrome as Related to Teaching Evaluations and Advising Relationships of University Teachers." *Journal of Higher Education,* 1994, 65(2), 183–193.

Britzman, D. P. *Practice Makes Practice: A Critical Study of Learning to Teach.* Albany: State University of New York Press, 1991.

Brookfield, S. D. "Independent Adult Learning." *Studies in Adult Education,* 1981, 13(1), 1–15.

Brookfield, S. D. *Developing Critical Thinkers: Challenging Adults to Explore Alternative Ways of Thinking and Acting.* San Francisco: Jossey-Bass, 1987.

Brookfield, S. D. (ed.). *Learning Democracy: Eduard Lindeman on Adult Education and Social Change.* New York: Routledge, 1988.

Brookfield, S. D. *Becoming a Critically Reflective Teacher.* San Francisco: Jossey-Bass, 1995.

Brookfield, S. D. "Clinical Reasoning and Generic Thinking Skills." In J. Higgs and M. Jones (eds.), *Clinical Reasoning in the Health Professions.* Oxford: Butterworth/Heinemann, 2000.

Brookfield, S. D. *The Power of Critical Theory: Liberating Adult Learning and Teaching.* San Francisco: Jossey-Bass, 2005.

Brookfield, S. D., and Preskill, S. *Discussion as a Way of Teaching: Tools and Techniques for Democratic Classrooms.* (2nd ed.) San Francisco: Jossey-Bass, 2005.

Brookhart, S. M. *The Art and Science of Classroom Assessment: The Missing Part of Pedagogy.* ASHE-ERIC Higher Education Report Series, 27(1). San Francisco: Jossey-Bass, 2000.

Brown, S., and Race, P. *Lecturing: A Practical Guide.* Sterling, VA: Stylus, 2002.

Buckley, F. J. *Team Teaching: What, Why, How?* Thousand Oaks, CA: Sage, 2000.

Butler, S. M., and McMunn, N. D. *A Teacher's Guide to Classroom Assessment.* San Francisco: Jossey-Bass, 2006.

Carlgren, I., Handal, G., and Vaage, S. (eds.). *Teachers' Minds and Actions: Research on Teachers' Thinking and Practice.* Bristol, PA: Falmer Press, 1994.

Casey, J. G. "Diversity, Discourse, and the Working-Class Student." *Academe*, 2005, *91*(4), 33–36.

Clark, C. M. "Teachers as Designers in Self-Directed Development." In A. Hargreaves and M. G. Fullan (eds.), *Understanding Teacher Development*. New York: Teachers College Press, 1992.

Cohen, R. M. *A Lifetime of Teaching: Portraits of Five Veteran High School Teachers*. New York: Teachers College Press, 1991.

Connelly, F. M., and Clandinin, D. J. *Teachers as Curriculum Makers: Narratives of Experience*. New York: Teachers College Press, 1988.

Connelly, F. M., and Clandinin, D. J. *Shaping Professional Identity: Stories of Educational Practice*. New York: Teachers College Press, 1999.

Conrad, R. M., and Donaldson, J. A. *Engaging the Online Learner: Activities and Resources for Creative Instruction*. San Francisco: Jossey-Bass, 2004.

Cranton, P. *Becoming an Authentic Teacher in Higher Education*. Malabar, FL: Krieger, 2001.

Cranton, P., and Carusetta, E. "Perspectives on Authenticity in Teaching." *Adult Education Quarterly*, 2004, *55*(1), 5–22.

Cross, K. P. "Classroom Research: Implementing the Scholarship of Teaching." In T. A. Angelo (ed.), *Classroom Assessment and Research: An Update on Uses, Approaches, and Research Findings*. New Directions for Teaching and Learning, no. 75. San Francisco: Jossey-Bass, 1998.

Cross, K. P., and Steadman, M. H. *Classroom Research: Implementing the Scholarship of Teaching*. San Francisco: Jossey-Bass, 1996.

Cross, W. E. Jr., Strauss, L., and Fhagen-Smith, P. "African American Identity Development Across the Life Span: Educational Implications." In R. Sheets and E. Hollins (eds.), *Racial and Ethnic Identity in School Practices*. Mahwah, NJ: Erlbaum, 1999, pp. 29–47.

Daloz, L. A. *Mentor: Guiding the Journey of Adult Learners*. San Francisco: Jossey-Bass, 1999.

Day, C., Calderhead, J., and Denicolo, P. (eds.). *Research on Teacher Thinking: Understanding Professional Development*. Bristol, PA: Falmer Press, 1993.

Dews, C.L.B., and Law, C.L. (eds.). *This Fine Place So Far From Home: Voices of Academics From the Working Class*. Philadelphia: Temple University Press, 1995.

Eisen, M. J., and Tisdell, E. J. (eds.). *Team Teaching and Learning in Adult Education*. New Directions for Adult and Continuing Education, no. 87. San Francisco: Jossey-Bass, 2000.

Evans, N. J., Forney, D. S., and Guido-Di Brito, F. *Student Development in College: Theory, Research and Practice*. San Francisco: Jossey-Bass, 1998.

Farrah, S. "Lecture." In M. Galbraith (ed.), *Adult Learning Methods*. Malabar, FL: Krieger, 2004.

Fein, A. D., and Logan, M. C. "Preparing Instructors for Online Instruction." In S. R. Aragon (ed.), *Facilitating Learning in Online Environments* (pp. 45–55). New Directions for Adult and Continuing Education, no. 100. San Francisco: Jossey-Bass, 2003.

Foucault, M. *Power/Knowledge: Selected Interviews and Other Writings, 1972–1977.* New York: Pantheon Books, 1980.

Frase, L. E., and Conley, S. C. *Creating Learning Spaces for Teachers Too.* Thousand Oaks, CA: Corwin, 1994.

Frederick, P. "The Dreaded Discussion: Ten Ways to Start." In D. Bligh (ed.), *Teach Thinking By Discussion.* Guildford, England: Society for Research into Higher Education/NFER-Nelson, 1986.

Freire, P. *Pedagogy of the Oppressed.* (Revised edition). New York: Continuum, 1993.

Fromm, E. *Escape from Freedom.* New York: Holt, Rinehart and Winston, 1941.

Fromm, E. *The Sane Society.* London: Routledge, Kegan and Paul, 1956a.

Fromm, E. *The Art of Loving: An Enquiry into the Nature of Love.* New York: Harper and Row, 1956b.

Gardella, L. G., Candales, B. A., and Ricardo-Rivera, J. "Doors Are Not Locked, Just Closed: Latino Perspectives on College." In M. A. Wolf (ed.), *Adulthood: New Terrain.* New Directions for Adult and Continuing Education, no. 108. San Francisco: Jossey-Bass, 2005.

Goldberger, N. R., Tarule, J. M., Clinchy, B. M., and Belenky, M. F. *Knowledge, Difference and Power: Essays Inspired by Women's Ways of Knowing.* New York: Basic Books, 1996.

Goodson, I. F. (ed.). *Studying Teachers' Lives.* New York: Routledge, 1992.

Gramsci, A. *Selections from the Prison Notebooks* (Q. Hoare and G. N. Smith, eds.). London: Lawrence and Wishart, 1971.

Greene, M. *Variations on a Blue Guitar: The Lincoln Center Institute Lectures on Aesthetic Education.* New York: Teachers College Press, 2001.

Grimmet, P. P., and Neufeld, J. (eds.). *Teacher Development and the Struggle for Authenticity: Professional Growth and Restructuring in the Context of Change.* New York: Teachers College Press, 1994.

Gunawardena, C. N. "Social Presence Theory and Implications for Interaction and Collaborative Learning in Computer Conferences." *International Journal of Educational Telecommunications,* 1995, *1*(2), 147–166.

Gunawardena, C. N., and Zittle, F. J. "Social Presence as a Predictor of Satisfaction Within a Computer-Mediated Conferencing Environment." *American Journal of Distance Education,* 1997, *11*(3), 8–26.

Guy, T. C. "Gangsta Rap and Adult Education." In L. G. Martin and E. E. Rogers (eds.), *Adult Education in an Urban Context: Problems, Practices, and Programming for Inner-City Communities*. New Directions for Adult and Continuing Education, no. 101. San Francisco: Jossey-Bass, 2004.

Habermas, J. *Autonomy and Solidarity: Interviews with Jürgen Habermas*. (Revised edition.) London: Verso, 1992.

Hall, S. *Culture, Media, Language: Working Papers in Cultural Studies*. New York: Routledge, 1991.

Hammersley, M. (ed.). *Controversies in Classroom Research*. Bristol, PA: Open University Press, 1993.

Hess, M. E. *Engaging Technology in Theological Education: All That We Can't Leave Behind*. Lanham, MD: Rowman and Littlefield, 2005.

Hoffman, J. *The Synchronous Trainer's Guide: Facilitating Successful Live and Online Courses, Meetings, and Events*. San Francisco: Jossey-Bass, 2003.

Hoffman, J. *Live and Online: Tips, Techniques, and Ready-to-Use Activities for the Virtual Classroom*. San Francisco: Jossey-Bass, 2004.

Hoggart, S. *On the House*. London: Pan Books, 1981.

hooks, b. *Teaching to Transgress: Education as the Practice of Freedom*. New York: Routledge, 1994.

Hopkins, D. *A Teacher's Guide to Classroom Research*. Bristol, PA: Open University Press, 1993.

Horton, M. *The Long Haul: An Autobiography*. New York: Doubleday, 1990.

Horton, M., and Freire, P. *We Make the Road by Walking: Conversations on Education and Social Change*. Philadelphia: Temple University Press, 1990.

Isenberg, J. *Going by the Book: The Role of Popular Classroom Chronicles in the Professional Development of Teachers*. New York: Routledge, 1994.

Jacobs, D. (ed.). *The Myles Horton Reader: Education for Social Change*. Knoxville, TN: University of Tennessee Press, 2003.

Jalongo, M. R., and Isenberg, J. P. *Teachers' Stories: From Personal Narrative to Professional Insight*. San Francisco: Jossey-Bass, 1995.

Johnson, S. D., and Aragon, S. R. "An Instructional Strategy Framework for Online Learning Environments." In S. R. Aragon (ed.), *Facilitating Learning in Online Environments* (pp. 31–43). New Directions for Adult and Continuing Education, no. 100. San Francisco: Jossey-Bass, 2003.

Johnston, C. A., and Dainton, G. *The Learning Connections Inventory*. Pittsgrove, NJ: Let Me Learn, 1997.

Kets de Vries, M.F.R. *Leaders, Fools, and Impostors: Essays on the Psychology of Leadership*. San Francisco: Jossey-Bass, 1993.

King, P. M., and Kitchener, K. S. *Developing Reflective Judgment: Understanding and Promoting Intellectual Growth and Critical Thinking in Adolescents and Adults.* San Francisco: Jossey-Bass, 1994.

Kolb, D. A. *Experiential Learning.* Englewood Cliffs, NJ: Prentice Hall, 1984.

Lewis, D., and Allan, B. *Virtual Learning Communities: A Guide for Practitioners.* New York: Open University Press, 2005.

Lindeman, E.C.L. "World Peace Through Adult Education." (Originally published 1945.) In S. D. Brookfield (ed.), *Learning Democracy: Eduard Lindeman on Adult Education and Social Change* (pp. 122–125). New York: Routledge, 1988.

Lindeman, E.C.L. "Adult Education and the Democratic Discipline." *Adult Education,* 1947, *6(3),* 112–115.

Lodge, D. *Nice Work.* New York: Viking, 1988.

Logan, J. *Teaching Stories.* St. Paul, MN: 1993.

Mamet, D. *Oleanna: A Play.* New York: Vintage Books, 1993.

Marcuse, H. "Repressive Tolerance." In R. P. Wolff, B. Moore, and H. Marcuse. *A Critique of Pure Tolerance.* Boston: Beacon Press, 1965.

Marcuse, H. *An Essay on Liberation.* Boston: Beacon Press, 1969.

Marton, F., Hounsell, D., and Entwistle, N. (eds.). *The Experience of Learning: Implications for Teaching and Studying in Higher Education.* (2nd ed.) Edinburgh: Scottish Academic Press, 1997.

Miller, J. L. *Creating Spaces and Finding Voices: Teachers Collaborating for Empowerment.* Albany: State University of New York Press, 1990.

Mills, C. W. *The Sociological Imagination.* New York: Oxford University Press, 1959.

Palloff, R. M., and Pratt, K. *Building Learning Communities in Cyberspace: Effective Strategies for the Online Classroom.* San Francisco: Jossey-Bass, 1999.

Palloff, R. M., and Pratt, K. *The Virtual Student: A Profile and Guide to Working with Online Learners.* San Francisco: Jossey-Bass, 2003.

Palloff, R. M., and Pratt, K. *Collaborating Online: Learning Together in Community.* San Francisco: Jossey-Bass, 2004.

Pascarella, E. T., and Terenzini, P. T. *How College Affects Students: Findings and Insights from Twenty Years of Research.* San Francisco: Jossey-Bass, 1991.

Palmer, P. J. *The Courage to Teach: Exploring the Inner Landscape of a Teacher's Life.* San Francisco: Jossey-Bass, 1997.

Paterson, R.W.K. "The Concept of Discussion: A Philosophical Approach." *Studies in Adult Education,* 1970, *1(2),* 28–50.

Perry, W. G. "Different Worlds in the Same Classroom." In P. Ramsden (Ed.), *Improving Learning: New Perspectives.* New York: Nichols, 1988.

Perry, W. G. *Forms of Intellectual and Ethical Development in the College Years: A Scheme*. San Francisco: Jossey-Bass, 1999.

Peters, R. S. (ed.). *The Concept of Education*. Boston: Routledge, Kegan and Paul, 1967.

Piskurich, G. M. (ed.). *Preparing Learners for E-Learning*. San Francisco: Jossey-Bass, 2003.

Polyani, M. *Personal Knowledge: Toward a Post-Critical Philosophy*. Chicago: University of Chicago Press, 1974.

Preskill, S. L., and Jacobvitz, R. S. *Stories of Teaching: A Foundation for Educational Renewal*. New York: Prentice Hall, 2000.

Race, P. (ed.). *2000 Tips for Lecturers*. London: Kogan Page, 2000.

Race, P. *The Lecturer's Toolkit: A Practical Guide to Learning, Teaching and Assessment*. London: Kogan Page, 2001.

Rogers, C. *On Becoming a Person: A Therapist's View of Psychotherapy*. Mariner Books, 1995. (Originally published 1961.)

Ryan, J., and Sackey, C. *Strangers in Paradise: Academics from the Working Class*. Boston: South End Press, 1984.

Sacks, P. *Generation X Goes to College: An Eye-Opening Account of Teaching in Postmodern America*. Peru, IL: Open Court Publishing, 1996.

Schubert, W. H., and Ayers, W. C. (eds.). *Teacher Lore: Learning from our Experience*. New York: Longman, 1992.

Shor, I. *Empowering Education: Critical Teaching for Social Change*. Chicago: University of Chicago Press, 1992.

Shor, I. *When Students Have Power: Negotiating Authority in a Critical Pedagogy*. Chicago: University of Chicago Press, 1996.

Shor, I., and Freire, P. *A Pedagogy for Liberation: Dialogues on Transforming Education*. Westport, CT: Bergin and Garvey, 1987.

Simon, R. I. *Teaching Against the Grain: Texts for a Pedagogy of Possibility*. New York: Bergin and Garvey, 1992.

Smith, E. "What is Black English? What is Ebonics?" (pp. 49–58). In T. Perry and L. Delpit (eds.), *The Real Ebonics Debate*. Boston: Beacon Press, 1998.

Snow, C. P. *The Masters*. New York: Scribner, 1951.

Steele, C. M. "Stereotype Threat and Intellectual Test Performance of African Americans." *Journal of Personality and Social Psychology*, 1995, 69(5), pp. 797–811.

Thomas, D. (ed.). *Teachers' Stories*. Bristol, PA: Open University Press, 1995.

Treisman, U. "Studying Students Studying Calculus: A Look at the Lives of Minority Mathematics Students in College." *College Mathematics Journal*, 1992, 23(5), pp. 362–372.

Van Ments, M. *Active Talk: The Effective Use of Discussion in Learning*. New York: St. Martin's Press, 1990.

Weinstein, C. E., Palmer, D. R., and Hanson, G. R. *Perceptions, Expectations, Emotions and Knowledge About College*. Clearwater, FL: H and H Publishing, 1995.

Weinstein, C. E., Schulte, A. C., and Palmer, D. R. *Learning and Study Strategies Inventory*. Clearwater, FL: H and H Publishing, 1987.

Welsch, K. A. (ed.). *Those Working Sundays: Female Academics and Their Working Class Parents*. Lanham, MD: University Press of America, 2004.

Index